Particularism and Universalism in the Book of Isaiah

Bible in History

Bible in History focuses on biblical interpretation in different ages and countries and is a series dedicated to studies of biblical exegesis as well as to research about principles of interpretation relevant to interpreters of the Bible. The series is open to studies focusing on philological and theological aspects of particular Bible passages but it also welcomes publications in the field of history of biblical interpretation that study the development of new ideas and their impact on interpretation of the text. Editions of textual variants as well as of influential old and modern commentaries are also within the scope of this series.

The series accepts publications in French and English.

Series published by
Joseph Alobaidi

PETER LANG
Bern · Berlin · Bruxelles · Frankfurt a. M. · New York · Oxford · Wien

Se-Hoon Jang

Particularism and Universalism in the Book of Isaiah

Isaiah's Implications for a Pluralistic World from a Korean Perspective

PETER LANG
Bern · Berlin · Bruxelles · Frankfurt am Main · New York · Oxford · Wien

Bibliographic information published by Die Deutsche Bibliothek
Die Deutsche Bibliothek lists this publication in the Deutsche National-bibliografie; detailed bibliographic data is available on the Internet at ‹http://dnb.ddb.de›.

British Library and Library of Congress Cataloguing-in-Publication Data:
A catalogue record for this book is available from *The British Library*, Great Britain, and from *The Library of Congress*, USA.

ISSN 1422-5972
ISBN 3-03910-597-3
US-ISBN 0-8204-7046-5

Hochfeldstrasse 32, Postfach 746, CH-3000 Bern 9, Switzerland
info@peterlang.com, www.peterlang.com, www.peterlang.net

Printed in Germany

Table of Content

Part II
Situating My Reading of Isaiah in the Larger Methodological Debate

Part III
Particularism and Universalism in the Book of Isaiah

Preface

This monograph represents a slight revision of a PhD thesis which was originally submitted to the Department of Studies in Religion, the University of Queensland, Australia, in 2002. The central focus of this research is a critical assessment of the polemical issues in Korea (religious pluralism and iconoclastic vandalism) from the biblical perspective of the book of Isaiah as a whole. This reserach seeks to present a full-fledged overview of how these controversial issues have driven the Korean Churches into a theological pitfall. It will also canvass how Isaiah's unitary themes – paradoxically characterised as both particularist and universalist – play a crucial role in evaluating these issues. From a Korean perspective, then, this study will offer negative implications not only for pluralist essayers who stoutly rebut the exclusive divinity of Yahweh, but also for naïve iconoclasts who are vigorously involved in the wilful vandalism of other religions.

All biblical quoatations, unless otherwise mentioned, are taken from the *New Revised Standard Version*. The Hebrew term, יהוה, is rendered as 'Yahweh' in this work, except the quotations from the *New Revised Standard Version* where the Hebrew word is rendered as 'LORD.'

I wish to express my appreciation to those who have encouraged me in the writing of this research. Firstly, my heartfelt thanks must go to my supervisor, Professor Edgar W. Conrad, for his painstaking supervision, which in practice has led to the completion of this work. His sophisticated insight and provocative criticism have left the deepest impact upon my academic pilgrimage. Without his sage and careful guidance, this research would not ultimately have been accomplished. I have never met such a mentor who is devoted to sacrifices on behalf of his students. It is a rare privilege to have studied under the tutelage of this scholar. I am indebted to Professor Philip Almond, Head of School of Philosophy, History, Religion and Classics, at the University of Queensland for his wise counsel and generosity.

I am also extremely grateful to Dr. William J. Dumbrell, Dr. Joseph E. Coleson, Dr. Jung-Woo Kim, Dr. In-Gyu Hong, Dr. Yung-Han Kim and Dr. Sang-Gyu Lee who presented papers for the conference hosted by the

Australia-Asia Theological Society in which I have been involved as Director. They have provided me with the opportunity to be engaged in a stimulating debate both in their papers and in personal conversation, which has led to an avenue to develop my theological insight. I wish to express my thanks to Rev. Matthew Man-Young Kim, Rev. Jung-Oh Joo, Rev. Kyu-Hyun Lee and Mr. David Kee-Chul Hwang for their financial support that enabled the society to continue to make a contribution to Asia and Australia's theological discussion.

I am indeed grateful to Dr. Paul R. House whose meticulous suggestions made this research well balanced. I would also like to thank my fellows, Dr. Hereward Tilton, Dr. Johnson Lim, Mr. David L. Little, Dr. Chul-Hyun Park, Dr. Man-Soo Choe and Mr. Kee-Moon Sung for being interested in my research with invaluable advice.

Finally, I should express a great deal of gratitude to my family for their love, encouragement and care, without which this study would not have emerged, and I wholeheartedly thank my loving wife, SaMi, whose sacrificial travail led me to experience the wondrous moment when my first beloved son, Edward Ha-Yoon Jang, was born.

Soli Deo gloria!

Seoul, S. Korea, July 2004
Se-Hoon Jang

Abbreviations

BBR	*Bulletin for Biblical Research*
BST	The Bible Speaks Today
BZAW	Beihefte zur ZAW
CB	Coniectanea Biblica
CCC	The Crossway Classic Commentaries
CR:BS	*Currents in Research: Biblical Studies*
Ch	Chronicles
Eerdmans	William B. Eerdmans Publishing Company
ET	*The Expository Times*
Deu	Deuteronomy
DSB	The Daily Study Bible
Ex	Exodus
Gen	Genesis
IDB	Interpreter's Dictionary of the Bible
Isa	Isaiah
IVP	InterVarsity Press
JBL	*Journal of Biblical Literature*
JBS	*Journal of Bible Sarangbang*
Jr	Jeremiah
Kgs	Kings
JETS	*Journal of the Evangelical Theological Society*
JSOT	*Journal for the Study of the Old Testament*
JSOTSup	*Journal for the Study of the Old Testament* Supplements
LXX	Septuagint
MT	Masoretic Text
NCBC	New Century Bible Commentary
NICOT	New International Commentary on the Old Testament
NIB	The New Interpreter's Bible
NT	New Testament
OBT	Overtures in Biblical Theology
OBS	Oxford Bible Series
OT	Old Testament
OTL	Old Testament Theological Library

SVT	Studia in Veteris Testamenti
Psa	Psalm
TynBul	*Tyndale Bulletin*
VT	*Vetus Testamentum*
VTSupp	*Vetus Testamentum*, Supplements
WBC	Word Biblical Commentaries
WMBC	Westminster Bible Companion
WBT	Word Biblical Themes
ZAW	*Zeitschrift für die alttestamentliche Wissenschaft*

Introduction

The past two decades in Korea have seen the proliferation of publications on the debate concerning religious pluralism, in which both pluralist and evangelical writers have been vigorously involved. Indeed, the more the opposing sides have issued a sharp challenge to their opponents, the more the debate on pluralism has intensified rather than declined. Significantly, since Sun-Whan Pyun, a pioneer of contemporary pluralism in Korea, was expelled from the Korean Methodist Church in 1992, the issue of religious pluralism in Korea has been so central that a growing number of Korean scholars have been actively engaged in an intense dispute over the issue.

Furthermore, over the last decades, the Korean religious community has witnessed outbursts of iconoclastic practices resulting in the irresponsible eradication of other religious relics and temples. This appalling tragedy indicates that the issue of an extremist attitude toward other religions is of decisive importance, matching developments in the global community. Most recently, the terrible incident of the Sept. 11 2001 attacks on the World Trade Centre in New York has struck people with horror and some circles have identified Islam as the enemy.

This research will therefore be concerned with the emerging conflict on the international scene, in which the modern global society, including the Korean religious community, has been embroiled with these two major polemical issues, religious pluralism and iconoclastic vandalism. This study will offer a critical assessment of these highly contested issues from a Korean perspective by looking at a number of Isaiah's central themes, which can be identified as particularistic and universalistic. The thesis then will seek to elucidate the contemporary implications of Isaiah's particularistic and universalistic themes for a pluralistic world, especially for the Korean religious communities.

In this thesis, which will be divided into three parts, the first section will aim to show how the controversial issues (religious pluralism and iconoclastic vandalism) grow out of the larger international scene, and will help readers to appreciate specific debates as they emerged in Korea. The first chapter of Part I will present an overview of how contemporary

Christians, including the Korean Churches, have been overwhelmed by one of the most contentious issues, religious pluralism. Indeed, liberal pluralist ideology has been a fiery fuse causing intense conflicts between conservative camps, which retain a singular commitment to the one God, and liberal writers who espouse a pluralist worldview. It will thus focus on an exhaustive look at how contemporary pluralist writers, including Korean pluralists such as Sun-Whan Pyun, a pioneer of a modern pluralist approach in Korea, stoutly rebut an exclusive position, and how evangelical circles respond to pluralist ideology with resistance, intolerance and criticism.

The second chapter of Part I will be concerned with the elucidation of how the notion of iconoclasm has enmeshed the Korean Churches in a predicament. The dramatic outbursts of iconoclastic vandalism are adding more fuel to the antagonism between Christianity and the civil community. In short, the first section of the thesis will deal with the debate on these problematic issues, which have driven a wedge between the Korean Churches and other religious groups, in the context of the broader international scene.

Part II of the thesis will present a reading of the book of Isaiah as a whole by focussing on its unitary themes, which can play a central role in assessing these two issues of religious pluralism and iconoclasm. This section will present a concise analysis of contemporary biblical methods in Isaiah study in accordance with the four classifications (traditional, redactional, canonical and literary approaches). In this section, specific emphasis will be placed upon the thematic approach that this thesis adopts. It will be argued that the book of Isaiah is to be understood as a unitary whole, not as an incongruous collection consisting of the three independent sources, such as First, Second and Third Isaiah. It will be maintained in this section that the central focal points such as the Holy One of Israel or Jerusalem/Zion, which are brought into prominence in Isaiah, serve as clues for reading the book of Isaiah as a thematic unitary whole.

In Part III of the thesis, attention will be explicitly drawn to the unitary themes in Isaiah, such as the Holy One of Israel, monotheism, the unique role of Torah, Zion, the New Creation and the New Israel. This final part of the thesis will offer a fully-fledged description of what is characterised as particularistic and universalistic themes in Isaiah. It will be shown that in the book of Isaiah, Yahweh is depicted as the sole God while His unfailing love reaches to non-Israelites, who abandon idolatry and go on a pilgrimage to Zion to pay homage to Him with special tributes. Though no god besides Yahweh can have the exclusive power to deliver the broken hearted from the hands of fatal forces, access to His sanctuary, Zion, will be universally available to all nations that will put their faith in the one Holy God and be dubbed the "New Israel". More remarkably, it is metaphorically portrayed in the book of Isaiah that the new people of God will be invited to participate in an epoch-making era in which the whole universe will be transformed into a new creation.

Consequently, this final section will offer a critical assessment of the polemical issues, religious pluralism and iconoclastic vandalism, in the light of Isaian unitary themes that can be characterised as particularistic and universalistic. On the one hand, therefore, it will be claimed in the final section that a religious pluralistic stance should be recanted in the context of the Korean Churches who regard the biblical Scriptures including Isaiah as the revealed word of God and retain unswerving commitment to Yahweh. On the other hand, a Korean understanding of universalist facets of Isaiah's themes will urge Christians to respond to people of different religious practices with lenience, tolerance and sacrifice rather than chauvinism, bigotry and self-righteousness. It will be asserted, therefore, that Christian iconoclastic vandalism leading to the wilful obliteration of other religious statues must be forsaken.

Part I

Situating the Thesis

The past two decades in Korea have witnessed a serious division between two opposing camps, exclusivists and pluralists. No one has found a way to quell the controversies swirling around them. In particular, both circles in Korea have produced a variety of publications by mounting a severe critique of their opponent. The writings appear to have become adversarial and argumentative with little attempt to attain a mutual understanding. The purpose of this thesis is to find a way to open up constructive communication between the opposing positions.

It is important for my approach that the bulk of Korean Protestant Churches hold the Bible in high esteem. These opposing sides on no account suppress the pivotal role of the Bible and its significance in the Korean Churches. Their positions are based on the common belief of the Korean Protestant Churches who have an unswerving commitment to the biblical texts. It appears, however, that these two rivals arbitrarily employ biblical texts to sustain their different and mutually exclusive views. Some fundamentalist theologians firmly argue the point that religious pluralism is fallacious from a particularist perspective in the Bible, while they devalue or evade what are unequivocally described as universal factors in the biblical texts. In contrast, pluralists highlight God's universal characteristics, but give short shrift to His unique attributes in order to espouse their liberal pluralist theology. It appears, unfortunately, that both camps cling to their biased biblical interpretation devoid of a comprehensive elucidation of how the two themes, particularism and universalism, are predominantly set forth in the Bible.

Misfortunes are never single or simple. Some extreme iconoclasts, who are devoted to Christianity, have been actively involved in irresponsibly destroying religious relics, including Buddhist images in temples. What is more, several enthusiasts have been intensely resistant to the erection of Tangun statues at public schools and deeply committed to the unlawful eradication of them in secret. As a consequence, this iconoclasm has been another major issue in Korean religious societies, which adds more fuel to the antagonism between Christianity and other religions.

It will be of decisive significance, therefore, to canvass the two extraordinary concepts, particularism and universalism, which are prevalent in biblical books and to assess these main issues (pluralism and iconoclasm) overwhelming the Korean Churches from the perspective of these ostensibly contradictory themes. Given the fact that these two central focal points, are observed more predominantly in the book of Isaiah than the rest of the biblical texts, there can be no doubt that the book of Isaiah as a whole plays a crucial role in evaluating these two major issues in cotemporary Korean religious societies.

This part of thesis will aim to offer a concise overview of how conservative Christians in the contemporary world, especially in Korea, run afoul of pluralists, who, without hesitation, discard the exclusive position. It will also focus on the elucidation of how enthusiastic iconoclasts enmesh the Korean Churches in difficulties.

Chapter 1

The Korean Churches and Religious Pluralism

Without question, the ill-fated inquisition forced by the Korean Methodist General Assembly on the late Sun-Whan Pyun,[1] which transpired in 1992, has been engraved on one's mind as an unheard-of tragedy in the Korean Churches.[2] He was expelled from the Korean Methodist Church due to the emphasis he placed on liberal pluralist theology. The great majority of the Korean Methodist ministers expressed disapproval of Dr. Pyun's radical position with respect to religious pluralism since he first addressed it in his provocative article, "Other Religions and Theology," in 1984.[3] Some Methodist leaders appealed to the Korean Methodist Church to decide whether religious pluralism is in tune with the basic axioms of the Korean Methodist confession.

As a result, the Korean Methodist Church held a special General Assembly to canvass support for the accusation against Dr. Pyun, and this Assembly found it unacceptable for the Methodist Church to accommodate his pluralist ideology. Without a meticulous examination of his claims about pluralism, the General Assembly barred Dr. Pyun from the Korean Methodist Church and thereby nullified his ordination. Consequently, his colleagues and other proponents, who promulgated his ideas at other theological seminaries and universities, censured the General Assembly for its decision. They deprecated its premature decision as improvident since it was lopsidedly led by the leaders of the Korean Methodist Church, and strongly insisted that it be re-evaluated. Meanwhile, some theologians pointed out that it was unreasonable for the General Assembly to decide

1 Sun-Whan Pyun held a doctoral degree in Theology from Basel University in Switzerland. Before facing his sudden death in 1995, he was dean of the Korean Methodist theological seminary until his resignation from the seminary following the decision of the General Assembly.

2 For further information about this inquisition, see *Ministry & Theology*, 6 (1992), 254–47.

3 This article appeared in one of the leading theological journals in Korea, *The Theological Thought*, 47 (1984), 687–717.

upon Dr. Pyun's expulsion without scrupulous investigation of his liberal pluralist theology. In contrast to those arguing for a reconsideration of the Assembly's decision, a large proportion of the Methodist ministers, who were convinced that Dr. Pyun tarnished their traditional Methodist legacy, entirely accepted the decision without hesitation. Other Protestant ministers and theologians also endorsed the arguments of the General Assembly in order to preserve their denomination's conservative stance from the liberal pluralist worldview.

Since this fateful inquisition took place, religious pluralism has been a major issue stimulating scorching debates between conservative exclusivists and liberal pluralists. Furthermore, it is noteworthy that Korean theological journals have published a number of significant articles about religious pluralism, which reflect how Korean religious pluralism has become polemical and contentious in the Korean Churches. Given the fact that these Churches have been embroiled in an intense controversy on pluralism, it is of vital significance to elucidate the impact of religious pluralism, especially of Dr. Pyun and his proponents' pluralist theology on them while noting the conservative responses to it.

In this regard, one finds it of decisive importance to embark on quests not only for the challenge of Korean pluralists but also for the vigorous response of Korean conservative evangelicals to it. Such dissonant voices are not at an ebb but continue to add more fuel to a blistering debate on pluralism. At this stage in the pluralist debate, it is important to deal not only with how Korean pluralism has taken a position against the Korean evangelical camp, but also with how Korean evangelicals have mounted an acute criticism of pluralist writers. In this sense, I will seek to offer an in-depth look at the conflict between Korean pluralists and their naysayers, who belong to the Korean evangelical camp after dealing with influential pluralist ideologies in the contemporary world and conservative evangelicals' responses to them.

1. Contemporary Christians facing religious pluralism

In order to understand the debate on religious pluralism in Korea, one finds it essential to trace the larger theological debate as it has emerged in the wider theological community outside Korea.

Over the past two decades, religious pluralism has been regarded as one of the most influential ideologies in the religious arena. Though the impact of inclusivism, which once dominated the 1970s, has not ceased,[4] the unblushing challenge of contemporary religious pluralism has been much more threatening to Christianity than the inclusive view ever was. Though conservative camps stoutly rebut this new belief system, its penetration has been so rapid that a growing number of Christian scholars increasingly sympathize with religious pluralists. Despite the propagation of this radical worldview, it is interesting that each of its proponents respectively offers its articulation in its various manifestations. There are, therefore, different voices elaborating its central point.

From the perspective of diversity, I now seek to focus on three leading contemporary religious pluralists by outlining their different underlying theories in order to show how religious pluralism gives short shrift to the contemporary Christian. Then I will draw attention to several conservative theologians who continue to adhere to the exclusive view in order to explicate how the contemporary Christian should be intensely resistant to religious pluralism in today's pluralistic global community.

1.1. Religious pluralistic voices in today's world

1.1.1. John Hick

Without question, John Hick is one of the most profound and prestigious religious pluralists today. He was born in Scarborough, Yorkshire, on 20 January 1922 and brought up in a family with long-standing ties to the

4 This theory is mainly advocated by Post-Vatican II Catholic scholars such as Karl Rahner who proposes a well-known inclusive view, "anonymous Christian," referring to all religious people who are ultimately to be saved by Christ despite the absence of the experience of Christian life. Likewise, this point is brought out by even some Protestant scholars, especially by a prominent Protestant inclusivist Clark Pinnock.

Anglican Church. During his earlier life, Hick underwent his first spiritual conversion, resulting in his accommodation as "a whole and without question the entire evangelical package of theology – the verbal inspiration of the Bible; creation and fall; Jesus as God the Son incarnate, born of a virgin, conscious of his divine nature, and performing miracles of divine power; redemption by his blood from sin and guilt; his bodily resurrection and ascension and future return in glory; heaven and hell."[5] In other words, at this stage, Hick's religious faith was predicated on the conviction that Jesus Christ is the unique Saviour, while all other religions are not salvific but false, and that unbelievers are inevitably driven to eternal perdition.

Then he began his ministry with the Presbyterian Church of England. He also involved himself in the study of philosophy and theology at several universities such as Edinburgh, Oxford and Cambridge. Hick taught the subject of the philosophy of religion at universities in both the United States and England and was appointed the H. G. Wood Professorial Chair in Birmingham University's Theology Department in 1967. The environment of Birmingham, marked by a multi-cultural, multi-racial and multi-faith lifestyle led Hick to a new radical conversion, which produced in him a paradigm shift to the theology of religious pluralism. Here he proposed a "Copernican revolution in the theology of religion," in two provocative books, *God and the Universe of Faiths* (1973) and *God has many names* (1980), which not only mount a severe critique of the traditional exclusive theory but also accommodate a God-centred model. In 1982, he moved to California in the United States to take up the Danforth Chair in the Philosophy of Religion at the Claremont Graduate School where his religious pluralism came to full bloom.[6]

Hick's Copernican revolution in the theology of religion

Having felt aversion to the traditional exclusive view that Jesus Christ is unique and that there is no salvation outside the church, Hick advocated his innovative religious pluralism by introducing a path-breaking theory

5 John Hick, "A Pluralist View," in *Four Views on Salvation in A Pluralistic World*, (eds.) Dennis L. Okholm & Timothy R. Philips (Grand Rapids: Zondervan Publishing House, 1996), 30; idem, *God Has Many Names* (Philadelphia: The Westminster Press, 1982), 15.

6 See John Hick, "A Pluralist View," in *Four Views on Salvation in A Pluralistic world*, 37–8.

referred to as a Copernican revolution. He argued that the Christocentric view is nothing more than a Ptolemaic position, which assumes that the earth plays a pivotal role as the centre of the universe. He uncompromisingly insists that just as the Ptolemaic view was inevitably replaced by a Copernican cosmology in which the centre of the solar system is not the earth but the sun, so the ecclesiocentric or Christocentric view that outside Christianity there is no salvation must be abrogated and substituted by a theocentric conception that "it is God who is at the centre and that all the religions of mankind, including our own, serve and revolve around him."[7] He maintains:

> The Copernican revolution in astronomy consisted in a transformation of the way in which men understood the universe and their own location within it. It involved a radical shift from the dogma that the earth is the centre of the revolving universe to the realisation that the sun is at the centre, with all the planets, including our own earth, moving around it. And the Copernican revolution in theology must involve an equally radical transformation of our conception of the universe of faiths and the place of our own religion within it.[8]

God-centred theory

Hick proceeds to accommodate a Kantian distinction between the noumenal world and the phenomenal world in order to enhance his God-centred model. According to the distinguished philosopher, Immanuel Kant, the noumenal world itself cannot be perceived by human consciousness since its existence transcends all of what is experienced in a terrestrial world, while the phenomenal world refers to the perceived object, a world that appears to reflect its real world. Similarly Hick claims that all religions are nothing but various phenomenal manifestations of the one noumenal Reality. Hick's point is that the different forms of all religions derive from their different consciousness or experience of a transcendent divine Reality or "the Eternal One" called God. Hick asserts, then, that all belief systems, including nontheistic religions such as Buddhism, point directly to the same God.

7 John Hick, *God Has Many Names,* 36.
8 Ibid.

Furthermore, following in Karl Jaspers' footsteps,[9] Hick seeks to focus on the reconstruction of the history of ancient religions, a history that is divided into two ages, the primitive age and the axial age. The former refers to a period when so called natural religion marked by various forms of worship associated with spirits, legendary figures, or territorial gods was dominant, a worship system that personifies the powers of nature. By contrast, the latter points to an era in which the human sophisticated sense of the divine Reality was expressed "in the teachings of any of the great spiritual masters, such as Isaiah or Jesus or Gautama or Muhammad or Kabir or Nanak,"[10] a period that dates from approximately 800 to approximately 200 B.C. Hick remarks:

> Thus the axial age was a uniquely significant band of time in man's religious history. With certain qualifications one can say that in this period all the major religious options, constituting the different forms of human awareness of the Eternal One, were identified and established, and that nothing of comparably novel significance has happened in the religious life of mankind since.[11]

According to Hick, then, the development of world religions is nothing less than the process of sophistication in the religious sense of the Eternal One expressed in different and particular cultures, languages, histories and so on. Hick comes to the conclusion that though a variety of forms of religion, which have their own individual founders and peculiar teachings, have existed in different cultural contexts, they are nothing more than different phenomenal manifestations of the one divine noumenon or the Eternal One. In this sense, Hick argues that the Ptolemaic ecclesiocentric or Christocentric position must be replaced by the Copernican theocentric view since all religions are just different experiential transformations of the same God, a point that indicates that all religions cling to the same Real/Ultimate/Divine.[12]

9 Hick consults Karl Jaspers' *The Origin and Goal of History* (Yale University Press, 1953), to reconstruct the history of all the myriad diversity of world religions. See ibid., 45.

10 Ibid.

11 Ibid., 46.

12 See John Hick, "A Pluralist View," in *Four Views on Salvation in A Pluralistic World*, 46–51.

1.1.2. Raimundo Panikkar

One can agree that Raimundo Panikkar is one of most influential and celebrated religious pluralists in today's world, though some oppose his identification as a pluralist. His mother was a Spanish Roman Catholic, while his father was an Indian Hindu. As a result, he was reared in the two different religious climates, which played a crucial role as an initial ground for nourishing his religious scholarship. Because of his interests in various academic areas, he holds doctorates in science (Madrid), philosophy (Madrid) and theology (Rome). He was ordained a Roman Catholic priest in 1946 and taught at Harvard University beginning in 1966. He then took up a post as professor of comparative philosophy of religion at the University of California in Santa Barbara in 1972, and retired in 1987.

The intra-religious dialogue among religions in the world

Pannikar has produced a prolific number of works both in philosophy and in religion. He identifies himself as a religious pluralist who seeks to lead the intra-religious dialogue in today's world.[13] Unlike John Hick who dilutes somewhat the distinctive traits of world religions, Panikkar does not besmirch all the myriad diversity of them but has great regard for the peculiar theologies of various religions and their significance. His focus on "an ecumenical ecumenism" clearly points to "unity without harming diversity."[14] The phrase, "an ecumenical ecumenism," not only refers to a unified movement among a range of churches or denominations in Christianity, but also includes intra-religious dialogue. It is noteworthy, here, that Panikkar prefers the use of the term, "intra-religious dialogue" rather than "inter-religious dialogue." He explains this point in this way:

> If interreligious dialogue is to be real dialogue, an intrareligious dialogue must accompany it, i.e., it must begin with my questioning myself and the relativity of my beliefs (which does not mean their relativism), accepting the challenge of a change, a conversion and the risk of upsetting my traditional patterns.[15]

He maintains:

13 For a further discussion of the notion of intra-religious dialogue, see R. Panikkar, *The Intrareligious Dialogue* (New York: Paulist Press, 1978).

14 Paul F. Knitter, *No Other Name? A Critical Survey of Christian Attitudes Toward the World Religion* (London: SCM Press, 1985), 153.

15 Raimundo Panikkar, *The Intrareligious Dialogue*, 40.

> The aim of the intrareligious dialogue is understanding. It is not to win over the other or to come to a total agreement or a universal religion. The ideal is communication in order to bridge the gulfs or mutual ignorance and misunderstandings between the different cultures of the world, letting them speak and speak out their own insights in their own languages.[16]

This new understanding of intra-religious dialogue prompts him to move beyond the inclusive position that God's self-disclosure is ultimately manifested in the historical Jesus through whom all religions can be salvific. Apart from the notion of the definitive normativity of Christ, which is articulated in the first edition of his *The Unknown Christ of Hinduism* (1964), Panikkar clearly expresses the adoption of a pluralist position without hesitation in the revised edition of the book (1981), in which a dramatic shift in his understanding of the religious worldview is made most apparent.

The notion of the universal Christ

Panikkar calls for a new alternative religious pluralistic view, that is, an "authentically universal Christology" or "cosmic Christ," a notion that is initially claimed in his best-known masterpiece, *Unknown Christ of Hinduism,* which was first published in 1964 but entirely revised in 1981.[17] In order to heighten the need for the intra-communication between miscellaneous religious cultures or traditions, Panikkar proposes a new religious paradigm shift in the revised edition of the book by highlighting the concept of "an authentically universal Christology." To begin with, Panikkar resists the Christian's traditional confession that only the historical Jesus is able to embody the Christ. On this position he is unmovable, he goes on to assert that no singular historical event or person can be the only and ultimate manifestation of the Christ who transcends all historical events or facts that humans undergo in the phenomenal world.

Then he argues that the Christ is by no means confined to a specific historical figure such as Jesus or Budda. Accordingly, an attempt to minimise the Christ to the one figure such as the historical Jesus whom Christians embrace as the fully personified Christ is nothing more than the process of idolisation. While he sympathises with those Christians

16 Ibid., xxvii.

17 Raimundo Panikkar, *The Unknown Christ of Hinduism* (Maryknoll: Orbis Books, 1981, rev. ed.).

who take up the position that Jesus is an ultimate manifestation of Christ, he is strongly resistant to the suggestion that the historical Jesus of Nazareth is the sole and absolute form of Christ. Instead, he maintains that Jesus is nothing but an historical form of the real ultimate Christ. This point indicates that a Christian has no monopoly on Christ. In short, he believes, "salvation by faith is present in all religions. God uses them as the normal channels whereby their followers attain salvation; and Christ, the Lord, the Word has not been confined to the human Jesus but has been more widely at work."[18]

1.1.3. John B. Cobb, Jr.

It is commonly agreed that John B. Cobb, Jr. is a prominent scholar among pluralist writers today. He studied at the University of Michigan, the University of Chicago, and the University of Chicago's Divinity School. Then he was appointed professor of theology at the School of Theology at Claremont, California, and was once Director of the Centre for Process Studies at Claremont. Some contemporary pluralists, who maintain a God-centred scheme, label Cobb an inclusivist who remains adherent to a Christocentric stance. After observing the major differences between the miscellaneous characteristics of all religions, Cobb finds it essential to redefine the meaning of pluralism in a more fundamental way. He states:

> How odd I find it to be writing for a collection of essays in criticism of theologies espousing religious pluralism! Yet I have agreed to do so because of the very narrow way – indeed an erroneous way, I think – in which pluralism has come to be defined. By that definition of pluralism, I am against pluralism. But I am against pluralism for the sake of a fuller and more genuine pluralism.[19]

In this way, Cobb asserts without reluctance that his belief system is more fundamental pluralism than the existing theocentric model.

18 Frank Whaling, "Theories of Religion," in *The Blackwell Encyclopaedia of Modern Christian Thought*, (ed.) Alister E. McGrath (Oxford: Blackwell, 1993), 549.

19 John B. Cobb, Jr., "Beyond 'Pluralism,'" in *Christian Uniqueness Reconsidered: The Myth of a Pluralistic Theology of Religions*, (ed.) Gavin D'Costa (Maryknoll: Orbis Books, 1992), 81.

Reconsidering the meaning of pluralism

To begin with, he is not reluctant to point out a critical problem with a God-centred theory that places a heavy emphasis on the centripetal feature of the Transcendent/the Ultimate/the Eternal One that serves as the starting point of inter-religious dialogue. The primary argument of religious pluralists such as John Hick had been that the transcendent Reality is the essence or base of all religious experiences, and that all religious traditions and cultures are ultimately nothing less than different manifestations of this same common ground. Having criticized representative pluralists like John Hick for failing to notice a variety of dissimilarities between all religious worldviews, he overtly resists the fundamental thesis of a God-centred model because it functions as a condition of dialogue among the world's religions. Rather than taking a God-centred approach, he calls for the need to draw attention to the various discrepancies, incongruities, and mutual contradictions among all religions. He remarks:

> Consider the case of Buddhism and Confucianism in China. What of their relative value and validity? They coexisted there through many centuries, not primarily as alternate routes to the same goal, but as complementary. In crude oversimplification, Confucianism took care of public affairs, while Buddhism dealt with the inner life. Perhaps one might go on to say that they were about equally successful in fulfilling their respective roles, but that statement would be hard to support and does not seem especially important.[20]

In this regard, Cobb makes it evident that it is unnecessary for religious societies to focus on the adoption of theocentricism in order to foster communication between different religious traditions and cultures. Rather, he affirms that it is achievable to intensify the interaction between Christianity and other religions without adherence to the idea of common essence of all religions. He also finds it possible to establish the genuine pluralism, which differs entirely from a God-centred model supported by many contemporary pluralists such as John Hick.

Towards a mutual transformation through inter-religious dialogue

The impact of process theology, especially of the thought of the notable English philosopher and pioneer of process philosophy, Alfred North Whitehead, led Cobb to a turning point in his understanding of religions.

20 Ibid., 83.

According to process theology, the world is an integrated, interrelated, and interdependent organic whole that through a process of change reaches toward a zenith of its ultimate potential. Indeed, all entities are so mutable and changing that they affect others even while receiving influence from them, a process that enables them to move towards a full development. By analogy with the basic principle of process theology, Cobb seeks to stress the need of mutual transformation through inter-dialogue among religions while preserving the distinctive features of their ethic, culture, teaching, and tenet. He illustrates this point in the following:

> For example, all three traditions [Judaism, Islam and Christianity] borrowed extensively from Greek philosophy. Especially in the case of Christianity and Islam, this borrowing involved, for good and ill, a profound transformation. In the case of Christianity it can be argued that its ultimate victory over Neo-Platonism for the commitment of the intelligentsia of the late Roman Empire was due to its ability to assimilate the wisdom of Neo-Platonism, while the Neo-Platonic philosophers were not equally able to assimilate the wisdom of the Hebrew and Christian scriptures.[21]

Cobb comes to the realisation that each religion ought to encounter different traditions to learn from them, a process that generates a mutual transformation which enables all religions to meet their ultimate potential. Each religious group finds it unnecessary to accommodate the notion of a common essence of all religions by giving up its traditional confession and uniqueness in order to build up inter-religious dialogue. It is his conviction, therefore, that Christians are able to promote their self-transformation through mutual dialogue with other religious traditions, because "to learn from others whatever truth they have to offer and to integrate that with the insights and wisdom we have learned from our Christian heritage appears to be faithful to Christ."[22]

1.2 Conservative evangelical responses to pluralism

1.2.1. D. A. Carson

D. A. Carson is a learned New Testament scholar and one of the foremost theologians of our time. He is well known as the author of numerous

21 Ibid., 90.
22 Ibid., 91.

books and co-author of several works. D. A. Carson was the son of a Baptist minister and grew up in the Baptist tradition. He took his doctoral degree in N. T. from Cambridge University under the supervision of Prof. Barnabas Lindars,[23] and has taught for many years at Trinity Evangelical Divinity School in Deerfield, Illinois, USA. Currently he is research professor of New Testament at the school. While he is best known as a New Testament commentator, his interest in the subject of religious pluralism dominates his scholarship, a fact that is evident in his prolific articles on pluralism that eventually appeared in his magnum opus, *The Gagging of God: Christianity Confronts Pluralism* (1996). This ponderous book is divided into four parts concerned with several issues in association with the subject of religious pluralism.

Here I will not scrutinise the whole book in its entirety, but will specifically focus on the examination of the second part entitled "Religious Pluralism," which deals with the principal assumption of prominent pluralists that on purpose evades or invalidates the unique attributes of God whose divine revelation is made explicit in the Bible. Then I will canvass Carson's strenuous argument that the authority of Bible and the significance of its plot-line remain relevant to our modern society, especially to contemporary Christians who wholeheartedly embrace the biblical books.

The Bible and its authority

D. A. Carson mounts an acute criticism of what he understands to be the pluralist's distorted view on the biblical image of God. He seeks to bind the debate on religious pluralism to the authority of the Bible. He unreservedly contends that the God of pluralism has no affinities with the God of the Bible. According to some notable pluralists such as John Hick, as we have seen above, all religious ideologies, cultures, and traditions are equally responses to the Ultimate/the Reality/the Transcendent, that is, an unknown God. However, Carson firmly takes up the conviction that the full presentation of God is unambiguously set forth in the Bible, especially in its plot-line, which extends from Creation to New Creation plainly depicted in Rev. 21:1–22:5. He goes on to underline two points: "(1) The

23 As co-editor he was involved in publishing a festschrift for his mentor. See *It is Written: Scripture Citing Scripture: Essays in Honour of Barnabas Lindars*, SSF, (eds.) D. A. Carson & H. G. M. Williamson (Cambridge: Cambridge University Press, 1988).

God of the Bible is a God who acts and talks. He is personal. The Christian's view of the Bible is tied to the doctrine of God, who discloses himself in deeds and words. (2) The Bible is simultaneously the product of God's mind and of human minds."[24]

He affirms that the biblical image of God as Person, Transcendent and Sovereign, is extremely alien to the notion of an unknown Reality of religious pluralists. Carson labels such pluralists idolaters who adhere to an unnamed Eternal One that has nothing to do with the biblical portrait of God as Sovereign Creator, Redeemer and Restorer. He observes:

> The pluralist is an idolater, worshiping the created world more than the Creator... Pluralists are inconsistent in that they want to be understood univocally while insisting that ancient authors, let alone God himself, cannot be. There may be many religious experiences, but none of them deals with the heart of the human problem, the sin that is so deeply a part of our nature.[25]

He ventures, thus, that those who earnestly embrace the Bible must emphatically object to the pluralists' understanding of an unidentified Reality. Furthermore, he also forcefully opposes the inclusive position claimed by experts such as John Sanders and Clark Pinnock who presuppose the possibility of salvation for the sake of those who wouldn't have heard the good news about the work of Christ. It seems to him that such inclusivism seldom does justice to what the biblical books say not only about God's unfailing love reaching to all nations but also about His wrath on offenders. While inclusivists intend to tease out some inclusive expressions found in the biblical texts, Carson focuses on a package of the exclusive biblical passages that he thinks they misconstrue. Then he criticises inclusivists in this way:

> Judging by the Bible's story-line, one must strenuously object to readings of Scripture that infer from every reference to God's sovereign activity among the nations, evidence of God's saving work… Although Sanders and especially Pinnock often speak of the importance of faith, they rarely listen to what the New Testament has to say about the content of faith, about the object of faith.[26]

24 See D. A. Carson, *The Gagging of God: Christianity Confronts Pluralism* (Leicester: APOLLOS, 1996), 153.

25 Ibid., 278.

26 Ibid., 291, 296.

In this instance, he concludes that the more the liberal idea such as pluralism or inclusivism makes deep inroads into Christianity, the more the authority of the Bible, which never focuses on an unknown God but the God named Yahweh, is challenged and might even be destroyed.

Against pluralists' historical reconstruction

Here Carson's scrupulous analysis of the pluralists' historical reconstructions deserves consideration. Surprisingly, the pluralists' attempt to rebuild the history of ancient religions, including Judaism, utilizes the standard historical approach to the biblical texts. As indicated earlier, John Hick places emphasis on a significant period dubbed "the axial age" in which the major world religions came into existence. Hick argues, "While Abraham is the semilegendary patriarch of Judaism and the exodus is its founding event, yet surely the distinctive Jewish understanding of the Eternal One and the relationship in which this understanding was embodied were formed very largely by the great prophets of the axial period."[27]

Here Carson critically challenges Hick's attempt to reconstruct Israelite religion and its ancient history. In his analysis, this radical assumption not only abrogates the plot-line found in the Hebrew Bible, but also redates the Old Testament documents as late as the prophetic period. It seems to him that Hick's approach to the ancient religions tends to follow in the footsteps of historical criticism, especially of source theory, that intends to re-construct ancient Israelite religion. Then he turns to probe three main approaches to the Hebrew Scriptures, especially to its monotheism in order to demonstrate the significance of the story-line in the Bible, which "begins with monotheism and, owing to the Fall, witnesses to the corruption of the knowledge of God and therefore to the rise of assorted false religions and false gods and distorted notions of the one true God."[28]

Having scrutinized contemporary attempts to reconstruct Old Testament history and their shortcomings, Carson asserts that many historical reconstructions rarely devote attention to the plot-line set forth in the Old Testament. He maintains:

> Historical reconstructions that attempt to crowd so many of the Old Testament books into a relatively brief period from about Josiah to the end of the Exile tend to focus enormous attention on the fall and restoration of Jerusalem and its temple,

27 John Hick, *God Has Many Names*, 46.

28 D. A. Carson, *The Gagging of God: Christianity Confronts Pluralism*, 247.

> and de-emphasize the earlier step in the plot-line. And from a Christian point of view, of course, the plot-line must be continued into the new covenant if the old covenant is to be seen in its proper proportions.[29]

It is Carson's judgement that Hick's understanding of the origin of ancient Israelite religion has affinities with contemporary evolutionary approaches to religions that assume that the world religions develop from a simple belief system like animism into a sophisticated religion related to monotheism. In this sense, Carson comes to the conclusion that one must be adamantly opposed to the pluralists' approach to Israelite history, which is a detriment to the Christian faith. At the same time he maintains that Christians must embrace the story-line in the Hebrew Bible that offers a full presentation of the one God called Yahweh.

1.2.2. Alister E. McGrath

It is commonly agreed in evangelical and non-evangelical circles that Alister E. McGrath is a considerable theologian who is committed to the revival of evangelicalism in a pluralist society. By holding two doctoral degrees in science and theology from Oxford University, which he achieved while he was in his twenties, he became distinguished in the scholarly world at an early age. What is more, the proliferation of his publications on various and extensive subjects such as Reformation, Enlightenment, evangelicalism, postmodernism, religious studies, and so forth made him a leading evangelist in a short period of time. He is currently principal of Wycliffe Hall at Oxford University. He is also research lecturer in theology at the University, and serves as research professor of systematic theology at Regent College in Vancouver in Canada. Having taken up the subject of religious pluralism, McGrath seeks to pose a strenuous resistance to liberal pluralist ideologies in his stimulating book, *A Passion for Truth* (1996), which is rigorously based upon evangelical conviction.

Religious pluralism and its imperialism

McGrath centres his attention on the impact of western-centred academics on liberal pluralist theology. He finds it ironic that contemporary pluralism, which poses the fundamental objection to the exclusive faith claimed by Christian evangelism that Jesus Christ is not only the ultimate

29 Ibid., 247–8.

embodiment of God but also the unique mediator of salvation, is imperialistic. As pointed out earlier, recent liberal pluralists such as John Hick are totally committed to the vigorous defence of the notion of an unknown God conceived or experienced among the world's religions. According to them, this God-centred model functions as a starting point of inter-dialogue among the religions of the world. They maintain that the uncertain assumption that all religious traditions are no less than equally valid but different phenomenal manifestations of the same divine noumenon must be an inevitable condition of inter-religious dialogue.

Here McGrath has argued clearly and convincingly that an undeniable factor of imperialism is deeply harboured in this God-centred theory, a principle which is often illuminated in the famous story about blind people who rarely perceive the whole form of an elephant, but just experience its part. Then he claims:

> For some to assert that she or he sees the big picture, while Christians and others see only part, amounts to imperialism, unless it can be shown to be universally available, a public knowledge which is open to general scrutiny and critical evaluation... Writers such as John Hick have insisted that the obvious differences between the world 'religions' are due to their different perceptions of 'the Real.' Yet no empirical evidence of any substance has been offered for this assertion.[30]

Though both the great majority of Buddhists and Christians are loath to agree to the proposal that they equally worship the same ultimate Transcendent, modern liberal puralists continue to impose the notion of Deity or the Real on all religious believers. In addition, the claim that all the world's religions are nothing but different experiential forms of the same Reality is so uncertain and unverifiable that it is nothing less than a phenomenological claim. In other words, this dubious approach is biased toward an empirical assumption of the pluralist theorists that lacks demonstration. In this sense, McGrath has no doubt that an attempt to force religious believers to embrace such a phenomenological claim is little more than the vestiges of western oriented imperialism. He states:

> One of the most serious difficulties which arises from John Hick's model is that it is not individual religions which have access to truth; it is the western liberal pluralist, who insists that each religion must be seen in the context of others, before it can be evaluated. As many have pointed out, this means that the western liberal

30 Alister E. McGrath, *A Passion for truth: The intellectual Coherence of Evangelicalism* (Leicester: APOLLOS, 1996), 212–13.

> doctrine of religious pluralism is defined as the only valid standpoint for evaluating individual religions... Yet is not this approach shockingly imperialist?[31]

After considering obvious dissimilarities among the basic doctrines of each religion, McGrath firmly avers that it is totally illegitimate to hold the view that there is an essence of all religions, and that Christians and other believers, including Muslims, worship the same Divinity. This is because many religious pluralists fail to perceive the various and distinctive features existing among the world's religions. He points out further that Christianity and other religions such as Judaism are based on entirely different belief systems concerning the work of Jesus and His crucifixion. While adherents of Judaism do not identify Jesus with the final Messiah through whom the fullness of God's self-disclosure is manifested, Christians retain heartfelt loyalty to Jesus Christ by worshiping Him as the Son of God who became the unique Saviour.

One also finds it difficult to identify the point of agreement between the key doctrine of both Christians and Muslims. For Christians Jesus must be identified with the unique and final mediator of salvation, while Muslims deem Muhammed to be the great prophet through whom God's final self-disclosure is delivered. What is more, Islam embraces the Qur'an as the authoritative revelation of God, whereas Christianity regards the Bible as the ultimate inspired word of God. McGrath strongly insists that there can be dialogue between Christians and other believers, including Muslims and Jews, without dismissing the exclusive fundamental belief of each of these religions. Clearly, then, any attempt to impose a dubious liberal idea of an unknown God on each religion is undoubtedly imperialist.

The evangelical understanding of salvation

McGrath accepts the reformed position of John Calvin who makes a distinction between a knowledge of God the creator revealed through nature and a knowledge of God the redeemer manifested only through Jesus Christ in order to initiate his evangelical understanding of God. According to liberal pluralist writers, it is essential to take the theocentric approach that all religions are substantially oriented to the one divinity in order to promote inter-dialogue between the world's religions. Yet Mc-

31 Ibid., 219.

Grath makes the point that the Christian understanding of salvation is closely interwoven with the person and work of Jesus Christ. Having been intensely resistant to the radical assumption that all religions are just different but equally valid routes to the ultimate salvation, McGrath comments:

> There is enormous variation within the religions in relation to the nature of salvation. Christian conceptions of salvation focus on the establishment of a relationship between God (in the Christian sense of the term) and his people, and use a variety of images to articulate its various aspects. Underlying these convergent images of salvation is the common theme of 'salvation in and through Christ' – that is to say, that salvation is a possibility only on account of the life, death and resurrection of Jesus Christ, and that salvation is shaped in his likeness.[32]

In other words, the traditional Christian view is that all of humankind can only be saved through the work of Jesus Christ on the cross. Without the particularity of Jesus as the Christ, there can be no salvation. It is from this Christian worldview that McGrath concludes that the sole religion to proclaim the good news of salvation is Christianity. He asserts that it is only through a knowledge of Jesus Christ that salvation is available to all human beings who, without a knowledge of Jesus Christ, partially and indirectly perceive God's divine creatorship through nature but fail to acknowledge and worship Him as their maker. In this sense, he suggests that this evangelical position is at odds with a radical pluralist proposal that adherents of all religions are saved, whether or not they are committed to explicit personal faith in Jesus Christ.

1.2.3. R. Douglas Geivett and W. Gary Philips

R. Douglas Geivett and W. Gary Philips are regarded as leading young evangelicals who take a profound interest in the issue of contemporary pluralism. Geivett teaches philosophy at the School of Theology at Biola University, while Philips teaches Bible and theology at Bryan College. In recent notable papers, they countenance neither pluralism nor inclusivism, but advocate a particularistic view that salvation is dependent on an explicit faith in Jesus Christ and his work. This stance leads them to mount a powerful attack on modern pluralist theology. In particular, in a signifi-

32 Ibid., 232.

cant book[33] edited by Dennis L. Okholm & Timothy R. Phillips, which deals with the four principal understandings of salvation in a plurality of religion, they focus on a steadfast apologetic for biblical authority fatally challenged by pluralist essayists.

Particularism and the divine revelation of God

Geivett and Philips refuse to compromise with pluralists who repudiate the final authority of the Bible. It is their view that having been influenced by historical criticism, especially by higher criticism, liberal pluralist writers like John Hick strongly deprecate the claim that the Bible is the unique inspired Word of God. In response to what they see as an attack on biblical authority, they begin with what they perceive to be the revelation of God. They draw a distinction between general revelation and special revelation as sources of religious knowledge in order to enhance their evidential approach for defending particularism. They make the point that general revelation, by means of which God unveils His divine presence in the created world, functions in a crucial role by reflecting God's willingness to redeem humans from the profound abyss of their sin and its effects. In other words, this Christian natural theology stresses that this general revelation leads fallen humankind to anticipate a special revelation from God in connection with His specific remedy to the fateful predicament of humanity. They observe:

> General revelation supports the expectation of special revelation. General revelation also teaches us where and how to look for a revelation from God that addresses concrete human spiritual needs, so that the divine remedy can be recognised and appropriated by human persons.[34]

Geivett and Philips turn to an elaboration of what they understand to be the two key sources of special revelation, which show the diagnosis and prescription for all humans who are in a predicament caused by fatal sins. According to them, the two underlying elements, the Old and New Testaments of the Bible and the Incarnation of Jesus, are the chief sources of special revelation from God. They propose three central points in relation

33 See their article, "A Particularist view: An Evidentialist Approach," in *Four Views On Salvation In a Pluralistic World,* (eds.) Dennis L. Okholm & Timothy R. Phillips (Grand Rapids: Zondervan Publishing House, 1996), 213–270.

34 Ibid., 218.

to the Christian understanding of a particular revelation from God. First, they hold the view that the Bible shows the image of God as the personal Creator of the universe who rules and intervenes in all events and affairs of the universe and who has a particular regard for humankind made as His image.[35]

Then they proceed to take up the point that good news is available through the gospel of Jesus Christ who is the final and ultimate embodiment of God's merciful initiative. Furthermore, it is of vital significance to recognise that the unparalleled historical event, the resurrection of Jesus Christ, plays a central role in confirming this good news. In other words, it is noteworthy that unlike other religious traditions, which are seldom as dependent on a real historical fact as Christianity, the Christian faith is vigorously grounded upon the genuine historical fact of the resurrection of Jesus. They maintain:

> Thus, Christianity has little value as a religious story or myth if its record of the events surrounding the life, death, and resurrection of Jesus is not historically accurate. Christianity cannot be accommodated to the hypothesis of religious pluralism without such great distortion that it ceases to be Christianity.[36]

In contrast to religious pluralists strongly resistant to biblical authority, Geivett and Philips are committed to the vigorous defence of a special revelation from God, namely, the divine origin of Christian Scriptures, in which the foremost historical events, the life, death, and resurrection of Jesus Christ, are brought to witness.

The biblical evidences of a particularist view

Geivett and Philips are concerned, then, to show how the Bible, especially some chief passages such as Acts 4:12; John 3:16, 18; 14:6; 17:20; Romans 10:9–15 and so on, authenticate the particularist position that salvation is dependent only on an explicit faith in Jesus Christ who fulfils God's saving initiative to rescue all humankind whose nature is totally distorted by sins. Having expounded those expressions oriented on particularism, Geivett and Philips forcefully argue that such references to particularism found in the Bible neither support religious pluralism nor confirm inclusivism. Rather it is their judgment that these biblical texts lead

35 Ibid., 227.
36 Ibid., 228.

to the positive affirmation that salvation is available only through Jesus Christ who is God in the flesh and who mediates God's salvific will on behalf of sinful humanity. Furthermore, they raise a crucial question in the following way:

> If the pluralist is right, there is little danger in promoting either inclusivism or particularism. If the inclusivist is right, there is little danger in promoting particularism, though it would be risky to promote pluralism. But if the particularist is right – and, on the supposition of epistemic parity, he is about as likely to be right – then there is great danger in promoting either inclusivism or pluralism. If particularism is true, then pluralism and inclusivism offer dangerously misleading assessments of the human condition and of the prospects for resolving the human predicament.[37]

In other words, as thorough defenders of Christian particularism, Geivett and Philips conclude that the many biblical references to the particularist stance they espouse make it impossible to adopt pluralism or inclusivism. Thus they assert that salvation is available only through Jesus Christ whose historical life, death and resurrection are the locus of the Christian faith.

So far my discussion has been focused on a broad overview of the cutthroat debate between liberal pluralists and evangelical particularists. As noted earlier, Hick strongly insists that a theocentric approach that all religious traditions are no less than different experiential forms of the Real/Transcendent/Ultimate called an unknown God must be an essential condition for inter-religious dialogue. Panikkar continues to espouse his pluralist idea that the cosmic Christ is not exclusively experienced in Christianity but universally manifested in all religious groups. As a pioneer of dialogue between Christianity and other religions, especially Buddhism, Cobb places distinctive emphasis on process theology centred on mutual transformation through dialogue in order to enhance the genuine pluralism concerned with the inconsistencies, the discrepancies, and the mutual exclusions among the religions of the world.

On the other hand, Carson stoutly resists any aspects of pluralistic worldview that dilute the authority of the Bible where God is portrayed as the unique personal divine named Yahweh. Also he poses fundamental objections to the pluralist's attempt to reconstruct ancient Israelite history found in the Old Testament resulting in the rejection of its story-line.

37 Ibid., 245.

McGrath assiduously resists liberal pluralism that imposes a theocentric view on all religious believers, while himself retaining a singular commitment to the uniqueness and finality of Jesus Christ. Geivett and Philips convincingly claim that salvation is dependent on an explicit faith in Jesus Christ who serves as the ultimate and final embodiment of God.

Given the fact that each rival mounts a severe criticism of the opposing side, it goes without saying that it behooves these two rivals to claim their religious worldview and to dismiss their opponent's position. It can be seen that the deeper they are absorbed in their particular belief system, the more they are increasingly at odds with each other. Sadly, as will be expounded in the next chapter, this intense conflict between liberal pluralists and conservative writers at last comes to a head in the Korean Churches, especially the Korean Methodist Church which is experiencing theological discord due to the challenge of religious pluralism.

2. The Korean Churches as a battlefield for debates on pluralism

Until recently, Korean Protestant Churches have been overwhelmed by a fiery debate about religious pluralism between two opposing sides, conservative theologians and other scholars who pursue the thought of the late Sun-Whan Pyun. A Protestant theologian Pyun was the first to address contemporary pluralism in 1984.[38] Korean theological journals have published notable articles[39] about religious pluralism which reflect how

38 Dr. Pyun addresses his theology in the original article presenting religious pluralism, "Other religions and Theology", which was published in one of the theological journals in Korea, *The Theological Thought*, vol. 47, No. 4 (1984), 687–717.

39 Three well-known theological journals in Korea, *Ministry & Theology*, *The Theological Though*, and *Christian Thought*, have printed many articles on religious pluralism since the 1980s. The list of these articles classified according to publishers is as below. The list of articles published in *Ministry & Theology* is the following: Carl E. Braaten, "Preaching the Gospel in a religiously plural age", vol. 11 (1989), 156–162; Eryl Davies, "Unknown Christ", vol. 8 (1991), 42–67; Dong-Joo Lee, "Religious pluralism", vol. 8 (1991), 68–87; Chang-Kyun Mok, "Religious Catholic Church", vol. 8 (1991), 88–98; Il-Ung Jung, "Religious plural culture and Christian education", vol. 8 (1991), 99–110; Bong-Lin No, "Current situation of religious plu-

Korean religious pluralism is a sensitive and striking issue in the Korean Churches, especially in the Korean Protestant Church. In this section, it will be spelled out how Korean liberal pluralists launched a powerful attack on conservative camps that retain a singular commitment to the exclusive divinity of Yahweh. Also attention will be drawn to responses to them by the evangelical sides.

ralism in Korea", vol. 8 (1991), 124–33; Hak-Jin Na, "Christianity in a plural religious circumstance", vol. 8 (1991), 134–57; Ho-Jin Jun, "Religious pluralism and the uniqueness of Christ", vol. 8 (1991), 158–75; Sin-Kun Lee, "Religious pluralist's understanding of resurrection", vol. 4 (1992); Young-Han Kim, "Religious pluralism and Korean indigenous theology", vol. 7 (1992), 61–90; Steve Franklin, "The uniqueness of Christ as hope and the punisher", vol. 10 (1992), 34–54; Chris Wright, "Religious pluralism and The uniqueness of Christ", vol. 10 (1992), 55–72; John A. Viser, "The identity of Jesus in post-modern world", vol. 10 (1992); Moon-Kyun Lee, "Religious pluralism and the response of Korean Churches", vol. 6 (1997); Special section, "Religious pluralism", vol. 2 (1999). The list of articles in *The Theological Thought* is the following: Sun-Whan Pyun, "Other religions and theology", vol. 47, No. 4 (1984), 687–717; Ok-Sung Cha, "Study on dialogues and co-operations between religions in the religious-pluralistic Society", vol. 69, No. 2 (1990), 529–558; Jin Kim, "The reality and the request", vol. 75 (1991), 1070–1113; SYMPOSIUM, "Religious pluralism, what is a problem?" vol. 79 (1992), 881–887; SYMPOSIUM, "Theory and praxis in religious pluralism", vol. 93 (1996), 7–42; Kyung-Jae Kim, "Antagonism and universality in MinJung Theology vs religious theology, vol. 93 (1996), 43–65; Chan-Soo Lee, "Theology of other religions", vol. 93, (1996), 64–88; In-Sik Choi, "Korean Church and mission in religious pluralism", vol. 93 (1996), 89–119; In-Sik Choi, "New mode of the mission in the plural society", vol. 102 (1998), 80–104; Sang-Jik Lee, "An analysis of conflicting factors between the conservative Church and religious pluralism in Korea and the search for an alternative interreligious dialogue", vol. 101 (1998), 180–217. The list of articles in *Christian Thought* is the following: Eric J. Sharpe, "The historical understanding of religious pluralism", vol. 11 (1992), 141–149; Kwang-Sun Suh, "Post-modernism and theological movement", vol. 4 (1993), 35–43; Young-Han Kim, "Reformed theology in post-modern age (1)", vol. 1 (1994), 122–138; Young-Han Kim, "Reformed theology in post-modern age (2)", vol. 2 (1994), 153–170; Ei-Gon Kim, "Jonah's syndrome of condemnation of religious pluralism", vol. 2 (1994), 226–232; Jung-Soo Hong, "Post-modern theology and Korean Christianity", vol. 7 (1994), 19–28; Paul F. Knitter, "The Christian theology must be the dialogue theology", vol. 8 (1994), 88–105; Kang-Nam Oh, "Some analogical models for religious pluralism", vol. 7 (1995), 68–92; Kyung-Jae Kim, "Hermeneutics for the establishment of Korean theology", vol. 9 (1996), 61–74; Karl-Josef Kuschel, "Christology, is it insufficient for dialogues with religions?", trans. Jin Kim, vol. 3 (1997), 104–124.

2.1. The challenge of Korean religious pluralism

2.1.1. Sun-Whan Pyun

It is widely known among Korean religious scholars that the late Sun-Whan Pyun was the Protestant theologian who initially embraced the liberal theology of pluralism and became its leading proponent. He was born in JinNamPo, Korea, in 1928 to a farmer who inherited traditional Confucianism from his father.[40] During his four years of primary school, Pyun had the opportunity to read several books about great men or sages such as Socrates, Buddha, and Confucius that his brother, who once lived in Tokyo, Japan, gave him on his way to Korea. At that time, he was influenced by their teachings and insights into the mystery of life. However, at the age of eighteen, he became a Christian, embracing Jesus as Lord. This was due to the crucial impact of Rev. Suk-Ku Sin whose preaching placed emphasis on two themes: "loving nation" and "believing Jesus".

Indeed, despite his involvement in ministry, Rev. Sin was deeply implicated in the Korean independence movement as a member of the forlorn hope, and was regarded as a leading patriot who was committed to an anti-Japanese movement. Yet his great achievement was an attempt to construe and defend the gospel in the context of eastern religions. His powerful message on inter-faith dialogue among eastern religions exemplified a Korean indigenous theology. Under the influence of Rev. Sin, then, Pyun came to reconsider the gospel in the context of eastern religions.[41]

In 1948, Pyun was admitted to a Methodist school called 'Sung Wha Theological Seminary,' which, at that time, suffered persecution under the communists. The Korean War, which broke out in 1950, drove him down to Pusan, the southern and second biggest city in Korea, which was rarely under military attack by North Korean armies. In 1951 he continued to study at the Korean Methodist theological seminary at which Prof. Yoon-Sung Bum taught Paul Tillich's "Systematic Theology". Then he enlisted in the army in 1953 and served as a chaplain for several years. After military service, he entered the Korea Theological Seminary, which

40 Sun-Whan Pyun, "My theological discipline," in *Religious Pluralism and the Korean Theology*, (ed.) Publication Committee (Chunan: The Korean Theological Study Institute, 1992), 15–16.

41 Ibid., 18.

was the only theological institution to provide a postgraduate course, and there encountered the Neo-Orthodox Theology initiated by Karl Barth, who draws attention to the word of God ultimately revealed in Jesus Christ. In 1958 he was influenced by the teachings of Dr. Bong-Rang Park, who held a doctoral degree in Theology from Harvard University, and under whose supervision he was confronted with the essence of Barth's theology centred on the divine revelation of God in the Bible. Yet he at once raised the question of how the particularity of the word of God could be in accord with the universality of the revelation of Jesus Christ. It was not until he studied in Switzerland that he was moved away from Barth's exclusive position that a knowledge of God is to be gained through Jesus Christ.

During his stay at Drew University in the U.S., Pyun was heavily influenced by learned existentialist theologians, such as Carl Michalson and Fritz Buri, who proposed the vigorous adoption of the idea of Rudolf Bultmann, a renowned New Testament scholar during the Twentieth century. He sympathized with Bultmann's claim that mythical and inscrutable events in the New Testament, including a range of miracles, the divine work of Jesus and the resurrection, must be 'demythologized' in order that the *Kerygma* be made relevant to contemporary Christians. He then came to the conviction that Bultmann's demythologising approach enables us to comprehend salvation from the contemporary perspective. In 1971 he moved to Basel, Switzerland, to study under the supervision of Prof. Fritz Buri, who had been profoundly influenced by a distinguished existentialist, Karl Jaspers. He sought to bring his academic interest to bear on inter-faith dialogue between eastern and western religions, as is evident in his completed doctoral thesis, "The Finality of Christ in the Perspective of Christian-Zen Encounter (1975)."

Simultaneously he began to give countenance to a pioneer of inclusivism, Karl Rahner, whose views are summarized above. Rahner proposed the notable theory of the "anonymous Christian," which refers to a person who is not evangelised but is saved because of the unfailing grace of God reaching to even non-Christians. Yet Pyun immediately came to find it inappropriate to hold steadfastly to an inclusive view in a pluralistic world, in which one bears witness to religious pluralism's deep inroads into Christianity.

Towards a theocentric non-normative Christology

It was not until the controversial article, "Other religions and theology," appeared in 1984 that he was entirely immune to an inclusivist position. Having taken a pessimistic view of an inclusive theory, Pyun contended that inclusivism is no less than a hidden relic of religious imperialism since it fails to be immune to a Christocentric view that somewhat belittles other religions. He asserts:

> When one takes theology into consideration in relation to other religions, it is significant to overcome a religious imperialism (exclusivism) that seeks to label other religions satanic and that mounts a severe curse on them. In addition, it must be abandoned to accommodate a fulfilment theory that regards other religions as a preparation for the gospel. Christianity in a religiously pluralistic world must take an equal stance toward other religions with mutual respect.[42]

Having shown the greatest reluctance to espouse exclusivism or even inclusivism, he began in earnest to pose the vigorous adoption of a theocentric position dubbed "Copernican revolution in the theology of religion" sustained by pluralist writers such as John Hick. Prior to an attempt to enunciate a pluralist perspective, his particular attention was drawn to the three idols he thought the Korean Churches ought to eradicate. To begin with, it must be argued that it is improper to evaluate Korean traditional religions from a western religious perspective, an influential western-centred view so biased that it inevitably leads the greater part of Korean Churches to take an imperialist stance toward non-Christian religions. Furthermore, he emphasises that the Korean Churches not only need to abrogate the traditional but obsolete mission model, which is too exclusive to remain relevant in a pluralistic world, but also need to be in co-operation with other religious believers and secular humanists in order to restore humanity.

At this time, Pyun takes up the positive affirmation that Korean theology ought to instigate iconoclasm so that the Korean Churches can be liberated from an ecclesiocentric approach. It is true, he notes, that it has been claimed within Christianity that outside the church, salvation is unavailable. Yet it is thought-provoking that more recently, the Catholic Church has received the Rahnerian notion of "anonymous Christian,"

42 Sun-Whan Pyun, "Other religions and theology" in *Dialogue between religions and Asian theology: Sun-Whan Pyun Collection I*, (ed.) Sun-Whan Pyun Archive (Chunan: The Korean Theological Study Institute, 1996), 180.

pointing to universality of salvation for the sake of non-Christians. Pyun then maintains that it must be considered that the church is not the exclusive community that yearns for salvation but the proclaimer of God's universal salvific will.

Subsequently he resists an extreme exclusivist theology, arguing that early western missionaries were no less than religious and cultural imperialists who sought to impose their western worldview on Korean indigenous religions and cultures. In other words, he comes to the realisation that one of the traditional Christian axioms, "there is no salvation outside the church," has exerted an adverse effect on Korean communities and has driven a wedge between Christianity and other indigenous religions in Korea. Then he affirms, "The Korean Church seldom comes to realise that the mission slogan, 'only Jesus!' gives rise to scandal and has become an object of criticism from the intelligent."[43] Having taken a pessimistic view of exclusivism or even inclusivism, Pyun initially holds a pluralist view called "the theocentric, non-normative Christology," which is well expressed in a highly contested article, "Dialogue between Christianity and Buddhism."[44] Here I will focus on the elaboration of his pluralist perspective.

A theocentric pluralist theology

There is no doubt that a theocentric approach advocated by liberal pluralists such as John Hick undergirds his radical theology of religious pluralism. According to Pyun, it is a misconception to espouse Jesus as the unique mediator who serves as the embodiment of God, an exclusive position that rams a Christ-centred view down another believer's throat. In other words, it is quite mistaken to retain an unswerving commitment to a Christ-centred view. Rather, it should be pointed out that God is at the centre of all religions; therefore they are nothing less than different but equally valid ways of salvation. Then he strongly expresses his espousal of a theocentric view, maintaining that this theory is essential in conciliating Christianity with other religions. Chan-Soo Lee points out:

43 Ibid., 194.

44 Sun-Whan Pyun, "Dialogue between Buddhism and Christianity," in *Encounter Between Buddhism and Christianity: Sun-Whan Pyun Collection II*, (ed.) Sun-Whan Pyun Archive (Chunan: The Korean Theological Study Institute, 1997), 108–131.

> The God to which he (Sun-Whan Pyun) refers is not a God on which Christianity can have a monopoly. Though it is called "God" in the Christian language, as John Hick pointed out, realistically it has an affinity with the Ultimate or the Eternal One. The God is the transcendent Reality, which no one monopolises.[45]

Pyun sympathises with the chief thesis of John Hick, his so called "Copernican revolution in the theology of religion," i.e., just as planets belonging to the solar system undoubtedly revolve around the sun, so "God" is at the centre of all religions and all religions revolve around a single god. Then he asserts that like other religions, Christianity is nothing but a religion reaching to truth and love. His basic concern is to argue that religious aspirations to attain salvation by all means come true, since all religious traditions and cultures are little less than different phenomenal experiences of the one divine noumenon; or in another words various experiential manifestations of the same God.[46] He maintains:

> Christianity is, of course, sufficient to save Christians. Yet many of the world's religions that serve as gifts of God's grace are needed to save all mankind. No particular religion or religious leader takes possession of salvation; rather salvation is the divine one, which only belongs to God... All religions of the world revolve around the sun of truth, the Real.[47]

When one is immune to the colonial understanding of God implanted by missionaries, it can be seen that God has acted for the sake of all the people in the history of humanity. Though many names standing for the Ultimate internally seem to refer to different gods, they point to the same one God.[48]

Indeed, he demands that the Korean Churches should recant their particularist or inclusivist position. He proposes a vigorous defence of a pluralist thesis that every desire, every aspiration, every longing for the object of religious worship is nothing less than a yearning for the same God above the world's religions. Furthermore, he articulates a new understanding of the universal people of God intricately bound up with theocentri-

45 Chan-Soo Lee, "The theology of other religions," in *The Religious Theology of Sun-Whan Pyun*, (ed.) Sun-Whan Pyun Archive (Chunan: The Korean Theological Study Institute, 1996), 156.

46 Sun-Whan Pyun, "Inter-religious dialogue for one hundred years and its prospect," in *Dialogue between religions and Asian theology: Pyun Sun-Whan Collection I*, 47–55.

47 Ibid., 49–50.

48 Sun-Whan Pyun, "Other religions and theology", 192.

cism. Having taken great interest in a prevailing pluralist theory that regardless of their superficial dissimilarities, both Christianity and other religions are equally valid, Pyun maintains that all religious believers, including Christians, are essentially identical and embrace the one same God that is at the centre of all religions.[49] That is to say, he reaches the conclusion that since each religionist has faith in the Eternal One, no religion can have a monopoly on salvation and no one can claim the superiority of a particular religion. This point enables him to affirm that each religious believer who remains faithful to the Eternal One deserves to be a member of the Kingdom of God.[50]

A pluralist Christology

Sun-Whan Pyun also opposes a traditional Christian proposition that the historical Jesus is the unique normative Christ, debunking its imperialist attitude toward non-Christians. He then goes on to emphasise a 'non-normative Christology' embraced by pluralist writers such as Raimundo Pannikkar whose best-known book, *The Unknown Christ of Hinduism*, especially its totally revised edition (1982), which offers an in-depth look at a pluralist Christology. Pyun initially seeks to make a sharp distinction between the historical Jesus and the cosmic Christ who is present in the midst of all religions. In his judgement, it is of decisive significance to realise that salvation is on no account dependent on an explicit faith in a specific historical figure like the Nazareth Jesus. Rather he understands that salvation is available to all religionists whose miscellaneous mediators are little less than equally valid but different manifestations of the cosmic Christ. Having been stuck on the notion of a 'cosmic Christ' to which Pannikkar clung, Pyun notes, "Christ is the ontic mediator between God and creature as the universal Savior... Jesus is not the revealed name but reveals the Supername. The heavens and earth result from such an unknown divinity."[51] It is claimed that the cosmic Christ is never confined to a particular historical figure such as the Nazareth Jesus as the exclusive salvific norm for all mankind. Then Pyun offers a lucid illustration in

49 Sun-Whan Pyun, "Dialogue between Christianity and Buddhism," in *Encounter Between Christianity and Buddhism: Sun-Whan Pyun Collection II*, 128.

50 Chan-Soo Lee, "The theology of other religions," 162–3.

51 Sun-Whan Pyun, "Other religions and theology," 204–5.

which the non-normative nature of the universal Christ is demonstrated. He remarks:

> Free grace based on free will, which originates from Christ, is inherent in the heart not only of Christians but also of Muslims and Gentiles. The world's religions are closely tied to the universal Christ who is not eccentric.[52]

In this way, Pyun issues an unbending challenge to the Korean Churches whose particularist position is at variance with his liberal pluralist view. However, the more he called for a paradigm shift to a pluralist approach, the more he suffered a fervent rejection by exclusivists. Yet, he did not so much recant his prime thesis about religious pluralism as unbendingly express the need to accommodate it to hearten inter-religious dialogue among the religions of Korea. Despite his frontier spirit, his liberal pluralist perspective drew him into the vortex of inquisition, which was an unparalleled calamity in the history of the Korean Churches. However, Pyun was not and is not the only one to make this pilgrimage. Indeed, several sympathisers who collaborated with him continue to espouse his position in a rather similar way while turning against their naysayers who rebut a pluralist worldview.

2.1.2. Kyung-Jae Kim

Undoubtedly, one of the most renowned and influential religious pluralists in Korea is Kyung-Jae Kim. He was born in 1940 in Kwang-Joo, a major city in Korea. His conversion into Christianity, which occurred when he read the Bible at an early age, led him to enrol in the Korea Theological Seminary, where he came under the tutelage and influence of a celebrated liberal theologian, Jae-Joon Kim, who was a pioneer of Korean historical criticism. After graduating from this seminary, he continued to pursue advanced study in both theology and philosophy at several schools. His academic career was advanced at the Claremont Graduate University in U.S.A. After the completion of his Ph.D. studies, he returned to Korea to teach the subject of cultural theology at several universities and seminaries. He is currently professor of theology at the Korea Theological Seminary and regarded as a prominent pluralist in contemporary religious societies in Korea.

52 Ibid.

A pluralist view on God

Since the unfortunate inquisition forced by the Korean Methodist General Assembly on Pyun, which took place in 1992, Kim has followed in the footsteps of Pyun and made a deep impact of pluralist ideology on Korean religious scholarship. To begin with, Kim calls into question that the biblical God, Yahweh, is entirely divorced from the God of Korean ancestors.[53] He vigorously resists the use of a particular term for God like "Yahweh." In other words, he disavows the fact that our forebears did not know the name of God revealed in the biblical books and thereby were damned to eternal perdition. He claims:

> I believe that the God of comfort, mercy, encouragement, deliverance and creation is the God who was present in the midst of our ancestors in a period when they met with suffering or pleasure. I do not believe that the God of the Bible, the unique God who creates the whole creation, was first known at the In-Cheon harbour where the first missionary arrived.[54]

He goes on to be critical of the dualistic understanding of revelation claimed by a number of orthodox theologians: that is, special revelation and general revelation. He gives short shrift to the view that traditional relics originating from Korean history and religious experience should be dealt with under general revelation that has so deteriorated that it is poisoned and only leads to idolatry. Then he argues that the exclusive affirmation that only the Bible should be reckoned the special revelation is intolerable. This is because this exclusive understanding of revelation results from lack of knowledge of other religions or a superficial understanding of them.

Kim continues to offer a metaphorical illustration of spring water in order to spell out his pluralist worldview. He explains that if we continue to dig a well in our houses, we would find spring water that issues from its original vein. In this way, it is circuitously pointed out that all religious experiences in a global society are nothing more than the different but equally valid responses to the ultimate Reality. In other words, it is inferred that all religious practices and teachings are merely the different ways of conceiving and experiencing the one ultimate divine reality.

53 Kyung-Jae Kim, *Christian Spirituality in a Religious Pluralist Age* (Seoul: DaSan-GulBang, 1992), 164.

54 Ibid., 167.

Toward a theology of liberation

Having considered the need for religious pluralism, Kim is deeply committed to a religious theology of pluralism concerned with the liberation of humans and of ecology.[55] He finds it of paramount importance to note that all religions should focus on the establishment of human liberation and ecological and environmental concerns. His main thesis is that every religion should have an altruistic concern to deliver both humans and the earth's ecology from a series of calamities, such as the oppression, destitution, pestilence and natural catastrophe that have been part of our life.[56] In other words, it is stressed that all religionists need to look for a precise remedy for the specific ills of humanity and for the destruction of ecological environment.

He maintains that one cannot unconditionally claim one's own religious legacy without any concern for the liberation of life or ecology. It is true that despotism and autocracy have despised human dignity, and that the crisis of ecology has overwhelmed the contemporary world due to an exploitation of nature. Kim empathically argues that each believer needs to demonstrate belief by seeking to overcome a series of social difficulties such as environmental complications, ecological disasters, and defamation of human value. He believes that all religious worldviews need to move from an anthropocentric perspective, which places emphasis on humanity, to a biocentric approach. Indeed, all religionists need to attend to the restoration of nature and the liberation of human life. This environmental approach serves as the ideal corrective for a despotic anthropocentric view. In this sense, Kim comes to the conclusion that the ultimate goal of each religion is to establish freedom, justice, peace and ecological liberation rather than to focus on its exclusivistic teaching and mission.

2.1.3. Jung-Bae Lee

Jung-Bae Lee seeks to blend Korean indigenous theology with religious pluralist ideology. When he entered at the Methodist theological seminary in Seoul that serves as the cradle of Korean indigenous theology, he came under the tutelage of Sun-Whan Pyun, the modern pioneer of religious pluralism. Indeed, Pyun's courses in religious studies helped Lee formula-

55 Kyung-Jae Kim, *Discourse for Cultural Theology* (Seoul: The Christian Literature Society of Korea), 86–88.

56 Ibid., 88.

te the critical framework in which he was to study, teach and write. After graduating from the seminary with Th.B. and M.Div., he left for Switzerland to take postgraduate courses at the University of Basel. The years at the University provided a very stimulating background for Lee's academic career and brought a dramatic new development in his life. He was both challenged and stimulated by the teaching of Fritz Buri and Heinrich Ott and embarked on quests for Korean indigenous theology. His efforts culminated in his receiving a Th.D. degree in 1986. With his doctoral degree in hand, Lee returned to Korea and took up his duties as professor of theology at Methodist theological seminary. He presently lectures in both religious studies and theology at the school.

A critique of indigenous theology and Minjung theology

In his provocative book, *Indigenisation and Ecological Culture*, Lee draws attention to the nub of two major theologies in Korea, indigenous theology and Minjung theology, and mounts an acute criticism of them. Firstly, Lee notes that in the last twenty years there has been an increasing disillusionment among a growing number of theologians, especially Minjung theologians, with indigenous theology. It is seen that a number of Minjung theologians denounce indigenous scholars for neglect of duty to dissuade autocratic powers from trampling on the right of personal liberty. The central difficulty with indigenous theology is the way in which it seldom takes into account social phenomena and their political issues.[57] In other words, indigenous theology shows indifference to a variety of socio-political problems, including an infringement upon personal rights. Lee comments:

> As Minjung theologians criticise, indigenous theory that fails to realise political and economical problems marked by suffering and suppression is nothing more than a non-historical movement, which adopts or connives at current political ideologies that give short shrift to civil liberties.[58]

On the other hand, the basic assumption of Minjung theology centred on socio-political issues in the present context is also seen as somewhat problematic and unattainable. This is because this perspective fails to learn

57 Jung-Bae Lee, *Indigenisation and Ecological Culture* (Seoul: JongLo Book House Company, 1991), 218–9.
58 Ibid., 219.

tolerance, respect, and mutual understanding toward other religions from indigenous theology and to recognise that liberation for human rights can on no account be accomplished by only a certain particular religion and its ideology. Then he calls for a paradigm shift from indigenous theology and Minjung theology to Korean culture theology oriented on nature and history.

Toward Korean culture theology

Lee finds it essential to shift our attention from a theocentric theory to a religious theology of liberation.[59] He argues that it is important to have a concrete grasp of Korean religions and their dynamic powers centred on human liberation. It must be granted, furthermore, that Korean theology helps these religions put their liberation theology into practice, a process that results in the mutual reformation between religions. In other words, Lee calls for a considerable shift from a God-centred scheme to a liberation theology of religions that plays a crucial role in fostering dialogue and cooperation between religions.

Nevertheless, Lee immediately comes to the realisation that the liberation theology seldom remains immune to a human-centred view. According to him, with rare exceptions, many religious worldviews are deeply influenced by western historicism that places emphasis on 'human liberation'. Lee emphatically contends that Korean theology needs to repudiate an attempt to illuminate Asian theologies from a western view oriented to human freedom, while extending the scope of religious concern for liberation to ecology.[60] In order to call for a need for ecological and environmental concerns, Lee draws attention to the Priestly writer and his focus on the term, *shalom*, found in the tradition of creation in the Old Testament Scriptures. He believes that the creation belief set forth in the Priestly source leads us to see the concept of the Sabbath as the foremost event associated with the peaceful relationship between humanity and creation. He goes on to insist that a human-centred view of creation attaches too much importance to humankind made in God's image who alone can have a fellowship with Creator, but somewhat dilutes the relationship between creation and God. Lee understands that possessing God's image and exer-

59 Ibid., 167–8.

60 For a detail of his ecology theology, see Eun-Sun Lee & Jung-Bae Lee, *Post modernism and Christianity* (Seoul: DaSanKulBang, 1993), 343–46.

cising dominion, rather than being seen in authoritative or hierarchical terms, suggests gracious actions towards creation. Therefore, one finds it of vital significance to see the image of God in terms of accountability toward one's fellow creatures and the rest of creation.

Finally, Lee seeks to offer a harmonic approach dubbed 'Korean culture theology' that coalesces a theology of liberation into an ecological perspective. This perspective dilutes overemphasis on pluralist ideology devoid of human liberation and environmental concerns. Rather this approach claims that despite the need to espouse a pluralist worldview that seeks to treat all religions as the same valid manifestations of the 'ultimate divine reality,' all religions need to focus their attention on 'human predicament' as well as 'environmental problems.' Then he concludes that the starting point of Korean culture theology is to consider contemporary socio-political difficulties and ecological problems and to show an in-depth look at how to settle them.

It has been seen that Korean pluralists are intensely resistant to an exclusive position that Yahweh is unique and the one God. Despite distinctions made between their arguments on pluralism, Pyun and his supporters such as Kim and Lee respectively concede that the religious traditions and teachings are little more than different ways of conceiving and experiencing the ultimate divine reality. This pluralist worldview eventually leads to the vigorous response of the Korean evangelical camp to pluralists.

2.2. *The conservative responses to Korean religious pluralism*

2.2.1. Dong-Joo Lee

Dong-Joo Lee is a leading woman scholar whose chief field of emphasis is mission theology in Korea. Particularly, she is well known as the theologian who has mounted a severe attack on Korean pluralists, especially on Sun-Whan Pyun. In fact, she played a crucial role in ejecting Pyun from the Korean Methodist Church and has continued to battle with the proponents of religious pluralism by offering a full defense of exclusivism.

After receiving the B. M. degree from Ewha Womans University, Dong-Joo Lee moved to Germany to enter Heidelberg University, from which she earned the Th.M. degree. During this time, she was licensed by the Baden state Church. She then moved from Heidelberg to Tübingen to begin her Th.D. studies and received her Th.D. degree from Tübingen University. After returning to Korea, she soon realised religious pluralism had become a pervasive, rapid and dramatic development throughout the Korean Churches.

Having voiced concerns that the proliferation of publications on religious pluralism had challenged and considerably influenced the Korean evangelical circles, Lee began to think that it was time to offer full-fledged responses to them. In particular she came to recognize that it was within liberal pluralist camps that the influence of Pyun, regarded as a pioneer of contemporary Korean pluralism, was felt most widely. She then increasingly viewed Pyun as an enemy, and as a detriment to Christian faith. She offered a vigorous criticism of him, while espousing a particularist position. Indeed, her strenuous view led to her emergence as the most challenging rival to Pyun.

Criticism of Sun-Whan Pyun's pluralism

Lee's wide-ranging argument against Korean pluralism, especially Pyun's pluralistic theology, is most clearly expressed in two booklets entitled *Asian Religions and Christianity*[61] and *Contemporary Theology of Mission*.[62] In these booklets she also offers an in-depth look at the intrusion of syncretism into Korean Churches. In *Asian Religions and Christianity*, she continuously and extensively battles the proponents of liberal pluralist ideology. It is significant to observe that in this book, she seeks to make a place for dealing with Pyun's pluralistic syncretism, though this effort seems to be substantially designed to overturn it.

In particular, her attention is drawn to Pyun's attempt to foster dialogue between Christianity and Buddhism. She focuses on the investigation of his understanding of God associated with the thoughts of Asian religions. According to a well-known Indian religious scholar, Khin Maung Din, it is futile for Christianity to come into conflict with Buddhism since Asian spirituality simultaneously views God not only as Person but also as Non-Person. In other words, from an Asian perspective, a western-

61 Dong-Joo Lee, *Asian Religions and Christianity* (Seoul: Christian Literature Crusade, 1998).

62 Dong-Joo Lee, *Contemporary Theology of Mission* (Seoul: Christian Literature Crusade, 1998).

centred view of God is so imperialistic that it is inappropriate to espouse it. Rather, in light of an Asian understanding of God, both Christianity and Buddhism experience the ultimate divine reality, which cannot be confined to a particular religion.

Lee realises that the influence of Asian religious writers leads Pyun to impose this Asian understanding of God on the Korean Churches and to claim that the world's religions are nothing less than different responses to the 'One Eternal'. Then she opposes Pyun's attempt to view the Christian God as a manifestation of 'the Ultimate' that all religions embrace. She argues that it is incongruous to equalise the theistic worldview found in Christianity with atheistic belief systems marked by Buddhism. Further she insists that Pyun's understanding of God is alien to the description of the unique God found in the Bible. Those who embrace the biblical texts, therefore, should not align themselves with him.[63]

She then focuses on Pyun's Christology in association with the notion of the 'cosmic Christ'. She argues against the notion of a 'universal Christ' who is present in the midst of all religious cultures and worshipping communities. Such a view is mainly claimed by Indian pluralists such as Panikkar or Din, whose ideas Pyun has taken up. Her criticism of Pyun on this point is:

> His [Sun-Whan Pyun's] notion of the 'universal Christ' indicates that 'Christ' is manifested among oriental religions. Sun-Whan Pyun's Christology never defines Jesus Christ as the Only Son of God, but as a non-historical and trans-historical, abstract Christ who is separable from Jesus and comparable with the 'Saviours' of Buddhism and Hinduism. This 'Christ' is not Jesus Christ to whom the Bible points but a 'different Christ' or the 'false Christ', and the Bible teaches that such a 'different Christ' is the eschatological 'anti-Christ'.[64]

She defies the notion of a 'universal Christ' claimed by Pyun. As noted earlier, Pyun, who was heavily influenced by Panikkar, asserted that the 'anonymous Christ' is behind the world's religions. Accordingly, Pyun argues that salvation in Hinduism is dependent on this 'Christ'. In other words, salvation understood by the Asian indigenous theologians that Pyun often quoted is self-fulfilling, dependent not just on Jesus Christ but on the 'unknown Christ' that is present within other religions. Yet Lee's rejoinder to those who embrace that 'Christ', including Pyun, is unswer-

63 Ibid., 86
64 Ibid., 88.

ving: "Though God not only commanded us to proclaim the Good News (Mt. 24:14; Acts. 1:8) in the world (1 Peter 3:19; 4:6), He already announced His plan to penalise those who disbelieve in Jesus Christ according to their deeds (Rom. 2:5–6). God has never promised salvation to those who do not trust Jesus Christ and resist the forgiveness of sin."

Subsequently, she seeks to debunk Pyun's understanding of the Spirit, and points out that his notion of 'the Spirit' is seldom divorced from the concept of 'Spirit' tied to the Buddhistic Christian theology of Lyun de Silva, a leading religious scholar, who espouses a monistic Buddhism that draws no distinction between human spirit and God's spirit.[65] Then she points out that his viewpoint on the Spirit is closely interwoven with an atheistic understanding of spirit that leaves room for a theanthropic approach to the Spirit. She maintains:

> The biblical 'Spirit' is neither the spirit of the world, nor the spirit of human or other religions, but the promised 'Holy Spirit' given by God from the heaven to those who have put their faith in Jesus Christ. This 'Spirit' is not the spirit that is present in the midst of indigenous religions hostile to Christianity, which equalise the human with the nature of Supreme. Rather an attempt to idolise the spirit of humanity stems from the original sin.[66]

Given the fact that Pyun's radical pluralist view led him to leave traditional faith, she concludes that it is indeed legitimate to embrace the Bible and its proclamation on the uniqueness of Jesus and to give short shrift to this liberal theology.

2.2.2. Ho-Jin Jun

One of the most celebrated theologians specialising in missiology within Korean conservative scholarship is undoubtedly Ho-Jin Jun. He grew up in an ardent Presbyterian tradition, from which his pious faith has gradually evolved. This religious upbringing led him to enter Koshin University and to go on to Koshin Theological Seminary. This school has been a stronghold of conservatism and has inherited the spirit of anti-Shinto Shrine worship in the Japanese occupation. His conservative background led him to apply for admission to Westminster Theological Seminary, which was formed as an alternative to Princeton Theological Seminary in

65 Dong-Joo Lee, *Contemporary Theology of Mission*, 25–6.
66 Ibid., 90.

the 1930's. He received a Th.M. degree from this seminary. He continued his studies at Fuller Theological Seminary, a leading evangelical school in the U.S.A., and was awarded a D.Miss. After returning to Korea, as a conservative evangelical, he became director and president of Korea Evangelical Theological Society, a position he filled with vigour, working to inspire evangelicalism in Korean theological scholarship. Having been keenly engaged with the position of the World Evangelical Fellowship, which poses a fundamental objection to a pluralist worldview, Ho-Jin Jun devoted particular attention to the subject of religious pluralism. He sought to counter the impact of pluralism that gradually penetrated the Korean Churches.

The Bible and pluralism

Having come to understand the issue of religious pluralism, Ho-Jin Jun drew a singular distinction between Christian and pluralist views on the Bible. He pointed out that Christians embrace the Bible as the inspired word of God that serves as the norm of faith and action, while pluralism intensely opposes this high view of Scripture. He was concerned to show that a pluralist theology diluted the divine character and uniqueness of Jesus Christ by utilising a historical critical method. In other words, Ho-Jin Jun understands that pluralist writers espouse historical criticism which, with rare exceptions, dismisses the divine inspiration and authority of the Bible in order to mount a severe attack on exclusivists. He urges pluralists to consider that the Bible itself is opposed to religious pluralism. He strongly affirmes that though the election of Israel played a vital role as means of salvation for all mankind, Israel found it essential to retain a singular commitment to the one God called Yahweh without embracing other gods. This view is based on his observation that the Bible leaves no place for syncretism or pluralism. He remarks:

> Pluralists and liberal theologians construe contemporary Christianity as the outcome of western culture and regard the Bible as a collection of historical documents, which must be judged by human reason. Due to the fact that this position prefers contexts more than texts, it is inevitable to shift faith and theology according to times and contexts and there is no room for the absoluteness of Christianity. That is to say, the absence of authority of the Bible as the inerrant word of God generates a new radical theology... Yet Evangelicalism believes that it is not

> Christianity that brings the Bible into existence; rather it is the Bible that brings Christianity into being.[67]

He reminds readers that, without exception, the biblical books, especially the Old Testament, including Isaiah, relentlessly despise other religions as idolatry. It is of consequence to bring to bear on a discussion of religious pluralism the prophet Isaiah's poignant criticism that God has forsaken idolatrous Israel because she has been engrossed in eastern religions and their cultures. He concludes that one should learn a crucial lesson from the biblical texts that eastern cultures and religions are under the wrath of God, who loathes polytheism and religious pluralism.

A Christian monotheism and Christology

It is interesting that Korean pluralists, who consistently follow in the wake of contemporary liberal writers such as John Hick, give short shrift to the image of God as Person. This is because they have no doubt that such an attempt to personify God is nothing less than an outcome of western theology. The great majority of religious pluralists affirm that though the gods of all religions are ostensibly different, they are substantially and realistically nothing but one and the same God. Yet Ho-Jin Jun disavows such a theocentric approach, since the God of religious pluralism is so divorced from that of oriental religions such as Hinduism or Buddhism. He points out that the mutual discrepancies among the world's religions are so central that it is illegitimate to impose the notion of 'Transcendent Being' on all religious believers. In addition, he devotes attention to the expression, 'cosmic Christ' manifested not only in the Nazareth Jesus, but also in certain strands of Hindu thought.

According to pluralist writers such as Paul Knitter, it is essential to construe exclusive expressions found in the New Testament, including Acts 4:12, as the language of love or a confession, which should only be applied to the age of early Church but should never remain relevant in a pluralistic world. Jun makes it clear, however, that Christianity has embraced the divine nature of the historical Jesus and His lordship and that Jesus Christ is the way for salvation and has become the scandal for non-

67 Ho-Jin Jun, "Religious Pluralism in Evangelical Perspective," in *Bible and Theology vol. 11*, (eds.) Sung-Soo Kwon, et al. (Seoul: Christian Wisdom Press, 1992), 32–33; See idem, *Religious Pluralism and Mission Strategy for Other Religions* (Seoul: The Korean Society for Reformed Faith and Action, 1993), 68–69.

believers. Jun then urges his readers to recall that Christianity has identified Jesus Christ with God, the Mediator, and the Supreme Being over the heaven and earth, and the unique *Logos*.[68] Jun argues that without faith it is impossible to espouse the uniqueness of the Christian claim that Jesus is the sole divine mediator. It is suggested, therefore, that this Christian position is to be preserved only through faith.[69] In this regard, Jun comes to the conclusion that since the biblical books leave no room for religious pluralism, whoever embraces them must disavow this liberal religious worldview that abrogates not only monotheism but also the uniqueness and finality of Jesus Christ.

2.2.3. Yung-Han Kim

It is extensively known within Korean evangelical circles that Yung-Han Kim is a learned scholar who specialises not only in post-modern thought but also Korean culture and religion. He was brought up under the influence of the Presbyterian tradition. At the age of twenty, he entered Seoul National University where he earned a B.A. degree. He then moved to Germany to take postgraduate courses at the University of Heidelberg. The years at the University brought a dramatic new development in his academic career. He studied philosophy and received his Ph.D from the University. Kim continued his Th.D. studies in modern theology at the same University. Two doctoral degrees in hand, he returned to South Korea and took up his duties as professor of Christian studies at SoongSil University. Seeing that religious pluralism had marked the acme of the liberal critical assault on traditional doctrines of Korean Christianity, including the uniqueness and finality of Jesus Christ, he embarked on studies about contemporary pluralist approaches to religions.

A critical reaction to Korean pluralist theology

In a provocative article, “Religious Pluralism & Korean Indigenous Theology,”[70] he mounted an acute attack not only on contemporary pluralist essayists such as S. T. Samartha, R. Pannikkar, John Hick, and Paul Knitter, but also on Korean scholars who are committed to religious pluralism

68 Ibid., 73.

69 Ibid.

70 Yung-Han Kim, “Religious Pluralism & Korean Indigenous Theology,” *Ministry & Theology*, 7 (1992), 61–90.

or indigenous theology. It appears, however, that the majority of his criticisms of Pyun are seldom dissimilar to those of Dong-Joo Lee whose arguments are discussed above. Therefore, my concern here is to show how Kim presents a devastating critique of Korean liberalists such as Dong-Sik Ryu and Kyung-Jae Kim.

Kim brings his focus to bear on the thought of Dong-Sik Ryu,[71] a pioneer of Korean indigenous theology. It goes without saying that one of the most important hallmarks of Ryu's religious scholarship is his attention to the *'Pung Ryu'*[72] theology or teaching. Ryu understands that the aim of *'Pung Ryu'* theology is to construe the gospel of Jesus from the perspective of *Pung Ryu.* According to Ryu, the *'Pung Ryu'* teaching encompasses the three major religions (Confucianism, Buddhism and Zen) and its source lies in the teaching of heavenly gods, which originates from faith in them. Ryu argues that Jesus is identified with the man of *Pung Ryu* who embodies *Pung Ryu.* Yet Kim was intensely resistant to this ingenious but dubious theory concerned with *Pung Ryu.* Kim firmly challenged:

> Here Dong-Sik Ryu transforms the Jesus of gospel, who is both the real God and the real man, into that of *Pung Ryu.* He [Ryu] begins not with the Triune Christian God but with a pantheistic thought of the *Pung Ryu* teaching in order to blend the former with the latter.[73]

In his discussion of the *Pung Ryu* teaching, Kim seeks to spell out Ryu's argument about it. Ryu contends that the *Pung Ryu* teaching is inextricably tied to the three principal elements of Korean spirituality: that is, *Han*, *Mut* and *Sam.*[74] In his elucidation of the three terms, *Han* is defined not only as the 'oneness' but also as the 'wholeness'. Given the fact that *Han* is likened to a Creator dubbed God, it can be argued that our ancestors

71 Dong-Sik Ryu studied at Boston University in the U.S.A. After returning to South Korea, he taught at both Korean Methodist theological seminary and YeonSe University for many years until his retirement. Despite his ripe old age, he devotes his energies to writings on Korean indigenous theology without pause.

72 This Korean term refers to Korean traditional elegance and taste or refinement, and represents the Korean religious spirituality. For a further analysis of the word, see Dong-Sik Ryu, "Love and Peace of a Journeyer of the Heaven," in *Korean Religion and Korean Theology: Essays in Honour of Dong-Sik Ryu's Seventieth Birthday*, (eds.) Kyoe-Jun Lee, et al. (Chunan: The Korean Theological Study Institute, 1993), 13–32.

73 Yung-Han Kim, "Religious Pluralism & Korean Indigenous Theology," 78.

74 Dong-Sik Ryu, "Love and Peace of A Journeyer of the Heaven," 20–22.

identified with *Han*'s nation embraced God. Ryu proposes a speculation on *Mut* that means Korean traditional beauties and serves as an indigenous word appropriately referring to *Pung Ryu*. It is noteworthy, likewise, that the Korean term, *Sam*, which connotes life or lifestyle, is understood to be an abbreviation of the Korean word, *Saram* that means human. Here Ryu is keen to formulate a distinctively indigenous approach to Christianity in relation to *Han*, *Mut* and *Sam*.

Positioning himself over against the traditional doctrine of the Trinity, Ryu carefully delineates his indigenous theology concerned with the Trinity of *Pung Ryu* by likening the Christian God to *Han*, the Spirit to *Mut*, and Christ to *Sam*. He avers that despite the contradictions, the mutual exclusions and the differences between miscellaneous religions, God identifies all religionists with His children.[75]

Having considered Ryu's various theories in all their aspects, Yung-Han Kim is highly concerned about this contextualization of the Christian faith in the Korean indigenous context and comes to the conclusion that Ryu's religious worldview is inextricably tied not only to syncretism, but also to religious pluralism. He goes on to contend that given the thesis of Ryu that all entities, including religious spirituality, are in the process of evolution, both a liberal pluralist ideology and the theory of evolution are deeply rooted in his worldview.

Having dealt with Ryu's indigenous theology, Kim turns to examine the thought of a leading cultural theologian Kyung-Jae Kim. Kyung-Jae Kim is not so much unwavering in his commitment to what is really fundamental in Korean Christianity as willing to propose a liberal pluralist ideology, a stance that deviates from and challenges the Korean evangelical camp. According to him, God is on no account confined to a specific god like Yahweh whom Christianity embraces as the unique God. This is because Yahweh is a mere territorial deity of Israel. He seeks to liken God to the fountain of water to describe his central focus on pluralism. He illustrates by this saying that if each man respectively digs a well, which stems from its fountain, to get potable water in each different area, then all religions are superficially different but ultimately valid responses to the same God.

Yet Yung-Han Kim immediately raises an objection against Kyung-Jae Kim's radical view on God. Yung-Han Kim points out that it is inap-

75 Yung-Han Kim, "Religious Pluralism & Korean Indigenous Theology," 79.

propriate simply to identify Yahweh with a god of the ancestors. Rather it is essential to view such an indigenous god in the light of Yahweh and Jesus Christ, a process that enables us to purge indigenous religions from detrimental elements such as shamanism, pantheism, and Satanism. This position is, as will be dealt with later, marked by his reformed theology of religion that is clearly articulated in his book, *The 21st Century and Reformed Theology, vol 2*.

A reformed theology of religion

Yung-Han Kim affirms the deep need for a mutual respect that plays a crucial role in fostering dialogue between religions while embracing the uniqueness and finality of Jesus Christ. It is thought provoking here that Kim's reformed theology eschews an exclusive position that, as fundamentalists believe, somewhat belittles other religions and unconditionally labels their practices superstitions. Yet he repudiates a liberal pluralist stance that emphasizes an open-ended attitude toward other religions, but rebuts key principal doctrines of Christianity, including the uniqueness of Jesus. He maintains:

> A reformed attitude takes an inclusive attitude toward other religions. This is because they are general revelation from God. As general revelation from God, other religions point to the transcendent God and help to cultivate spirituality and morality. Yet the general revelation is so corrupted that it cannot teach us about the true God because of the fall of humanity. Therefore, other religions must be illuminated in the light of the gospel that Christ is the unique embodiment of God and the final mediator for salvation of humankind. And they need to be taught to know the true God as the Trinity.[76]

Kim makes it evident, then, that it behooves a reformed theology to emphasis the four principles for dialogue among religions. Firstly, it is required to have an in-depth look at other religions and to foster dialogue between them with a mutual respect.[77] Secondly, it is appropriate to take an open-eared attitude toward other religions and to learn valuable spirituality and morality embedded in them. In other words, what is true dialogue

76 Yung-Han Kim, *The 21st Century and Reformed Theology, vol 2: The Postmodernism and Reformed Theology* (Seoul: Publishing House of the Presbyterian Church of Korea, 1998), 70.

77 Ibid., 74.

is to learn from the other.[78] Thirdly, in reality, inter-religious dialogue is inevitably accompanied by the conflict between gods that each religion embraces. Yet this conflict is not a libel on each other but persuasion or advice, which is concomitant with impact and love.[79]

Finally, a reformed approach to religions needs to retain a deep commitment to Jesus Christ and to demonstrate the superiority of Yahweh in an objective way. Then he draws the conclusion that "a reformed dialogue is not only 'an apologetic dialogue,' but also 'a dialogical apologetic'."[80] That is to say, a reformed theology or dialogue that Kim addresses does not force others to embrace Christian faith, but introduces the uniqueness and finality of Jesus with mutual respect by trusting the work of the Spirit who leads people to conversion. In this sense, inter-religious dialogue is intrinsically the conflict between spirits behind personalities, the battle between worldviews and the combat between gods.

3. Evaluation

The study has shown how Korean pluralists issue a vigorous challenge to the Korean evangelical camp. Also, it has been spelled out how Korean evangelicals firmly disavow religious pluralism, arguing that it is inappropriate for the Korean Churches to accommodate it. Indeed, the past decade has witnessed a deep and long-standing chasm between liberal pluralists and conservative evangelicals within the Korean Churches. It is noteworthy, here, that in spite of scorching debates between these two opposing sides, a large proportion of them belong to the Korean Churches who hold unswervingly to a high view of Scripture and embrace the Bible as the word of God. Still, it seems to me that these two camps have not offered a full-fledged argument on the subject of religious pluralism in the light of the Bible.[81]

78 Ibid., 74–5.

79 Ibid., 75.

80 Ibid.

81 Recently, a few articles on the issue from a biblical perspective have been published in Korea. See Tae-Soo Yim, "Religious Pluralism and Indigenization from the Perspective of Old Testament," *Christian Thought*, 465 (1997), 117–125; Jung-Woo

For instance, Pyun and his defenders claimed a liberal pluralist theology that all religions are nothing less than different but equally valid manifestations of the Transcendent in order to foster dialogue with other religions. Yet it should be pointed out that his argument about pluralism is dependent not on the Bible itself but on western scholarship. It is not surprising, therefore, that even one of his pupils labels his pluralist model a 'mosaic theology,' since it is fundamentally dependent on western or eastern scholars such as John Hick, Paul Knitter and Raymundo Panikkar.[82] The point made here is that no matter what he argues, the many ramifications of his pluralism are seldom immune to a western-centered worldview and its imperialism.

On the other hand, evangelical writers who are deeply devoted to the authority of the Bible regard it as the most central heritage of the church. The vast majority of them firmly insist that it is inappropriate to be committed to the adoption of religious pluralism since it wreaks havoc with the authority of the Bible, which has no room for pluralism. It is surprising, however, that regardless of their position based upon the Bible, they have not offered a thorough and painstaking treatment of pluralism from a biblical perspective. Many of their views are also based on Western expressions of Christianity. In other words, given the fact that the Korean Churches hold to the view that the Bible is the word of God, the issue of religious pluralism must be considered and evaluated in the light of the Bible. It can be seen that while the mainstream of evangelists, including Dong-Joo Lee, Ho-Jin Jun and Yung-Han Kim, emphasise the central role of the Bible in the Korean Churches, they have not presented a thoughtful look at how to assess a liberal pluralist worldview from a biblical perspective.

In my judgement, the more evangelicals espouse the Bible to reject pluralist views, the more they should focus on the meticulous investigation of what is the biblical position on pluralism. In this sense, it is urgently needed to offer an in-depth look at how to evaluate the issue of religious pluralism from a biblical perspective in the context of the Korean Churches who have been entangled in it.

Kim, "Religious Pluralism and an Exegesis on the First Commandment," *Ministry & Theology*, 2 (1998), 58–68.

82 Sung-Do Kang, *Religious Pluralism and Salvation* (Seoul: The Christian Literature Society of Korea, 1997), 119–113.

Chapter 2

The Korean Churches and Iconoclasm

Over the past several months, all global communities have been filled with fear due to the unheard of calamity that took place on September 11, 2001, in New York. Muslim fundamentalists hijacked domestic airliners, two of which were crashed into the World Trade Centre. The twin towers fell to pieces, killing hundreds of people, a tragedy that struck terror into the hearts of the American people. Sadly, one misfortune accompanied another. The U.S. military attacked Afghanistan to catch the ringleader of the attacks and his adherents. As a result, a host of Afghan people inevitably took refuge in neighbouring countries to flee the missile attacks that killed many innocent refugees. The fact that this ill-advised terrorism has deeply upset all religious communities indicates that religious zealotry is a contentious issue in contemporary pluralistic global societies.

The last 20 years in Korea has also seen outbursts of iconoclasm, causing chaos in contemporary Korean religious society. In particular, idol-breaking has been a controversial subject for Korean Churches. Several Christian iconoclasts have been impetuously involved in the eradication of Buddhist images in temples, believing that they were justified in doing so. As a consequence, the majority of Buddhists have responded with rage, criticism and ill will to these fanatics, labelling their behaviour as vandalistic. On the other hand, some Christian fundamentalists have been engaged in the reckless destruction of statues of Tangun, the legendary progenitor of the Korean people and founder of Korea's oldest kingdom. This zealous attitude has caused great social discord.

In this regard, the aim of this chapter is to show how the Korean Churches have been embroiled in the issue of iconoclasm, which has antagonised relations between Christianity and other religions. This issue will be critically evaluated from the perspective of Isaiah's universalist themes in the following chapters.

1. Christian iconoclasts and the destruction of Buddhist images

1.1. Idol breaking and incendiarism

Since 1984 when Buddhist images in *Moo Ryang Sa* and *Il Sun Sa* temples were defaced with paint and had red crosses drawn on their murals, Christian extremists have been recklessly involved in the destruction of Buddhist statues and temples.[1] In 1987, a Christian fanatic belonging to the *Tam Ra* church in Je Ju Do (the biggest island in Korea) plotted to destroy several Buddhist sanctums in a temple, resulting in the two main sanctums being burnt to ashes. He was prosecuted and put in jail. In 1995, a Protestant minister sneaked into a Buddhist sanctum of *Chung Young Sa* temple in Jin Hae, and devastated its properties. According to a witness to this incident, the Christian iconoclast yelled out that worshiping these images was nothing less than idolatry and that he would go to heaven for his attempt to destroy them. Subsequently, in 1998, an arsonist set fire to a Buddhist temple in Seoul, and inflicted a great loss on the temple.

One incident followed another. More recently, an unheard-of affair transpired on June 26, 1998 in Je Ju Do. A Christian zealot, Soo-Jin Kim, crept into *Won Myung Sun Won* temple and recklessly knocked the heads off 750 granite statues. This act of vandalism was perhaps the most audacious iconoclast attack that had ever taken place in Korea, and it threw all Korean religious societies into consternation. As a result, Korean Buddhists almost lost patience with these attacks, and the deep hostility between the two religions (Christianity and Buddhism) came to a head.

1.2. The deep chasm between Christianity and Buddhism

Taking a militant stand against these attacks, a number of Buddhist leaders sought to form a special committee to take measures to cope with the situation. They decided to release details of these illegal acts through leading newspapers, magazines and broadcasting stations in order to show

1 For details of how Korean fanatics have been involved in the destruction of Buddhist images, see *Christian Thought*, vol. 479 (1998), 56–64.

how they had suffered great losses. Given that the situation grew worse, the Korean Churches could not hesitate to express their condolences to the Buddhists over the idol breaking and incendiarism. On August 7, 1998, KNCC, a representative Christian association, publicly and explicitly censured these fanatics for the negligence of their duty to preserve Buddhist statues as national relics. Many Christian leaders also heard with regret that Buddhists had suffered great losses from such vandalism and felt that it was a great pity that things should have come to this. Dr. Jong-Sung Lee, a leading theologian in the Korean Presbyterian Church (Tong Hap), stated:

> It is said that recently, there has been antagonism and conflict between Christianity and Buddhism. The hostility between the two religions caused in civil society, the army and the religious world, has not come to an end. It is not easy to do away with this conflict since these two religions have their own subjective worldview. Given that we live in a religious pluralistic world based upon the spirit of democracy, however, it is unacceptable to tolerate religious authoritarianism and despotism… If Christianity believes the Lordship of Jesus Christ as the absolute truth, it is essential to respond with love, patience and respect to non-evangelicals until they embrace the truth. Since God is love, violence and aggression are not tolerable.[2]

Even laymen thought that it was a matter of sincere regret that such incidents had happened so frequently. Nevertheless, the great majority of Korean Buddhists were still sceptical about the Korean Churches' response. Being concerned about such long-standing and confrontational divisions between the two major religions in Korea, the Ministry of Culture and Tourism sought to arrange for a special meeting to intercede between the conflicting religions so that they could reach an amicable settlement. On August 27, 1998, five Christian leaders met seven Buddhist representatives to confer with them about problems between Christianity and Buddhism.

However, both circles in no way could make a compromise to solve the long-term hostility between them. This is because the Buddhist camp understood that this iconoclasm had been perpetrated by a well-organised group while the Christian side assumed that only a handful of vandals were responsible for the incidents. Sadly, Christian iconoclasts never renounced idol breaking but continued to focus on the demolition of Bud-

2 Ibid., 66.

dhist statues, a form of iconoclasm that has been contentious in Korean religious societies.

2. Vandalism of the images of Tangun

2.1. The Hanmunhwa Movement Federation of Korea and its 'Tangun' project

The ongoing conflict concerning iconoclasm of Tangun statues between a civil group, the Hanmunhwa[3] Movement Federation of Korea (HMFK), and the Christian community has been a controversial issue in Korean religious societies. At the core of this bizarre conflict is a mythical figure, Tangun, concerning early Korean history.[4] A religious group known as HMFK was launched on June 12, 1998 with 300 participants, including the Venerable Wol-Ju (chief of the Buddhist Chogye Order), Ji-Ha Kim (a celebrated Korean poet) and other social leaders. Hyung-Rae Lee, spokesman for the organization, stated, "Tangun is the legitimate founder of Korea. He is not just a fictional figure. However, the ancient Korean tales of Tangun were severely distorted by the Japanese colonialists in an

3 This Korean term refers to native Korean culture.

4 The ancient Korean myth of Tangun first appeared in the *Memorabilia of the Three Kingdoms* (samguk yusa), an unofficial history written by the monk Il Yon (1206–1289), who attempted to create an ideology that would educate the people and foster universal love at the end of the 13th century. In the Tangun legend found in 'the Memorabilia of the Three Kingdoms, he was the son of Hwanung, the son of Heavenly King, Hwanin. Hwanung had a keen desire to descend among the humans. Hwanin allowed his son's descent to the terrestrial world, along with a retinue of 3,000 subjects and three gods in charge of wind, rain, and the clouds. After descending to the earthly world, Hwanung built the Sacred City in Mt. Taebaek, which is now Mt. Paekdu in North Korea. Though he had to marry a woman, no woman existed at that time. One day a tiger and bear approached Hwanung and requested to be turned into human beings. Hwanung said if the tiger and bear could live only on garlic and mugwort for 100 days in the dark of a cave, they would become human. The tiger was not able to complete the task, but the bear succeeded and was transformed into a woman called Woongnyo. She married Hwanung and gave birth to Tangun, who founded the Old Choson kingdom in Pyongyang in North Korea in 2333 B.C. and ruled it for more than 1,000 years.

effort to destroy the national spirit." With the aim of reviving the founding values of Korea represented by Tangun and applying them in modern Korean society, HMFK began donating 2.5-meter bronze figures of Tangun to public buildings and schools.

2.2. *Churches' response to the Tangun project*

Despite HMFK's attempt to make Tangun a state symbol to revive Korea's spiritual roots, this legendary progenitor has been at the centre of a religious brawl. Indeed, the HMFK's plan to put up more than 360 Tangun statues across the country in schools and public parks drew outrage from individual Christians and met with strong resistance from Christian groups.[5] Local Christian organisations issued petitions to stop this campaign, calling the plan a plot to idolize the mythical figure. Churches resisted the HMFK movement, calling it a bid to establish a state religion by erecting iconic figures. According to Christian groups, Tangun is nothing more than a mythical figure born to Hwangung, the son of a heavenly king, and Woongnyo, a bear woman. In other words, Tangun is merely a fictional figure whose existence cannot be historically reconstructed. Jae-Ha Ryu, general-secretary of the Korean National Council of Churches (KNCC) said:

> The existence of Tangun has not been proven. They [HMFK] are just trying to cover the nation with mythical idols. Erecting a religious symbol in public places is illegal and, worse, their act will develop a false view of history among our children.[6]

He added:

> HMFK's intention is to expand its membership by exerting an undue influence on impressionable young people... Based on superiority of native values, ultra-national doctrines might lead to extreme patriotism and a tragic end since they deny foreign cultures in the age of globalization.[7]

5 Jung-Woo Kim, "The conflict between the mythical Tangun and the historical Tangun and the scope of religious tolerance," in *Journal of Bible Sarangbang*, vol. 9 (1999), 3–6.

6 *The Korea Herald*, July 9, 1999.

7 *Korean Times*, July 4, 1999.

In this regard, it is inappropriate to display the images of Tangun at local schools and public areas and to create a national religion based on an uncertain myth. Churches continued to argue that a rash attempt to erect the statues in public institutions is a violation of the constitution, which guarantees freedom of religion. Then they staged protests and sent letters to schools to dissuade them from putting an object of worship in public institutions. However, HMFK on no account sympathized with the Christians' response to the Tangun campaign. Chi-Hun Han, a spokeman for HMFK said, "Without knowing the spirit and philosophical foundation on which Korea was built, we cannot make further progress in a world which is now dominated by Western values."[8] They announced that building the images of Tangun has nothing to do with a violation of the constitution. They also insisted that the schools accepted the Tangun images as being beneficial for educational purposes. Inevitably, this religious dispute over Korea's mythical figure came to a head, a serious dispute between HMFK and the Christian community that culminated in the vandalism of fanatics who are involved in attacks on Tangun statues in provincial schools.

2.3. Vandalistic attacks on the images of Tangun

On June 1999, three seated Tangun statues, made of bronze and other metals, were intentionally beheaded, defaced with paint or completely destroyed in elementary and middle schools in Yoju, Kyonggi Province.[9] Indeed, the public were transfixed by the awful images of Tangun in the schools. Christian vandals, who give short shrift to 'Tangun worship', were suspected of perpetrating the attacks. In response to this vandalism, HMFK issued a statement expressing its rage on the insensible and violent acts. Min-Jong Sin, spokeswoman for the organization, said:

> Tangun has existed in our 'collective unconscious' as the origin of Korea's national identity. It has survived oppression by Japanese colonial rulers and the rejection of some religious extremists.[10]

Misfortune never comes alone. On December 12, 1999, seven Protestant ministers, who dismissed 'Tangun worship' as a form of idolatry and de-

8 Ibid.
9 *Weekly Chosun*, August 28, 2001.
10 *The Korea Herald*, July 9, 1999.

nounced the HMFK campaign as an attempt to create a national faith around the iconic figure, were actively involved in destroying Tangun images in South Kyongsang Province.

As a consequence, on May 24, 2001, two of them were prosecuted for vandalism and thereby sentenced to two years' penal servitude for it. A district court announced that while it was possible to try to dissuade the government from letting the statues be placed in public schools, it was unlawful to perpetrate such vandalism to destroy the statues without legal proceedings. Sadly, these acts of vandalism did not disappear, and remain a controversial issue that has damaged relations between HMFK and the Christian community.

So far it has been shown how the issue of iconoclasm has enmeshed the Korean Churches in difficulties and how Buddhists and HMFK have responded to the vandalistic acts committed by several Christian extremists. The iconoclasm continues, however, and no authority has intervened to settle the issue. At this point, one finds it of vital consequence to assess the ongoing iconoclastic behaviour from a biblical perspective. In this sense, this research emphasises the book of Isaiah, especially its universalist themes, to offer critical implications for this issue in the last part of the research.

Part II

Situating My Reading of Isaiah in the Larger Methodological Debate

As indicated above, over the past two decades, Korean religious pluralism has been an intense fuse to spark a severe conflagration accompanied by scorching disputes between conservative theologians and their opponents supportive of religious pluralism. Indeed, this deep-seated and long-standing division between both sides has intensified rather than declined. While there have been fiery controversies between the two camps, each side has tended to mount an intense assault on its adversaries. As a result, there has been very little dialogue or genuine argument between the two camps.

Interestingly, both of these opposing circles respectively, with a rare exception, share the view with a host of Korean Churches that the Bible is to be held in high esteem and embraced as the word of God. Still, it is ironic that no one among these two camps, both of whom belong to the Korean Churches, has offered a wide-ranging and meticulous look at how to appraise Korean religious pluralism from a biblical perspective. In fact, while Korean pluralist writers have been deeply committed to God's universal characteristics marked by His wide-reaching presence in the midst of all the world, including all religions, evangelical theologians appear to have been solicitous to emphasis His particular traits such as His incomparability or His uniqueness.

It is must be pointed out, however, that, in spite of strongly held views, no-one from either of the two sides has produced a study that offers a clear-cut treatment of religious pluralism in the light of the Bible. No one has looked closely at universalism and particularism in the Bible and how biblical views can be informative to the present debate. In this sense, this research will aim to offer a scrupulous look at how to view religious pluralism from these two central themes found in the Bible, especially the book of Isaiah. This is because the two central themes, particularism and universalism, are predominantly embedded in the book of Isaiah as a whole.

In addition, it must be considered that the book of Isaiah has been regarded as one of the most beloved biblical books read by Korean Christians since several of its passages are often cited by New Testament writers, especially the Synoptic authors who tend to link its messianic prophecies to Jesus. In this regard, it is of vital consequence to assess the two issues (religious pluralism and iconoclasm) in the light of the book of

Isaiah, especially its particularist and universalist motifs.[1] Therefore, this section will seek to show my strategy for reading Isaiah as a preliminary stage to the specific elucidation of the two core themes, particularism and universalism in Isaiah, which play a central role in evaluating the issues in the context of the Korean Churches.

1 While it would be important to study particularism and universalism in the larger biblical perspective, the limits of this study confine me to the book of Isaiah. I hope to turn to these broader perspectives in future studies.

Chapter 3

Strategy for Reading Isaiah

As mentioned earlier, this research will aim to probe several central themes concerned with the two concepts, particularism and universalism, deeply rooted in the book of Isaiah. My interpretive strategy based upon the literary approach is divorced from the usual historical-critical interpretive methods. My interest is to view the book of Isaiah as a literary whole rather than to attempt to identify and to explore the original materials deriving from the eighth century prophet, Isaiah ben Amoz, or from the so called Second Isaiah or Third Isaiah.

It is vitally significant to note that in the past two decades, there has been a dramatic move in Isaianic studies to focus on the book of Isaiah as a whole. In other words, it is noteworthy that a group of recent biblical interpreters increasingly tend to understand the book of Isaiah as a whole without embracing the three-book theory proposed by Duhm and followed by most other mainstream scholars for over a century. In order to place my reading of Isaianic research in perspective, it will be of consequence to sketch current trends of Isaianic studies centred on the cohesiveness of the book of Isaiah.

1. Wholistic Reading of the Book of Isaiah in Recent Research

Since Bernhard Duhm, an influential German scholar, whose commentary on the Book of Isaiah was published in 1892,[1] the Book has been sepa-

1 *Das Buch Jesaia* (HKAT 3.1; Göttingen; Vandenhoeck & Ruprecht, 1892); Before Duhm's three-book theory, critical scholars such as J. C. Döderlein (1775) and J. G. Eichhorn (1780–83) also addressed the presupposition that the book of Isaiah is a composition encompassing independent books.

rated into three independent books.[2] His scheme postulates that chs. 1–39 must be the work of the eighth century prophet of Jerusalem, Isaiah ben Amos, that chs. 40–55 were written by anonymous prophet of the Babylonian exile identified as Deutero-Isaiah, and that chs. 56–66 are writings of a prophet called Trito-Isaiah who perhaps lived in the postexilic period.[3] This hypothesis has been influential in the scholarly world and in particular has dominated Isaiah studies.

During the past two decades, however, biblical interpreters have begun to shift their scholarly interest from the notion of three Isaiahs to reading the book as a whole. Unlike Duhm and those who walk in his footsteps, they regard the present text as containing a literary cohesiveness. The book of Isaiah has not come to us in divided segments but as a literary whole. Most recently, a growing number of biblical commentators have been involved in the discussion of the unity of the book by focusing on the book as a whole. It can be seen, however, that in spite of their deep commitment to the unity of the book of Isaiah, these contemporary scholars not only manifest various interpretations but also offer different approaches to the entire book understood as a whole. Roy F. Melugin comments on this interpretive phenomenon correctly as below:

> Why these differences? They do not differ because they possess different texts of Isaiah or because major new archaeological evidence available to some but not others accounts for differences in interpretation. Instead, each of these scholars employs a somewhat different strategy for interpretation.[4]

2 For an analysis of Duhm's view on the book of Isaiah, see Christopher R. Seitz, *Zion's Final Destiny: The Development of the Book of Isaiah* (Minneapolis: Fortress, 1991), 1–14.

3 Ronald E. Clements, *Old Testament Prophecy: From Oracles to Canon* (Louisville: Westminster John Knox Press, 1996), 78; Christopher R. Seitz, *Zion's Final Destiny: The Development of the Book of Isaiah* (Minneapolis: Fortress, 1991), 1–2; Marvin A. Sweeney, *Isaiah 1–39* (Grand Rapids: Eerdmans, 1996), 41.

4 Roy F. Melugin, "The Book of Isaiah and the Construction of Meaning", in *Writing and Reading the Scroll of Isaiah: Studies of Interpretive Tradition*, eds Craig C. Broyles & Craig A. Evans (Leiden: Brill, 1997), 39; cf. also P. R. House, *Old Testament Theology* (Downers Grove, IVP, 1998), 273–74; For a discussion of the difference between synchronic and diachronic reading of the book of Isaiah, see Rolf Rendtorff, "The Book of Isaiah: A Complex Unity. Synchronic and Diachronic Reading," In *New Visions of Isaiah*, (eds.) R. F. Melugin & M. A. Sweeney, JSOTsup214 (Sheffield: JSOT Press,1996), 32–48.

These scholars seek to approach the book as a whole by employing different interpretive procedures, which stem from their particular strategies, which they bring to the text.[5] Since each of these scholars elaborates a wholistic reading of Isaiah with his/her own methodological perspective, it is of vital significance to articulate these various strategies and to elucidate the differences between them. In order to achieve this task, this study will attempt to offer an in-depth look at how to assess these different approaches under four classifications that are steering current studies of the unity of the book of Isaiah: traditional, redactional, canonical and literary approaches.

1.1. The traditional approach

This approach is firmly affiliated with a pre-critical understanding focusing on the single authorship of the book of Isaiah. The 'one-prophet' theory, which is typical of the traditional approach to Isaiah, takes it for granted that the whole book must be the product of the eighth-century prophet, Isaiah ben Amoz.

Several more recent conservative biblical commentators have shown their approval of this model as their main methodological approach to Isaiah research. They have not slavishly but mainly followed in the footsteps of E. J. Young, a leading conservative biblical interpreter, who published a three-volume work on Isaiah[6] over three decades ago. They have tended to preserve this scheme oriented to the single authorship of the book while espousing Young's primary principle. Thus this research will seek to look more closely at two contemporary conservative theologians, John N. Oswalt and J. A. Motyer, who represent the traditional view on the unity of Isaiah by looking at what is their eloquent response to the historical critical view on the composition of Isaiah.

In his book, *The Book of Isaiah: Chapters 1–39*, John N. Oswalt firmly rebuts Duhm's three-book thesis and takes up the conviction that Isaiah,

5 For a considerable analysis of these strategies, see Edgar W. Conrad, *Reading Isaiah,* OBT (Minneapolis: Fortress Press, 1991), 3–33.

6 E. J. Young, *The Book of Isaiah* (3 vols, Grand Rapids: Eerdmans, 1965–72). For further information on Young's academic career, see Allan Harmon, "Edward Joseph Young," in *Biblical Interpreters of the 20th Century: A Selection of Evangelical Voices*, (eds.) Walter A. Elwell & J. D. Weaver (Grand Rapids: Baker Books, 1999), 189–201.

the son of Amoz, is responsible for the whole book. He critiques the historical critical approach to the book of Isaiah that has predominated in Isaiah studies since Duhm published his epoch making commentary on Isaiah. First of all, Oswalt points out that a greater part of the historical critics who espouse Duhm's hypothesis by no means arrive at a uniform agreement regarding the date and authorship of the book. Rather they set forth a variety of notions about the final composition of the book. He goes on to observe, "It is very difficult to obtain agreement among scholars as to the date and authorship of any but a few chapters of the total book."[7]

In addition, having taken into consideration that Duhm's criteria downplays the message of the book of Isaiah, he argues that "since it is agreed that the prophet can speak only to his immediate historical context and even then not in specific prediction, much of religious argument of the book is reduced to rhetoric, and faulty rhetoric at that."[8] Finally, he eloquently insists that the thesis of multiple authorship cannot be adopted in the light of the theological and ideological unity of the book. He maintains, "It must be asked whether the hypothesis of a complex redactional process functioning over several hundred years can satisfactorily account for that unity, especially since there is no evidence that such a group process existed."[9] It is clear, therefore, that Oswalt is deeply devoted to the notion of one individual author, the prophet of Jerusalem, Isaiah the son of Amoz, by whom the entire book was written.

Oswalt seeks to overcome the problem of differences between the style and historical context of chs. 1–39 and those of chs. 40–66 (a factor that has led scholars to argue for two or three Isaiahs) in the following way. He maintains that the different styles in chs. 1–39 and in chs. 40–66 result from different subjects and different phases in the prophet's life. As Oswalt understands it, Isaiah wrote chs. 1–39 and 40–66 at two times of his life and on two different subjects. He remarks:

> Thus, it is not at all beyond the realm of possibility that some years after the completion of what are now chs. 1–39, new visions of God's greatness, particularly as it related to a future era, provoked in Isaiah a new style consistent with the broadened vistas he was now seeing. A similar case in point seems to be the gospel of

7 John N. Oswalt, *The Book of Isaiah: Chapters 1–39,* NICOT (Grand Rapids: Eerdmans, 1986), 24.

8 Ibid, 24.

9 Ibid, 25.

> John and the book of Revelation, if tradition is correct that the two books should be attributed to the same person.[10]

Interestingly, however, he does not preclude the possibility of compositional works, that is, the whole book was edited or transmitted by others who ministered with the prophet of Jerusalem.[11] It must be pointed out, here, that his argument becomes contradictory. While he appears to disclaim the editorial process of the book by maintaining the single authorship, he nevertheless opens the plausibility of redactional transmission.

In my judgement, it is problematic to speak of both single authorship and redaction since the two methodological approaches clearly are not in accord with each other. Inasmuch as Oswalt presumes the existence of editorial or transitional materials added by others, it is impracticable to sustain the one-prophet thesis. Regardless of his brilliant observations and serious interpretation of the book highlighting single authorship, Oswalt inevitably makes a problematic assumption by entertaining both the notion of single authorship and redaction.

I wish now to turn to the viewpoint of J. A. Motyer, an eminent conservative theologian who, in his reflections on Biblical theology has engaged the book of Isaiah. Like Oswalt he attributes the authorship of the book of Isaiah to the eighth-century prophet, Isaiah ben Amoz of Jerusalem. Firstly, espousing the observations of O. T. Allis,[12] he holds the view that the three-book interpretation initiated by critics was heavily influenced by nineteenth-century rationalism.[13] Historical critics who maintain Duhm's rationalist criteria postulate that the book of Isaiah alludes to three different stages in which conceivably three different individual authors worked. Also, they advocate two presuppositions: (1) the existence of a 'school' of Isaianic disciples, which perhaps added some materials to the original literature, and (2) the work of an editor, who creates a final composition by collecting and arranging the various materials.[14]

As a result, they conclude that it is inappropriate to sustain the wholeness of Isaiah since the present book of Isaiah contains three independent

10 Ibid, 26.

11 Ibid.

12 For a further analysis of his biblical method, see John H. Skilton, "Oswald T. Allis," in *Biblical Interpreters of the 20th Century: A Selection of Evangelical Voices*, (eds.) Walter A. Elwell & J. D. Weaver (Grand Rapids: Baker Books, 1999), 122–130.

13 J. A. Motyer, *The Prophecy of Isaiah* (Leicester: IVP, 1993), 25.

14 Ibid., 30.

works implying various historical settings. However, Motyer prefers to consider the whole Isaianic literature as "originating from an 'organizing mind' (Isaiah's) at the beginning rather than from an anonymous editor and a company of disciples-preachers in the fifth-century."[15] Subsequently he argues that the oldest manuscript dating back to 100 BC demonstrates the synthesis of Isaiah since "the first two lines of chapter 40 (which is where many scholars say the book should be divided) come without any break in the text at the bottom of the column on which chapter 39 ends."[16] Furthermore, he imputes the entire book to Isaiah of Jerusalem in order to recover the overall cohesiveness of the book of Isaiah. Then he draws the conclusion that it follows naturally to adopt the overall unity of Isaiah based on a single authorship of the book.

He further argues that the New Testament quotes several passages of the text of Isaiah, which means that "the New Testament writers and Jesus took Isaiah to be the author of the whole book that bears his name."[17] Consequently he appears to maintain that the name of Isaiah used in the New Testament quotations from Isaiah must refer to the eighth-century prophet Isaiah. Thus, he resolutely defends a single authorship attributing the book to the authorship of the prophet Isaiah, the son of Amoz, by stressing the authority of the New Testament.

Yet, it is questionable whether his conclusion that in order to recover the unity of the book, a single authorship of Isaiah must be sustained. There could be several alternate ways to corroborate the unity of Isaiah without such a traditional approach concerned with single authorship. Recently, there are many scholars who are willing to search for the overall literary cohesiveness and the theological unity of the text by utilizing different methodological strategies.[18] While witnessing to the unity of Isaiah

15 Marvin E. Tate, "The Book of Isaiah in Recent Study", In *Forming Prophetic Literature: Essays on Isaiah and the Twelve in Honor of John D. W. Watts*, (eds.) James W. Watts & Paul R. House, JSOTSup 235 (Sheffield: Sheffield Academic Press, 1996), 27.

16 J. A. Motyer, *Isaiah: An Introduction and Commentary* (Leicester: InterVarsity Press, 1999), 27.

17 Ibid., 34.

18 Marvin E. Tate, "The Book of Isaiah in Recent Study", In *Forming Prophetic Literature: Essays on Isaiah and the Twelve in Honor of John D. W. Watts*, JSOTSup 235, (eds.) James W. Watts & Paul R. House (Sheffield: Sheffield Academic Press, 1996) 43–50. Here Tate discusses four interpretive strategies in association with the one-book interpretation including the following: Thematic and Intertextual Continuities, Redactional Analyses and Literary Readings.

by utilizing various interpretive procedures, they find it unnecessary to embrace the assumption of a single authorship, a theory that remains a nucleus of the traditional approach. Paul R. House summarizes these interpretive trends in the following way:

> At this point critical and conservative scholars alike are dealing with texts as they have been received in the Hebrew canon. Some of these writers are interested in the literary unity of the text, some in the book's theological coherence, some in its editorial structuring and some in its role as canonical document. Disagreements over authorship issues remain a significant point of contention, but this difference no longer precludes discussion of matters that reflect Isaiah's theological unity.[19]

Though scholars set forth varying solutions concerning the issues of authorship, a growing number of them concentrate on the unity of the text as containing a literary and theological cohesiveness. As a result, it is not mandatory to push for one individual author of Isaiah in order to demonstrate the book's wholeness. It is my judgment, therefore, that the direction of our interpretive reading must advance forward to the holistic reading of the present text without being sidetracked by authorship issues. Moreover, because people such as the Jews, pose a fundamental objection to the authority of the New Testament, the suggestion ascribing a single authorship to the New Testament's authority would be problematic to those who do not belong to Christian communities, and who embrace only the Old Testament as canonical.

1.2. The redactional critical approach

Unlike conservative biblical commentators such as John N. Oswalt and Alec Motyer who are deeply committed to the single authorship of the book of Isaiah, others are more concerned with the creative manipulation of an editor responsible for shaping the text into a unified whole. Unlike older historical critics,[20] who look for authentic oracles in the text used by

19 P. R. House, *Old Testament Theology* (Downers Grove: IVP, 1998), 273–274.

20 Form critics, for example, separate between authentic oracles and non-authentic oracles that may be late additions inserted into previous material by an editor. They then attempt to identify its authenticity from the literature by concentrating on genre, historical background and literary units. For a discussion of older historical criticism, see Edgar W. Conrad, *Reading Isaiah,* 6–12; Marvin A. Sweeney, *Isaiah 1–39* (Grand Rapids: Eerdmans, 1996), 10–14.

redactors who collected and added to the original work of the prophets, they argue that it is a composite work containing different kinds of materials but shaped into a unified final form. They are committed to the intention of an editor, who has become a kind of 'author' shaping the text as a whole. They search for the meaning of the text in Isaiah's unity, which they understand to be an intentional and redactional design by an editor. This methodological approach has been employed by redactional critics such as R. E. Clements, Rolf Rendtorff and Marvin A. Sweeney. Here, I will aim to analyse their interpretive strategies and comment on them.

Disavowing the single authorship of the book of Isaiah, R. E. Clements understands the whole book of Isaiah to be the fabrication of an anonymous redactor. Like older historical critics, however, he does not believe the redactional shape of the book of Isaiah to be the result of purely mechanical collection. Clements remarks:

> All of these considerations are sufficient to indicate that the overall structure of the book shows signs of editorial planning and that, at some stage in its growth, attempts were made to read and interpret the book as a whole. There are also many indications, however, to show that the contents of the book have passed through a number of stages of ordering and redaction and that what we now have is the result of a process of editing and addition. It would be possible to suppose therefore that the kind of editorial unity which now binds chs. 1–39 with chs. 40–66 belongs to a late, and relatively superficial, stage in the book's compilation.[21]

Clements argues forcefully, then, that both chs. 1–39 and 40–66 taken together manifest a kind of editorial unity since they are intentionally combined by the creativity of a series of redactors. Consequently he observes that themes such as "Israel's blindness and deafness",[22] "a light to the nations"[23] and "Zion as symbol and political reality",[24] function as

21 R. E. Clements, "The Unity of the Book of Isaiah" in *Old Testament Prophecy: From Oracles to Canon* (Louisville: Westminster John Knox Press, 1996), 96.

22 R. E. Clements, "Beyond Tradition History: Deutoro-Isaianic Development of First Isaiah's Themes," in *Old Testament Prophecy*, 78–92.

23 R. E. Clements, "A Light to the Nations: A Central Theme of the Book of Isaiah," in *Forming Prophetic Literature: Essays on Isaiah and the Twelve in Honor of John D. W. Watts*, (eds.) James W. Watts and Paul R. House, JSOTSup 235 (Sheffield: Sheffield Academic Press, 1996), 57–69.

24 R. E. Clements, "Zion as Symbol and Political Reality: A Central Isaianic Quest," in *Studies in the Book of Isaiah: Festschrift Willem A. M. Beuken*, (ed.) J. Van Ruiten and M. Vervenne, Bibliotheca Ephemeridum Tehologicarum Lovaniensium CXXXII (Leiden: Leuven University Press, 1997), 3–17.

evidence of editorial unity. According to Clements, these themes are spread throughout the entire book and are significant keys suggesting it to be a composite and unified work. These themes set forth in chs. 1–39 are also found in chs. 40–66. This fact indicates that chs. 40–66 develop the themes of chs. 1–39.

Furthermore, Clements underscores the redactional function of chs. 36–39, which connotes the creative work of an editor. He argues that chs. 36–39 are the latest material and were put between chs. 1–35 and chs. 40–66 to function as a bridge connecting them. In other words chs. 35–36 make "a suitable conclusion for the first half of the book by introducing an abbreviated summary of the message of hope which occupies the second half."[25] Thus, the first half of the book, which prophesies the demise of Jerusalem, is followed by ch. 40, which begins with oracles concerning the deliverance of Israel. Therefore the two parts of the book (chs. 1–35 and 40–66) are bound together by chs. 36–39, which suggests an intentionally composite work put together by scribes. In summary, Clements concludes that the overall cohesiveness of the book of Isaiah must be based on editorial activities that have creatively manipulated the collected sources into an organized whole.

Rolf Rendtorff, a leading German scholar, does not so much slavishly adopt the older historical-critical approach of reading Isaiah as three separate books; rather he analyses the book of Isaiah by searching for key words as evidence indicating the wholeness of the book. In particular, his redactional approach to the book of Isaiah has drawn the attention of many scholars since it is so divorced from that of existing historical critics. He takes up the observation that some key words indicate the unity of the book of Isaiah since they are widespread throughout the book. First, he notes that core words in chs. 40 such as "comfort", "the glory of the Lord" and "iniquity", are reiterated everywhere in the whole book.

> In that day you will say: I will praise you, O LORD. Although you were angry with me, your anger has turned away and you have *comforted* me. (12:1) *Comfort, comfort* my people, says your God. (40:1) As a mother *comforts* her child, so will I *comfort* you, and you will be *comforted* over Jerusalem. (66:13)

And they were calling to one another: "Holy, holy, holy is the LORD Almighty, the whole earth is full of *his glory*," (6:3); And *the glory of the*

25 R. E. Clements, "The Unity of the Book of Isaiah," 96.

LORD will be revealed, and all mankind together will see it. For the mouth of the LORD has spoken." (40:5); "Arise, shine, for your light has come, and *the glory of the LORD* rises upon you. (60:1); "And I, because of their actions and their imaginations, am about to come and gather all nations and tongues, and they will come and see *my glory*." (66:18)

According to Rendtorff, these core words are keys for understanding the way the entire book is connected. They disclose the linkage combining chs. 1–39, chs. 40–55 and chs. 56–66 with each other. Furthermore, he states that notions such as "Zion/Jerusalem", "Holy One of Israel" and "Righteousness", are main concepts which link the three sections thereby forging Isaiah into one final product.[26]

Here, unlike Clements who observes that chs. 40–55 develop themes and notions in chs. 1–39, Rendtorff points out that chs. 40–55 are the common base for the two other parts of the book (chs. 1–39 and 56–66) because both are oriented to it. Accordingly, he makes it clear that "chs. Xl–lv form the core of the present composition from which and toward which both of the other sections have been shaped and edited."[27] Therefore, chs. 40–55 form the compositional core of the book of Isaiah and neither chs. 1–39 nor chs. 56–66 can be understood apart from it.

Marvin A. Sweeney underscores the creative handling of the editors who composed the book of Isaiah in its final form. He takes up the conviction that the literary characteristics and ideas in the present text stem from the intention of the anonymous redactors. Subsequently, he takes into consideration that "the overall structure, genre, setting and intention of the book in its final form must be studied in order to identify the per-

26 Rolf Rendtorff, *The Old Testament: An Introduction* (London: SCM Press, 1985), 198–95. More recently he stresses the importance of the function of ch. 6 and 56:1. See his *Canon and Theology*, OBT (Minneapolis: Fortress, 1993), 146–69, 170–80, and 181–89.

27 The quotation comes from Edgar W. Conrad, *Reading Isaiah*, 17. Rolf Rendtorff emphasises the dominant role of Second Isaiah in the book of Isaiah in the following way: "the book of Isaiah has not been composed by the combination of three independent 'books', but is a work with many strata and a lengthy history behind it. It has two specific focal points: the activity of the prophet Isaiah in the second half of the eighth century and the collection of the sayings of a prophet or preacher, who remains anonymous, towards the end of the Babylonian exile. The latter's proclamation of salvation became the starting point for a wider collection in which Isaiah's message of judgment was continued and met a response in the message of salvation at the time of the exile, and was taken up and developed in the post-exilic period." (See his *The Old Testament: An Introduction*, 200).

spectives and literary character of the final redaction."[28] Thus, though the book of Isaiah has an editorial history of 400 years, it is clear that the present final form of the book can be regarded as a single literature based on this redactional work.[29]

Furthermore, the structure of the literature is concerned with several themes. In particular "judgment" and "restoration," which are major themes in the book, play a dominant function in the book of Isaiah as a whole. According to Sweeney, chs. 1–39 predict coming judgment and ensuing restoration, while chs. 34–66 claim that the renewal is about to commence, which means that the punishment has already ended.[30] Then he offers a scrupulously detailed analysis of how both chs. 1–39 and 34–66 are linked with each other through the themes of "Judgement" and "Restoration", themes which are set forth in the entire book.[31] Besides these themes, Sweeney also presents other concepts to corroborate the theological and literary cohesiveness of the book of Isaiah such as the following:

(1) The lexical associations between chs. 1 and 65–66
(2) The portrayal of Babylon as the symbol of world power arrayed against in both halves of the book
(3) The transitional function of chs. 36–39
(4) The theme of a new exodus
(5) The theme of Israel's blindness and deafness
(6) The theme of "justice" and "righteousness"[32]

Sweeney's concern is to show that these themes are conclusive features demonstrating the unity of Isaiah. Yet Sweeney's view, like that of Clements and Rendtorff, on the literary coherence of the book of Isaiah is based on the authorial intention of the redactor. They understand the oneness of the book according to the redactor's authorial intention. Redactional critics, including Sweeney, postulate that this editorial or redactional unity developed as result of the creative manipulation of redactors, who created the book as it developed through time (diachronically). They

28 Marvin A. Sweeney, "The Book of Isaiah in Recent Research," *CR: BS* 1 (1993), 147.

29 Ibid.

30 Mavin A. Sweeney, *Isaiah 1–39,* 41.

31 For a detail analysis of this issue, see his *Isaiah 1–39*, 41–44.

32 Ibid., 41–42.

do not understand the unity of the book of Isaiah as a synchronic whole apart from matters concerning its redactional intention.

It can now be seen that redactional critics demonstrate the synthesis of the book of Isaiah highlighting the creative design of redactors whose intentions are in fact not intrinsic to the text but imposed from the outside. Now I want to comment further on their main theories and interpretive methodologies. First of all, unlike old critics who devote their attention to the authentic words of the prophet contained in the text, redactional critics such as Clements, Rendtorff and Sweeney are entirely concerned with the intention and theology of editors. Unlike old critics who consider the text as a collection edited mechanically, they draw attention to the redactional unity of the text based on the artful handling by redactors. However, these scholars draw a great distinction between the intention of the prophet as author and the intention of the editor.

If the editorial design results from redactional intention, then, it is impossible to detect the original intention of the prophet. The creative design of the redactor means that the original words of the prophet could be manipulated. The editor's intention, on which the critics focus, is problematic, however. They are actually doing nothing more than projecting their own assumption about intention into the minds of the redactor(s). Clements argues, for instance, that Isaianic materials were revised for those who survived when Jerusalem fell to Babylon in 587 B.C. He proceeds to observe that a late redactor reworked the previous writings, since it is inevitable that these survivors not only listened to reasons for the current devastation but also to the message of hope.[33]

However, Clements' reasoning is problematic. There is no way of knowing whether survivors had such needs or whether a late editor actually revised the text. Clements' argument is just nothing more than his own tentative conjecture about the meaning of the text projected into the past. Sweeney also attempts to make a structural analysis of the book of Isaiah, especially of chs. 1–39, in the light of the redactional intention. However, these structural frames are constructed by Sweeney, which he attributes to a past redactional design. Melugin supports this criticism of Sweeney's presentation of structure:

> Yet the structure is not "in" the text; it is rather a construct shaped by Sweeney. He has not discovered a structure; he has created one. To be sure, Sweeney's presenta-

33 R. E. Clements, *Old Testament Prophecy*, 101–102.

> tion of structure can be tested as to how well it "fits" the text. But even if Sweeney's structure seems to "fit" the text, it is quite possible that a somewhat different conceptualization of structure might also fit the text equally well.[34]

Indeed, the dates and the process of editing as well as the redactional structure of the text that redactional critics propose are based on their own construction of the text as readers. They assume that redactional intentions are found "in" the text. As Conrad points out,[35] however, they do not discover the editors' intentions but create them by utilizing their own interpretive strategies.

1.3. The canonical approach

The canonical approach is one of the major interpretive methodologies initiated by critical scholars who, since the early 1970s, saw flaws in historical criticism. Canonical critics downplay the diachronic reading of the historical approach and highlight the text in its present form as the locus of interpretation.[36] In particular, they seek to find the unity of the Isaianic text emphasising its final form. This canonical methodology has been employed by significant scholars such as Brevard S. Childs, J. A. Sanders, Christopher R. Seitz and Paul R. House. Here I will seek especially to focus on the canonical analyses of Childs, Seitz and House.

In his article, "The Canonical Shape of the Prophetic Literature," having commented on several problematic defects of the historical approach,[37] Childs points out that historical critics are not concerned with

34 Roy F. Melugin, "The Book of Isaiah and the Construction of Meaning," 48.

35 Conrad comments on redactional intentions that critics such as Sweeney present in the following way: "The redactors' intentions are no more inherent in the text than those of the prophet. His own interpretive strategies, imposed from outside the text, have shaped the text and have yield intentions." (Edgar W. Conrad, *Reading Isaiah*, 20).

36 For a detail of basic theories of canonical approach, see Carl R. Holladay, "Contemporary Methods of Reading the Bible," in *The New Interpreter's Bible* (Nashville: Abingdon Press, 1994), 134–35.

37 Here it is important to note Childs' critique on the historical critical method. He remarks that "first of all, the legacy of the literary-critical method in distinguishing between 'genuine' and 'non-genuine' oracles has continued to interject a pejorative category into the discussion. Secondly, the form-critical analysis has increasingly atomized the literature and continued to rest much of its analysis upon fragile and often highly speculative theories of original settings. Thirdly, the redactional and so-

the present form of the text that the community of faith has adopted as an authoritative canon.[38] Calling for a radical alternative interpretive method to historical criticism, especially to redactional criticism, then, he underscores the necessity of the canonical approach.[39] In particular, Childs focuses on a canonical understanding of Second Isaiah by presenting it as a new theological context for understanding First Isaiah. Second Isaiah is understood as a word of promise that the prophet of Jerusalem, Isaiah ben Amoz, announced to Israel. This interpretation comes about because "the present non-historical setting into which the canon has placed these traditions is a highly reflective, theological context."[40] In the narrative of Cyrus (44:28–45:1), for instance, the original historical context is kept to a minimum. In other words, Second Isaiah presents Cyrus as a theological reflection rather than a historical individual. The message of Second Isaiah, which originally had its setting in the context of the sixth century,

---

ciological methods have tended to politicize the biblical material and render it into a type of political propaganda. As a result, little success has been achieved in interpreting the prophetic books as Scripture of the church which accords to the Bible an authoritative role in the formation of the Christian life". ("The Canonical Shape of the Prophetic Literature," in *Interpreting the Prophets*, [eds.] James Luther Mays & Paul J. Achtemeier [Philadelphia: Fortress Press, 1987], 41–42).

38 Childs maintains that "theological reflection on its actualization has been built into the structure of the canonical text. The modern hermeneutical impasse has arisen in large measure by disregarding the canonical shaping. The usual critical methodology of restoring an original historical setting often involves stripping away the very elements which constitute the canonical shape. Little wonder that once the text has been anchored in the historical past by 'decanonizing' it, the interpreter has difficulty applying it to a modern religious context!" (Ibid., 43–44).

39 Brevard S. Childs responds with a clear voice to a redactional approach to the book of Isaiah to make a sharp distinction between his interpretive method and redactional criticism. He says, "I agree with the modern redactional stress on the multilayered quality of the biblical text. However, in my opinion, it is fully inadequate to find the unity of this book in a succession of redactional layers, each with its own agenda, which are never ultimately heard in concert as a whole. To end one's critical analysis by outlining a seventh-, sixth-, and fifth-century redactional succession, each with an absolute dating, fails to reckon with the book's canonical authority as a coherent witness in its final received form to the ways of God with Israel. Ultimately, the analysis of distinct layers and compositional growth must be used to enrich the book as a whole, rather than to fragment it into conflicting voices of individual editors, each with a private agenda. In the end, it is the canonical text that is authoritative, not the process, nor the self-understanding of the interpreter." (Brevard S. Childs, *Isaiah,* OTL [Louisville: Westminster John Knox Press, 2001], 4).

40 Ibid., 325.

takes on an eschatological dimension in the context of the eighth-century prophet. Therefore the new context of Second Isaiah now presented as the message of Isaiah, should be understood in its context as a message concerned with God's plan for salvation oriented to all of history. No longer should it be understood as a message for those in exile. This way of interpreting indicates why Childs understands the book of Isaiah to be a cohesive writing in the canonical context.

However, Childs' canonical approach raises several problems. First, though he attempts to set up canonical analysis to overcome what he identifies as the flaws of historical criticism, he does not go beyond the hypotheses of the historical scheme. In other words, he continues to adhere to Duhm's theory of three Isaiahs. Second, while drawing great attention to Second Isaiah, Childs does not expound the canonical function of Third Isaiah. Regardless of these defects, however, his attempt to establish the synthesis of the book of Isaiah from the canonical perspective not only invigorated Isaianic research but gave vitality to other scholars such as Seitz who developed his own canonical approach.

Seitz, Childs' former student and colleague, embraces the canonical approach as his primary method. Though Seitz presents his interpretive methodology as "Canonical Critical"[41] his reading of the book of Isaiah is somewhat dissimilar from Childs' canonical approach. In addition, his understanding of the wholeness of Isaiah is divorced from modern biblical interpretive methodologies that place emphasis on the role of the reader in interpretation. He asserts:

> It seems to me that two mistakes have followed from an emphasis on reading the book of Isaiah as a unity. The first is that a unified book must mean a single reading and just one as the goal of modern interpretation. The second is that unity is only something imposed by readers. As we have seen, "unity" is not a literary claim for single, tightly constructed uniformity of perspective. Rather, it is a concept meant to constrain emphasis on multiplicity of perspectives in a single work. This constraining has not been artificially imposed by later readers armed with a theory of Isaiah's authorship. Rather, it flowed from the historical process that stretched back through time, ultimately to bump into the prophet Isaiah himself,

41 Christopher R. Seitz, "Isaiah 1–66: Making Sense of the Whole," in (ed.) Christopher R. Seitz, *Reading and Preaching the Book of Isaiah*, (Philadelphia: Fortress Press, 1988), 105.

> regarded by the community as coherent and trustworthy and above all as God's man.[42]

In particular, he introduces an analogy of a North Carolina farmhouse[43] in order to illustrate how the text exhibits itself as a whole. The interior of the building has separate rooms. Though this house displays the traces of modification, it is not the result of merging independent houses together. This analogy makes it clear that the "farmhouse was the product of 'redaction,' i.e., that the latest form of the house was the product of earlier architectural arrangements, and that the house was not the result of merging several independent houses but rather by adding to a single original house."[44]

It is his conclusion, therefore, that the book of Isaiah is not so much a work containing three independent books as a final form derived and edited from its original materials. Based on this understanding of the text in its final form, Seitz is intensely resistant to historical critics who state that the entire book of Isaiah is a literature consisting of three separate collections. He offers a current challenge to the three books theory by showing how the text can be understood as a single text growing by addition:

1. There is only one superscription, or opening rubric.
2. There is only one narrative telling of the commissioning of a prophet in the book (i.e., Isaiah, in chap. 6).
3. The literary boundaries between 1, 2, 3 Isaiah are not marked in any special way. [45]

In sum, Seitz comes to the conclusion that the book of Isaiah comes to us as a single book in a final form; not as three separate books though it has been revised in the editorial process.[46]

42 Christopher R. Seitz, *Word without End: The Old Testament as Abiding Theological Witness* (Grand Rapids: Eerdmans, 1998), 128.

43 Ibid., 108–109.

44 Roy F. Melugin, "The Book of Isaiah and the Construction of Meaning," in *Writing and Reading the Scroll of Isaiah: Studies of an Interpretive Tradition,* (eds.) Craig C. Broyles & Craig A. Evans (Leiden: Brill, 1997), 42.

45 C. R. Seitz, "Isaiah 1–66: Making Sense of the Whole," 109.

46 For a discussion of the unity of the book of Isaiah in detail, see his *Word Without End: The Old Testament as Abiding Theological Witness,* 113–29. For a comment on Seitz's view of the unity of Isaiah, see Roy F. Melugin, "Introduction," in *New Vision of Isaiah,* (eds.) Roy F. Melugin & Marvin A. Sweeney, JSOTSup 214 (Sheffield: Sheffield Academic Press, 1996), 16–17.

Paul R. House, an evangelical scholar, has published a significant work, *Old Testament Theology* (1998), viewed from a canonical perspective. In this book, he not only embraces the book of Isaiah as a final canonical form but also as part of the whole canon. He then proceeds to lay great emphasis upon the theological unity of the book of Isaiah as a whole. Accordingly, he presents several themes as focal concepts characterising the unity of the book: God's holiness, monotheism, the New Exodus, Yahweh's rule over history, and the coming Davidic Savior. He also makes a clear representation of the structure of the book based on monotheism:

> The God who condemns and calls: Isaiah 1–12
>
> The God who eliminates prideful Nations: Isaiah 13–27
>
> The God who secures the Remnant: Isaiah 28–39
>
> The God who saves through a suffering Servant: Isaiah 40–55
>
> The God who creates New Heavens and Earth: Isaiah 56–66

Here it is important to note that House does not rely on Duhm's three books theory but demonstrates the theological unity of the book from the canonical perspective. Further, his approach is unique in that he attempts to attribute the subject of the overall message of the book to one God by focusing on monotheism. Subsequently he utilizes the theory of intertexuality in order to find some linkages between the Isaianic text and other books in both the Old Testament and the New Testament. However, Paul House draws a sharp distinction between his approach and other canonical analyses in association with the nature of biblical authority. In a careful discussion of Seitz's canonical methodology in his *Old Testament Theology*, unlike other canonical critics, including Seitz, House seeks to offer his high view of Scripture regarding the Bible as the revealed, written word of God. He affirms:

> Still, I do not agree with Seitz on certain key issues... I do not share his reluctance to equate the Bible with God's word... I believe Seitz undermines his statements about the text's authority and coherence. The Bible's authority rests on the extent to which it is God's revealed, written Word... Though I appreciate Seitz's careful attempts to describe the unity of Isaiah, I do not share his opinion on the book's original author. Again, the authority of a text is in question whether it makes truth

> claims (such as authorship) that are not true... I believe the best canonical approach weds canonical theology and evangelical views of history.[47]

In this sense, it can be seen that House seeks to read the book of Isaiah from a canonical perspective, which lays weight on the final shaping form of the book of Isaiah as canonical, while remaining adherent to an evangelical view of biblical authority. In spite of a deep commitment to canonical approaches, each canonical interpreter respectively expresses a different view of the inspiration and authority of the Old Testament. In other words, neither Childs nor Seitz is as entirely devoted to a high appreciation of the Old Testament as the Word of God in the way House is.

So far I have dealt with some of the main points of specialists who focus on the unity of the book of Isaiah embracing canonical approaches as their own interpretive methods. Though these canonical perspectives are somewhat divergent, their primary focus is on the final form and the thematic theological unity of the book of Isaiah as well. However, there is growing recognition that some canonical critics such as Childs, who advocate a new interpretive scheme to go beyond the weakness of historical approach, seldom remain immune to historical analysis based on a diachronical analysis. Richard J. Coggins launches a powerful criticism of canonical critics, especially of Childs. In a provocative article, he remarks:

> There is also a curious kind of obscurantism in much of the 'canonical' standpoint. As I have just said, Childs's work is built upon the foundation of historical-criticism, yet he often in his more recent writing seems to want to kick away the ladder up which he has climbed. While I have been working on Isaiah I expected to find in his Introduction (to the Old Testament as Scripture) a great deal of help in terms of looking at the book as whole, but I was disappointed. He has a brief discussion, as one would expect, on the reception of Isaiah within the church as a single book, but there is nothing fresh, as far as I was able to discover, in terms of reading it as a unity. For Childs the assumption was that the viewpoint of historical criticism, proposing an extremely complex variety of backgrounds for the elements in the book, was right as far as it went, but having taken that on board what is next required is a great leap of faith to accept the church's traditional use of it as a whole.[48]

47 Paul R. House, *Old Testament Theology*, 558–9.

48 Richard J. Coggins, "New Ways with Old Texts: How Does One Write a Commentary on Isaiah?" in *ET* 9 (1996), 365.

In other words, canonical interpreters, including even Paul House, tend to pose no fundamental objection to a redactional approach which emphases the growth of the book through time.[49] In this regard, it comes as little surprise that the canonical approach sheds no light on the question of how one can be immune to a prevailing historical-critical method and successfully overcome its shortcoming. At last, biblical scholarship inevitably comes to witness the rise of a (new) literary criticism, which seeks to sever ties entirely with historical criticism and even collides head-on with it, a new paradigm shift in interpretation that opens an avenue to a new epoch in interpreting the book of Isaiah.

1.4. The literary approach

Since 1990 some scholars, who point out what they see as the flaws of both redactional and canonical approaches, have employed a literary approach for reading the book of Isaiah as a literary whole. This methodological approach does not accommodate the diachronical reading of the historical method but embraces the book as it is, not as it developed to form a literary whole. Further, this approach emphasizes the role of the reader to which earlier interpreters have paid little attention in interpretation.[50] This interpretive method has been utilized by specialists such as Edgar W. Conrad, Peter D. Miscall, Katheryn Pfisterer Darr and David M. Carr. Here attention is drawn to the works of Conrad, Miscall and Darr.

Edgar W. Conard seeks to detect the literary cohesiveness of the book of Isaiah by calling for a dramatic shift to a new interpretive paradigm. In particular, his reading of the book provides a new starting point for Isaiah research. First, he argues forcefully that many biblical scholars have disregarded the role of the reader who not only brings his/her own interpre-

49 Recently, redaction critics such Clements and Rendtorff are concerned with the canonical approach. This phenomenon indicates that both approaches are blended with each other.

50 Having recognised the significance of the role of reader in interpretation, David J. A. Clines concludes, "What has happened in Biblical studies, as likewise in many branches of literature, simply, is a shift in focus that has moved from author to text to reader." (David J. A. Clines, *What Does Eve Do to Help?: and Other Readerly Questions to the Old Testament*, JSOTSup 94 [Sheffield: Sheffield Academic Press, 1994], 9–10).

tive strategies to the text, but is also involved in the construction of the text's meaning.[51]

Further, he clearly disagrees with historical critics who claim that the meaning of text emerges only from authorial or redactional intention. Rather, he takes up the conviction that the textual meaning comes from the interplay between the text and the reader. That is to say, the meaning of a text emanates from the process of reading. Modern literary critics term such theory "reader response criticism".[52]

Subsequently, Conrad argues that one finds it essential to acknowledge the notion of the otherness of text, that is, that the text is an alien text from the past, and that to understand this text as alien it must be read as a whole.[53] It is significant to discover that for present readers, the book of Isaiah is an alien text passing from the past to the present. It is surprising to realise, however, that many historical critics and fundamentalists have reconstructed the text by dismissing its otherness in order to make it fit into contemporary notions of a text. They force it to fit contemporary notions of textual unity and cohesiveness. Conrad maintains that contemporary readers should read the book of Isaiah as a literary collage. His following statement leads us to understand his synchronical reading of Isaiah:

51 Edgar W. Conrad, *Reading Isaiah*, 3–5.

52 For a detailed discussion of reader response criticism in modern literary theories, see Stanley Fish, *Is There a Text in This Class? The Authority of Interpretive Communities* (Cambridge: Harvard University Press, 1980); see also Susan R. Suleiman and Inge Crosman, eds, *The Reader in the Text: Essays on Audience and Interpretation* (Princeton: Princeton University Press, 1980); (ed.) Jane P. Tompkins, *Reader Response Criticism: From Formalism to Post-Structuralism* (Baltimore: Johns Hopkins University Press, 1980). For an analysis of reader response theories in biblical interpretation, consult Anthony C. Thiselton, "The Hermeneutics of Reading in Reader-Response Theories of Literary Meaning," in *New Horizons in Hermeneutics* (Grand Rapids: Zondervan, 1992), 516–557; idem, "Reader-Response Theories and Biblical Theological Fiction," in Roger Lundin, Clarence Walhout & Anthony C. Thiselton, *The Promise of Hermeneutics* (Grand Rapids: Eermans, 1999), 152–182; Kevin J. Vanhoozer, *Is There a Meaning in This Text?: The Bible, the Reader and the Morality of Literary Knowledge* (Leicester: Apollos, 1998), 367–452; Moises Silva, "Contemporary Theories of Biblical Interpretation," in *NIB* (Nashville: Abingdon Press, 1994), 116–120.

53 Edgar W. Conrad, *Reading Isaiah*, 167–68; See also idem, "Prophet, Redactor and Audience," in *New Vision of Isaiah*, (eds.) Roy F. Melugin & Marvin A. Sweeney, JSOTSup 214 (Sheffield: Sheffield Academic Press, 1996), 315–16.

> The structural unity of a text such as Isaiah is not obvious to contemporary readers of the text. This is because the text has been read customarily by biblical critics as a largely disunified collection of material of disparate origin. It is possible, however, in a close reading of Isaiah to identify recurring rhetorical techniques and patterns that suggest its unity... The Book of Isaiah contains repetition in vocabulary, motif, theme, narrative sequence, and rhetorical devices such as rhetorical questions, pronominal shifts, and forms of address. This repetition creates cohesion in the text. The repetition in the text, however, is not literal; repetition is always repetition with difference. Variation in the recurrence of repeated elements in the text suggests movement and progression.[54]

Most recently, Conrad has sought to employ the theory of intertextuality to make some linkages between the book of Isaiah and the book of the Twelve.[55] Conrad observes that both Isaiah and the Twelve set forth a period of Assyrian dominion, a period when prophetic individuals are ordered by the Lord to write down their message. He goes on to note that in both books these written words are intended for another time.

He makes it obvious, further, that just as oracles written by prophetic figures in the time of Assyrian period were relevant for another time, like the Persian period, the two books are relevant for the present world. He argues, thus, "Our reception of those texts is not something that can be detached from our world any more that the prophetic 'books' or the book of Isaiah's vision can be detached from their reception in a Persian setting in the Book of the Twelve and in the Book of Isaiah".[56] In this regard, it appears to me that his representation of reading Isaiah and the Twelve leads to the conclusion that those books have been received from the past and remain available for the present time.

In sum, having pointed out the shortcoming of historical criticism that reconstructs the text according to contemporary conventions and manners, Conrad enables us to recognise the role of the reader, who utilises his/her own interpretive strategies to read the text, and calls for the necessity of reception of the book as a literary whole.

Like Conrad, Peter D. Miscall adheres to the literary approach and seeks to read Isaiah's text as a whole without adopting Duhm's assumption. Miscall aligns himself with the viewpoint of John D. W. Watts that

54 Edgar W. Conrad, *Reading Isaiah*, 30.

55 Edgar W. Conrad, "Reading Isaiah and the Twelve as Prophetic Books," in *Writing and Reading the Scroll of Isaiah: Studies of an Interpretive Tradition,* (eds.) Craig C. Broyles & Craig A. Evans (Leiden: Brill, 1997), 3–17.

56 Ibid., 17.

the book is a unified whole, a Vision. However, he rebuts Watts' conjecture that the whole book was finally composed in the reign of Artaxerxes I (435 B. C.). While Miscall assumes that the postexilic writer(s) used materials derived from the eighth century to produce a composite work, he is not concerned with exploring the texts' 'original prophetic speeches,' which would lead to reading the book in disconnected sections. Instead, Miscall, like Conrad, approaches the text as a cohesive literary work.

Furthermore, Miscall attempts to link the themes of Genesis 1 to those of the book of Isaiah through intertextual connections, a fact that indicates that Isaiah has to do with the representation of Genesis 1.

> Isaiah tropes on Genesis 1 at the start of his book and by the close has made clear his purpose: a new heavens, a new earth and a new book. "Remember not the beginning things... I am making something new" intones the prophet quoting the Lord. Among "the beginning things" not to be remembered is the report "In the beginning" which, in the Hebrew Bible, is also the title of the book of Genesis. The letters, words and themes of Genesis 1 are dispersed throughout Isaiah; this is a new creation, a new book, and not just a translation of Genesis 1.[57]

Subsequently, he scrutinises several metaphors such as 'light', 'darkness', 'water' and 'dry land' to detect some intertextual linkages between Genesis 2:4a and Isaiah.[58] Such an attempt to link Genesis and Isaiah by several themes opens up a provocative avenue in Isaiah research.

Katheryn Pfisterer Darr, a professor at Boston University in the U.S., also utilises a literary approach to the book of Isaiah. She does not embrace a diachronic reading of the text on which an historical critical approach is based but utilises a synchronic approach to the text grounded upon a reader-oriented reading. She insists, then, that the unity of Isaiah does not rely on the redactional approach but on the readers' synchronic reading because "sequential readers can interrelate texts in ways that redactors never envisioned." Consequently, her approach exemplifies a synchronic reading of the text of Isaiah.

> Consider, for example, Isa 2:5–22 with its threat that Yahweh "has a day" against "all that is proud and lofty" (vs. 12). These various symbols of grandiosity-cedars

57 Peter D. Miscall, "Isaiah: New Heavens, New Earth, New Book" in *Reading Between Texts: Intertextuality and The Hebrew Bible*. (ed.) Danna Nolan Fewell (Louisville: Westminster/John Knox Press, 1993), 48.

58 For a detailed analysis of those metaphors, see his "Isaiah: New Heavens, New Earth, New Book", 41–57.

> of Lebanon, high mountains, lofty towers-include the "ships of Tarshish," vessels proverbial for their size, beauty, and richly-laden holds. Whether redactors intended a connection between 2:16 and a sequentially much later text is, of course, impossible to prove. For the reader recalling this early threat, however, Yahweh's "day" comes with the opening words of Isaiah 23: "Wail, O ships of Tarshish, for your fortress is destroyed" (vs. 1a, repeated in 14). By Isa 60:9, those same ships, now in Yahweh's service, bring home Israel's most precious possession – its children, gold and silver.[59]

Influenced by the principal interpretive models of J. A. Darr who is a New Testament scholar as well as her husband, Darr introduces her own interpretive strategy as a reader-oriented method grounded on several critical premises. First, she insists that the text has rhetorical functions by agreeing with Burke who "stressed the persuasive nature of language". Second, she makes it clear that meaning emanates from "the dynamic interaction of both the rhetorical strategies of the text and the interpretive structures (a repertoire of conventions and expectations) of its reader" which means that meaning not only lies on "what the text brings to the reader but also on what the reader brings to the text".[60]

Accordingly, she fully agrees with literary critics such as Iser and W. Booth who emphasise "the dynamic interaction between text and reader in the temporal, conventional process of reading". Third, according to Darr, it is true that numerous components set forth in the text such as historical, social, linguistic and literary factors are still available for contemporary readers in the interpretation of ancient texts. In sum, Darr concludes that the unity of Isaiah is not based upon the intention of the redactor(s) but upon the synchronic reading of readers who utilise their own interpretive strategies on the text, and approaches the book of Isaiah as a cohesive literary work.

So far I have treated the principal interpretive methodologies of those who countenance a literary approach. The use of a literary approach has led to a dramatic shift to a new interpretive paradigm. Though some are concerned that this methodology overlooks historical facts in the text, this appraisal appears to be somewhat problematic. This is because experts who employ the literary approach do not so much give short shrift to the historicity of text; rather, they disavow the reconstructed history of text

59 Katheryn Pfisterer Darr, *Isaiah's Vision and the Family of God* (Louisville: Westminster John Knox Press, 1994), 22–23.

60 Ibid., 24.

offered by historical critics. Meanwhile, some believe that this literary scheme may result in an arbitrary reading of readers since it attaches too much importance to the role of the reader. Given the notion of otherness of the text, which Conrad asserts, however, this doubt can be resolved. Indeed, it should go without saying that the literary method not only points out the deficiency of historical criticism, which rebuilds the textual history in the light of rationalism, but also reinstates the overall unity of the text.

2. My approach to the book of Isaiah as a whole

So far emphasis has been placed upon the four primary interpretive methodologies engaged in Isaiah studies, especially those relating to the unity of the book. Also attention has been drawn to each method's defects and strengths. As the previous priority of historical criticism has been shown to be problematic, it must be stressed that it is impossible to know the intentions of the prophet or the redactor or to re-trace the historical development of the text. The book of Isaiah is not a window to reconstruct the history behind the text but a mirror to reflect our contemporary world.

In this sense, I believe that it is best to read the book of Isaiah as a whole without embracing the standard historical-critical reading that seeks to divide the book into three independent sources (First, Second and Third Isaiah). In this section, I want to focus on the elaboration of how to read the book of Isaiah as a whole.

2.1. Beyond a historical-critical reading of Isaiah

Without question, during the twentieth century the prevailing historical-critical approach to the Bible has dominated biblical scholarship. One can agree that the rise of historical criticism has been so influential that with rare exceptions, most biblical scholars are not immune to its impact. It is assumed by historical critics that the meaning of the biblical text is associated with the intentions of the author that play a significant role as clues for determining the inception of the text.[61]

The dominant historical-critical method also takes into consideration the historical context of a text as an essential factor in elucidating what was the intent of the original authors of the biblical books. It is presupposed that most of the biblical books originate from several original source documents. Most biblical texts are identified as an incongruous collection consisting of the different underlying sources. As a consequence, it is taken for granted that since most of the biblical books were composite, the original documents are to be recovered and understood by reading them against the different historical contexts, from which they arose. For instance, historical critics conclude that the book of Isaiah is to be dealt with as a composite work containing the three incoherent sources: First Isaiah, Second Isaiah (known as the Deutero-Isaiah) and Third Isaiah (called Trito-Isaiah), each of which originated in a different historical context.

As a consequence, since the early twentieth century, the theory of three independent sources has dominated Isaiah studies. It is interesting to note that even canonical criticism, or redactional criticism is, without exception, heavily influenced by this historical-critical reading of Isaiah. Canonical critics are not reluctant to accommodate the threefold division of the book of Isaiah by using First, Second and Third Isaiah as the starting point for understanding the canonical form of Isaiah. The recent redactional approaches to Isaiah are also committed to a thoughtful look at how the three Isaiahs function as the one edited book. In other words, both critical readings of Isaiah are not entirely divorced from such author-oriented historical criticism since their approach appears to grow out of the three Isaiahs' theory, which has been regarded as a starting point for interpreting the book of Isaiah.

It deserves to be considered, however, that over the last two decades historical criticism has faced a growing criticism among a host of biblical scholars.[62] More recently, as noted earlier, the rise of the new literary ap-

61 According to John Barton, the historical critical study of the Bible is concerned with the four main issues: (1) genetic questions (2) original meaning (3) historical reconstruction and (4) disinterested scholarship. See John Barton "Historical-critical approaches," in *Biblical Interpretation*, (ed.) John Barton (Cambridge: Cambridge University, 1998), 9–12.

62 Unlike historical critics, including canonical commentators, who bring their academic interest to bear on the text or the author but not the reader, a guild of contem-

proach, including a reader-response theory, which places particular emphasis on the interplay between the text and the reader, has opened the way to a dramatic shift in interpreting the book of Isaiah. In other words, the focal point of biblical interpretation has dramatically moved from author to text to reader. It is recognized that the meaning of a text emerges in the activity of reading in which the reader is involved. Fernando F. Segovia comments:

> In other words, literary criticism must come to terms with the fact that lying behind the identification and interpretation of the formal features of a text in text-dominant approaches and lying behind the different reading strategies in reader-dominant approaches is always the real reader – the flesh-and-blood reader, historically and culturally conditioned, with a field of vision fundamentally informed and circumscribed by such a social location. It is such a reader, out of such social locations, that engages in the reading and interpretation of texts, arguing for certain literary and rhetorical reconstructions of the text and employing in the process a variety of interpretive model-constructs.[63]

From this perspective, several acute challenges are raised against historical criticism. Firstly, in the light of contemporary literary theory,[64] one crucial problem facing historical critics is their failure to recognise that, rather than being passive receivers of a text discovering its meaning, as readers they become actively involved in shaping the meaning of text.

This point highlights the fact that the original intentions of the author are no longer inherent in the text but imposed by historical critics who, as readers, are involved in the creation of meaning, even with what they consider to be authorial intentions. Historical critical readers aim to read the biblical books such as Isaiah against what is argued to be their original historical background associated with components such as genre and set-

---

porary literary interpreters do not dismiss but devote attention to the interaction between the text and the reader in interpretation. See Katheryn Pfisterer Darr, *Isaiah's Vision and the Family of God*, 23–27.

63 Fernando F. Segovia, "And They Began to Speak in Other Tongues: Competing Modes of Discourse in Contemporary Biblical Criticism," in *Reading from This Place, Vol. 1*, (eds.) Fernando F. Segovia & Mary Ann Tolbert (Minneapolis: Fortress Press, 1995), 20.

64 For a concise survey of new literary approaches to the Old Testament, see Tremper Longman III, "Literary Approaches to Old Testament Study" in *The Face of Old Testament Studies: A Survey of Contemporary Approaches*, (eds.) David W. Baker and Bill T. Arnold (Grand Rapids: Baker Books, 1999), 97–115. See also *New Visions of Isaiah,* esp. 188–341.

ting *(Sitz im Leben)* in order to uncover the intentions of authors. From the perspective of the new literary approach, especially a reader-reception theory, however, this original historical context against which the original authors' intentions can be understood is reconstructed to conform to literary conventions arising in the world of the critics themselves. It is necessary to recognise, therefore, that historical critics' painstaking exploration for authorial intention is nothing more than their own elaborate but suppositional procedure grounded in their own contemporary conventions. David M. Gunn and Danna Nolan Fewell point out:

> In the same vein, but perhaps even more important, was the assumption that what was being expounded by the historical critic was, if not the correct meaning of the text, at least a step towards the correct meaning. There are two questions here. One is whether critics (readers) think of texts as having ultimately only a single right method of interpretation. For most historical critics the answer to both questions was, yes. The critic was seeking the right meaning, and historical criticism was the correct method by which to seek it. Historical criticism, indeed, was the summit of the interpretational pyramid. All those layers below were merely relics of bygone mistakes, centuries of wrong interpretations. (The arrogance of this position is, of course, breathtaking, but recognisably Western.)[65]

In this sense, one comes to the conclusion that historical criticism is not the exclusive way of discovering a textual meaning but little more than the outcome of sophisticated but presumptive hypotheses, an imperialistic enterprise that has been dealt with as a single way in which the meaning of the text is available. In my judgement, no interpretive method should have a monopoly on what a biblical text means.

Secondly, the historical-critical perspective leads to the problem that the access to textual meaning is not available to ordinary readers of the biblical books, but only to experts who are dexterous in manipulating such a biblical technique. The complexity of historical critical schemes has resulted in the long-standing chasm between specialists who have historical criticism at their fingertips and other readers who have little capacity to deal with it. Conrad argues:

> The historical-critical reading of biblical books such as Isaiah has employed reading strategies that, in radically reshaping the books, make them inaccessible to the average reader. Only professional historical critics can use reading strategies that

65 David M. Gunn and Danna Nolan Fewell, *Narrative in the Hebrew Bible* (Oxford: Oxford University Press, 1993), 8.

> require the identification of underlying sources, the differentiation between authentic and inauthentic words, the distinction between preexilic and postexilic layers of tradition, and so forth.[66]

Contemporary commentators have become aware of the recognition in critical literary theory of the role of the reader in interpretation. They maintain that the meaning of a text emanates from the interaction between the text and the reader. In this respect, a textual meaning is not solely dependent on the aesthetic sophistication of historical critical methods but emerges in the reading process in which the reader is actively engaged. In this sense, this insight into the role of the reader in interpretation has a negative implication for the complexity of historical criticism.

Thirdly, a fundamental question can be raised against historical criticism. One can question whether historical criticism leaves room for the relevance of biblical books for the contemporary world. One of the major contributions of historical criticism to biblical theology is that it enabled readers to be immune to the despotism of dogmatic theology and allowed the biblical literature to speak out of the past. One main difficulty with the historical critical method, ironically, lies in its attempt to reshape the biblical books by situating them exclusively in the past. For scholars in the dominant historical critical approach, the biblical texts are to be read against what is argued to be their original historical settings in order to determine the authorial intentions. All other meaning is to be subordinated to the original intentions of the author. However, this author-centred approach fails to show how the biblical Scriptures remain applicable to today's context. The focal point of recent biblical interpretations shifts from attempting to identify a clear portrayal of the life and times of the original author(s) to dealing with the biblical books as the text to reflect the issues of contemporary times.

It is recognised that the meaning of the text can be more fruitfully approached when the biblical books such as Isaiah are to be read from the perspective of one's own context. Having considered reader-response approaches, Richard J. Coggins offers a notable way of reading the book of Isaiah in his own situation.

> In other words, Isaiah is saying something very important to us about a similarity, comparability, between God's character and behaviour and human character and behaviour. And that demand for human righteousness is set alongside a demand for

66 Edgar W. Conrad, *Reading Isaiah*, 25.

> justice, so we are forced to see that it is not simply behaviour of the kind we call 'religious'; it must show itself in active concern for the poor and disadvantaged. If one of the assumptions and values of which I was speaking is the desirability of religious services, I get a nasty shock already in ch. 1 where I am forced to consider that justice for widow and orphan may be an even more basic demand.[67]

In short, the more the biblical books such as Isaiah are read in the present of the reader, the more their meanings and values can be enriched. For instance, from the contemporary perspective of some Christian communities like my own in Korea, the prophetic proclamations of God's yearning to restore the whole creation are being fulfilled in the present time. The prophetic events of God's salvific action on behalf of His people never recede into the dim past. Instead, the eschatological visions of what is meant for the future in the prophetic books are understood to be a reality that the contemporary Christians experience. This reflective way of reading the book of Isaiah that represents the perspective of my own interpretive situation, leads me to the conviction that the biblical texts need to be understood in my own present world.

2.2. *My reading of the book of Isaiah as a thematic unitary whole*

So far it has been demonstrated how historical criticism confronts three major and crippling disadvantages: It fails to see the significant role of readers in interpretation; its sophisticated approach to the determination of meaning is not available to the average readers; and its focus on the past obscures the relevance of the text in the contemporary community. When I aim to read the book of Isaiah as a whole, I am not concerned with the basic assumption of traditional historical method that the book of Isaiah should be divided into what is argued to be its underlying independent sources. For critics in the standard historical critical school, the book of Isaiah is dealt with as an incoherent combination of the writings of three prophets who perhaps ministered in different periods: First Isaiah (chapter 1–39 in eighth century B.C.E.), Second Isaiah (chapter 40–55 in the sixth

67 Richard J. Coggins, "New Ways with Old Texts: How Does One Write a Commentary on Isaiah?" in *ET* 107 (Edinburgh: T&T Clark, 1996), 367.

century B.C.E.), and Third Isaiah (chapter 56–66 later in the sixth century B.C.E.).[68]

On the contrary, I am not interested in dealing with the book of Isaiah as an incongruous combination of three individual sources that are to be read independently in order to determine original meaning. My concern is not to offer a historical critical analysis centred on an attempt to reconstruct the original historical settings against which the original authors' intentions are understood. My sympathy is with a literary approach, with reading the book of Isaiah as a whole, rather than with the reconstruction of the textual history and its process.

More recently, over the last two decades, biblical interpretation has witnessed a dramatic shift in Isaiah studies from the three-book approach to interpreting Isaiah as a whole, as a single book. With the rise of the new literary approach, several scholars have sought to read and interpret Isaiah as a whole, while uncompromisingly recanting the fundamental premises of the standard historical critical approach.[69] Special attention has been drawn to the literary structural,[70] rhetorical,[71] ideological[72] and thematic[73] facets set forth in the book of Isaiah, which function as key central clues for understanding the book of Isaiah as a whole. It is argued by some that explicit signals in the text shed light on how to see the book of Isaiah as a whole. In my own approach, further emphasis will be placed on these

68 For a further discussion of this issue, see Raymond B. Dillard & Tremper Longman III, *An Introduction to the Old Testament* (Grand Rapids: Zondervan Publishing House, 1994), 268–276. See also Edgar W. Conrad, *Reading Isaiah,* 6–12; Marvin A. Sweeney, *Isaiah 1–39*, 41–62. For different assumptions of the issue of this authorship, see Christopher R. Seitz, *Word without End: The Old Testament as Abiding Theological Witness,* 113–129; J. Barton, *Isaiah 1–39*, 13–43.

69 Edgar W. Conrad, *Reading Isaiah*, see esp. 3–33.

70 Ibid, see esp. 34–51.

71 Robert H. O'Connell, *Concentricity and Continuity: The Literary Structure of Isaiah* (Sheffield: Sheffield Academic Press, 1994).

72 Antti Laato, *"About Zion I will not be silent": The Book of Isaiah as an Ideological Unity* (Stockholm: Almgvist & Wiksell International, 1998), see esp. 50–63.

73 See Barry G. Webb, "Zion in Transformation: A Literary Approach to Isaiah" in *The Bible in Three Dimensions: Essays in Celebration of Forty Years of Biblical Studies in the University of Sheffield*, (eds.) David J. A. Clines, Stephen E. Fowl and Stanley E. Porter (Sheffield: Sheffield Academic Press, 1990), 65–84; William J. Dumbrell, "The Purpose of the Book of Isaiah", *TynBul* (1985), 111–128.

central signs[74] to gain an insight into the way in which the book of Isaiah is read as a unitary entity.

Firstly, one of the most noteworthy indicators of the unity of Isaiah is that there is only one superscription for the book of Isaiah marked by the expression, 'the vision concerning Judah and Jerusalem that Isaiah son of Amoz saw during the reigns of Uzziah, Jotham, Ahaz and Hezekiah, kings of Judah.' No matter how the vision of Isaiah is defined,[75] this initial title alludes to the fact that all parts of the book are closely linked with what the prophet Isaiah saw in his vision during the precise period from King Uzziah through the reign of King Hezekiah.

One might feel it inappropriate to agree with the thesis that the title in 1:1 introduces the whole book, since another apparent superscription appears in 2:1. Having drawn attention to what has traditionally been understood as two superscriptions, yet, Carr makes the following observation:

> Such labels [1.1 and 2.1] serve as separate meta-textual keys to the reader/hearer of the parameters of various macrostructural units. They are *meta*-textual because they help to mark major units of text and guide the reader/hearer in understanding them. In this case, the superscription in 1.1 seems to introduce the book as a whole, while the superscription in 2.1 introduces a major macrostructural unit of the book.[76]

In other words, while Isaiah 1.1 plays as a central key to introduce the whole of the book, Isaiah 2:1 is centred on a single unit in the book. From this perspective, Isaiah 1:1 can be understood to introduce the book as a whole. I understand that the vision of Isaiah designates the book to be a vision that is about the polarity of the destiny of Jerusalem; that is, the death of Zion and its glorious future. This inscription at the outset of the book of Isaiah suggests that the book be understood from the perspective of Isaiah's visionary oracles.[77] Briefly stated, the location of this initial

74 See Barry G. Webb, "Zion in Transformation: A Literary Approach to Isaiah", 67–72.

75 Watts seeks to relate this vision to the entire parts of the book as drama, while Conrad defines the vision of Isaiah as Isaiah 6–39 concerned with a certain time frame – from the death of Uzziah to the death of Hezekiah. See John D. W. Watts, *Isaiah 1–33*, 3–4; Edgar W. Conrad, *Reading Isaiah*, 117–9.

76 David M. Carr, "Reading Isaiah From Beginning (Isaiah 1) To End (Isaiah 65–66): Multiple Modern Possibilities" in *New Visions of Isaiah*, (eds.) Roy F. Melugin & Marvin A. Sweeney (Sheffield: Sheffield Academic Press, 1996), 197–8.

77 But I am not interested in identifying these editors or tracing a process of the title's editing and addition based on a historical-critical approach concerned with a textual

rubric at the beginning of the book suggests that the whole contents of 66 chapters have to do with the vision of the prophet Isaiah regarding the city of God, Jerusalem, and that the book is to be read as a whole.

Secondly, several key motifs, which are brought into prominence in the book of Isaiah, are understood to be evidence to read the book as a thematic unitary whole.[78] For instance, it is agreed among commentators who draw attention to Isaiah's focal points that one of the most overmastering themes set forth in the whole book is the notion of "the Holy One of Israel" which rarely appears in the rest of the Old Testament. Given the frequent occurrences of the expression, 'the Holy One of Israel,' in the book of Isaiah as a whole, it comes as little surprise that Isaiah can be seen as a book about a holy God.

It can be seen that the Holy One of Israel is revealed as Punisher who despises Israel's uncleanness resulting in His great grief (cf. 1:4; 5:18–19, 24; 30:8–14; 37:23–25), while He is also identified as Saviour who delivers the suffering people of God out of the hands of fatal forces (cf. 47:4; 48:17; 49:7). Also Yahweh is panoramically depicted as Restorer who will renew Zion as the cosmic centre to which the world will go up in a pilgrimage of worship from every quarter (60:9, 14). In short, the emphasis upon the holy divine is so central that it serves as a window on an overall message of Isaiah about a holy God. In addition, Yahweh's interest in and devotion to Jerusalem/Zion is given major emphasis throughout the book of Isaiah. As was shown earlier, the beginning and the end of the book are centered on Jerusalem. From the outset, Isaiah 1 paints a gloomy scene in which Jerusalem is depicted as a profane city like Sodom and Gomorrah, which is actively involved in ostensible sacrifice devoid of social justice, and confronts a call to repentance. On the other hand, Isaiah 66 shows a presentation of an epoch-making era in which Zion will be dramatically transformed as the cosmic centre of a new creation. The simultaneous but different emphasis on Jerusalem at the beginning and the end of the book indicates that Isaiah's overall prophecy is intimately

---

history. Rather, I am concerned with how this title plays a central role in seeing the book of Isaiah as a whole.

78 Many biblical interpreters call attention to the important thematic elements such as Zion/Jerusalem, the New Exodus, the divine kingship, the New Heavens and the New Earth and so on. See Tate, "The Book of Isaiah in Recent Study" in *Forming Prophet Literature: Essays on Isaiah and the Twelve in Honor of John D. W. Watts*, (eds.) James W. Watts and Paul R. House (Sheffield: Sheffield Academic Press, 1996), 45–6.

bound up with the fate of the historical Jerusalem and the eschatological transformation of Zion. In fact, the first half of the book of Isaiah begins in Isaiah 1 with the portrait of a decadent Jerusalem and ends in Isaiah 39 with a presage of exile directed against King Hezekiah and his city, Jerusalem. The second half of the book focuses its attention on the deliverance of Jerusalem that is craving for Yahweh's saving action on behalf of God's people. Furthermore, constant emphasis is placed upon the Zion theme, especially the prophetic vision of what is portrayed as a New Jerusalem, which functions as the world governmental centre of the divine kingship in the final section (Isaiah 56–66). In this sense, one finds it difficult to avoid the conclusion that the Jerusalem/Zion theme provides for a theological and thematic cohesion of Isaiah.

Finally, special attention has been paid to the interrelation between Isaiah 1 and 65–66 that function as a crucial marker for understanding the book of Isaiah as a whole. Conrad's approach to the texts (chapter 1 and 65–66) comes to the fore. He makes an insightful observation about what he calls 'the implied audience' who appears as 'we' in these sections, a first person plural voice that serve as a clue for understanding the relationship between the beginning and the end of the book. These links at the beginning and end suggest that the book is a literary whole. He remarks:

> What the "we" implies about itself in the two passages toward the end of the book parallels what the LORD says about the community toward the beginning of the book. The self-description of the "we" at the beginning and end of the book, with its counterpoint in the LORD's description of the community, provides further evidence about the structure of the book as a whole.[79]

It seems to me, yet, that Conrad's thesis that the appearance of the first person plural voice in 1:9–10 alludes to a deep and longstanding chasm between the implied audience of survivors and their rivals in the commu-

79 According to Conrad, it is noteworthy that there is the simultaneous appearance of the expression, "we" in both Isaiah 1 and 65–66. The two sections also point to the present context in which the division between the implied audience (the righteous) and its rivals (the unrighteous) has been made. This situation in the passage suggests that the implied audience marked by "we" has met with great setbacks to its aspiration such as unsocial behaviours, including the shedding of innocent blood abused by its opponents. Therefore, in the beginning and the end of the book, the "we" as the righteous exhort their rivals to hear the word of God, while anticipating the ultimate fulfilment of what is intended by Yahweh to punish sinners like burning worms and to renew Zion. See his *Reading Isaiah*, 83–116.

nity is not immune to a socio-historical reconstruction of the text grounded in a sophisticated hypothesis. Particularly, I am reluctant to sympathise with his conclusion that the implied audience as "we" in Isaiah 1 and 65–66 have already experienced a devastating punishment of God against Babylon.[80] It appears that this attempt to situate Isaiah 1 and 65–66 in an historical context like post Babylonian is nothing more than a product of the reconstruction of the text derived from a painstaking but conjectural premise. In contrast, my interest is to see the text as it is rather than to reshape the original socio-historical world of the text. I want to focus on the literary context in front of contemporary readers, needing no reconstruction whatsoever.

Apart from identifying the implied audience as the "we" and their original socio-historical situation in Isaiah 1 and 65–66, my concern is to concentrate on the phrase, "hear the word of God". This is because this expression is simultaneously found in the texts and plays a central role in understanding the book of Isaiah as a whole. Significantly, the beginning and the end of the book of Isaiah are concerned with an exhortation to hear the word of God addressed to those who are involved in carrying out sacrifices against God and involved in the shedding of innocent blood.

> Hear the word of the LORD,
> you rulers of Sodom!
> Listen to the law of our God,
> you people of Gomorrah! (1:10)
> Hear the word of the LORD,
> you who tremble at his word:
> "Your brothers who hate you,
> and exclude you because of my name, have said,
> Let the LORD be glorified, that we may see your joy!";
> yet they will be put to shame. (66:5)

As Conrad points out,[81] the coincident occurrence of the phrase, "hear the word of God" in Isaiah 1 and 65–66 suggests the importance of hearing the word of God for understanding the overall message of the book of Isaiah. For instance, the significance of the phrase is clearly illustrated in the Hezekiah narrative found in Isaiah 36–39. It is demonstrated in this narrative that the word of God plays a crucial role in ensuring the protection of Judah from invaders like Assyria and the survival of Jerusalem.

80 Ibid., 102; 116.
81 See his *Reading Isaiah*, 98–99.

Indeed, for Jerusalem, success or failure is solely dependent on hearing God's word. In this sense, the intended location of this expression at the beginning (1:10) and the end (66:5) of the book points to the fact that the future for a people of God, like Hezekiah and his people, is solely dependent on hearing God's word. Likewise, in the book of Isaiah, God's word serves as a negative word of judgment against evildoers like those who are engaged in hypocritical sacrifice that lacks social justice and righteousness and thereby confront a call to repentance. This point leads us to the conclusion that the overall message of the book of Isaiah has intimate relevance to the phase, which serves as a clue for reading Isaiah as a whole.

2.3. Hear the Word of God!

Here I wish to focus on the elucidation of how hearing the word of God in the Hezekiah narrative plays a pivotal role in understanding the overall message of the book of Isaiah. It is spelled out in the narrative that Zion's destiny hinges on hearing the Torah, the word of God. Here, close attention will be given to Ahaz's response to the prophet Isaiah's message centered on simple trust in Yahweh, which stands in stark contrast to that of Hezekiah.

Pekah of Israel and Rezin of Damascus conceived of a coalition to take a stand against Assyria (2 Kings 16:5–6; Isa. 7:1) and asked Judah to join the coalition. It appears, however, that the call for Judah's action against Assyria met with Ahaz' blunt refusal. This results in the Israelite-Syrian attack on Jerusalem from 734 B.C. to 715 B.C. Having had been actively engaged in the pro-Assyrian policy, Ahaz had no choice but to commit himself to the Assyrian king, Tiglath Pileser. In the midst of the tumultuous time, the prophet Isaiah addresses the king's fearfulness and calls for trust in Yahweh, the only remedy for this threat. The point Isaiah makes in this announcement is that this threat would ebb and finally recede so that Zion would be able to survive.

His message makes it clear, furthermore, that Jerusalem's future is solely dependant on whether she is resolute in turning back from Assyria to Yahweh who promises deliverance from the alliance of the Syrian and Israelite kings. In this sense, there is no doubt that Zion's destiny depends on hearing the word of God spoken through the prophet. Sadly, Ahaz's response to the giving of the sign indicates that he gives little attention to the word of God. The Ahaz narrative portrays him as a faithless king who pays no attention to God's word but puts his sole commitment in a pagan king.

The Hezekiah narrative throws the king's response to Isaiah's comforting oracle containing the 'fear not' formula into clear relief. It is indicated in these chapters that the deliverance of Judah from the destroyer has nothing to do with any political policies but rather with a trust in God's ability to care for his covenant people. As is the case of the Ahaz narrative, the Hezekiah narrative is associated with a national crisis in which the Judean king suffers from a military attack. Reminiscent of Isaiah's message to Ahaz in which the 'fear not' formula is shown, the prophet Isaiah delivers a comforting oracle containing the words, 'fear not' to Hezekiah. The point he makes in the oracle is that an impending destruction of the enemy is about to happen and that Hezekiah should remain firm in his commitment to Yahweh even in the midst of crisis. The Hezekiah narrative paints a miraculous deliverance from the Assyrian king in which what God said has dramatically been fulfilled. Here it is significant to show a further close look at chapters 36–37 concerned with the need for hearing the word of God, which plays a vital role in reading the book of Isaiah as a whole.

The Assyrian king poses a threat to Jerusalem and sends Rabshakeh from Lachish to Jerusalem with a large force to quell the city (36:2). Interestingly, the Assyrian commander's attention does not focus on military assaults but to a persuasive speech to destroy the city. As shown in 36:4–10, the Assyrian officer's message to servants from Hezekiah shows a parallel structure in which the uselessness of trust in three options (the Judean king, Egypt and Yahweh) is respectively emphasized.

A. The uselessness of trust in Hezekiah (verse 5)
  B. The uselessness of trust in Egypt (verse 6)
    C. The uselessness of trust in Yahweh (verse 7)
A'. The uselessness of trust in Hezekiah (verse 8)
  B'. The uselessness of trust in Egypt (verse 9)
    C'. The uselessness of trust in Yahweh (verse 10)

As indicated in the passages, the Assyrian officer affirms that the Judean king is so frail that he would not able to sustain his city. Then the rhetorical speech of the Assyrian commander contends that no matter what political ways are chosen the Assyrian king will succeed in the military attack. Finally he emphatically seeks to persuade the Judean people from vigorous resistance to the Assyrian army since even Judah's God, Yahweh allows the Assyrian army to attack the city. In short, the commander's words mock the Israelite's trust in their king, in Egyptian assistance, and ultimately in Yahweh as ridiculous. The commander speaks in Hebrew rather than in Aramaic in order that the Israelites are able to listen to what the Assyrian king said. The point he makes in the whole speech is that the Judean people must not hear the word of God but listen to the words of the Assyrian king. Ironically the commander mocks the people of the city for resting on the word of God, while he himself is fighting only with words. The commander never focuses on any military action in Jerusalem but only on persuasive speech. In other words, it is not a military war, but a war by words. To whose words shall the people of the city listen? The commander claims that survival is dependant on hearing the words of the Assyrian king.

Learning of the commander's message, Hezekiah tears his clothes, wears sackcloth and goes to the temple. Also he sends his servants to the prophet Isaiah with a penitent message.

> They told him, "This day is a day of distress and rebuke and disgrace, as when children come to the point of birth and there is no strength to deliver them." (37:3)

It should be noted here that the two ways of interpreting the verse deserve careful attention. One interpretation understands that Isa. 37:3, which functions as a penitent confession of a powerless monarch, indicates that Hezekiah feels remorse for relying on Egyptian assistance implied in the commander's speech. On the other hand, scholars such as Seitz claim that since the commander's charge of reliance on Egypt is nothing more than a groundless curse, this verse has nothing to do with Hezekiah's foreign alliances with Egypt. Seitz observes:

> Moreover, what is one to make of the factual nature of the Rabshakeh's address when he concludes his remarks on a note that is surely to be construed as bombast and manipulation? 'Is it without YHWH that I have come up against this place to destroy it? YHWH said to me, Go up against this land and destroy it' (18.25). Whether or not this item can be classified as historical, it clearly functions in the narrative to indict the Rabshakeh as a blasphemer. Given this, it is difficult to ac-

> cept the Rabshakeh's charge of reliance on Egypt as objective proof of Hezekiah's foreign policy.[82]

My sympathy, however, is with Darr who understands that Isa. 37:1–3 "functions as the confession of a now powerless monarch who, in violation of the expressed policy of Yahweh's prophet, has willfully chosen to rely on his own strength and that of his allies."[83] Given Hezekiah's unfaithful action in sending tributes to the Assyrian king as narrated in 2 Kings 18, it is probably inferred that Hezekiah rests on Egyptian assistance against the Assyrian army. In this sense, the commander's charges of Egyptian alliance seem to be grounded in fact, and Hezekiah's penitence appears to have to do with his foreign policy, especially his foreign alliance with Egypt. His conviction is that the Assyrian military attack is part of a divine punishment against his unfaithful action in alliances with Egypt. After receiving a message from the Assyrian commander, the Judean king now repents for what he has done by not trusting in Yahweh. Echoing a comforting oracle containing the words, 'fear not' delivered to Ahaz, Isaiah's message is communicated through his servants and reassures the desperate but penitent king. Isaiah said to them:

> Tell your master, 'This is what the Lord says: Do not be afraid of what you have heard-those words with which the underlings of the king of Assyria have blasphemed me. Listen! I am going to put a spirit in him so that when he hears a certain report, he will return to his own country and there I will have him cut down with the sword.' (37:6–7)

Given this situation, Hezekiah finds himself in a fix. For him there are only two options. He must decide which to choose. Either he should tread in the footsteps of his predecessor who downplayed trust in Yahweh; or he should listen to Isaiah's message, which calls his attention to the word of God who promises that Zion will survive notwithstanding the fact that the present situation seems to be one of despair. To whose words shall he listen? Hezekiah finally rejects the commander's call for hearing the words of the Assyrian king. He is adamant that the city of God will be saved since what God has promised through the prophet Isaiah will be faithfully fulfilled. Thus, he decides it is of no value to seek a political solution for deliverance from a military attack. Rather, he comes to the

82 Christopher R. Seitz, *Zion's Final Destiny*, 73.

83 Katheryn Pfisterer Darr, "No Strength to Deliver," in *New Visions of Isaiah*, 243.

conviction that there is no other way of passing a national crisis besides Yahweh whose words are to be heard. The language of 37:36–37 makes it clear that what God has said about the destruction of the Assyrian army relayed by the prophet Isaiah has dramatically been fulfilled.

> Then the angel of the Lord went out and put to death a hundred and eighty-five thousand men in the Assyrian camp. When the people got up the next morning there were all the dead bodies! So Sennacherib king of Assyria broke camp and withdrew. He returned to Nineveh and stayed there. (37:36–37)

In this sense, it should certainly be borne in mind that Hezekiah is described in chapters 36–37 of the book as a model of the righteous who hear the word of God. What is more, as indicated earlier, interest in hearing the word of God is also brought prominence into Isaiah 1 and 65–66. It is commonly agreed among scholars that these chapters serve as both the introduction and conclusion to the sixty-six chapters of the book. Given the inclusio form, Isaiah 1 and 65–66 function a significant role in reading the book of Isaiah as a unitary whole. Interestingly, it is implied in both chapters that the deep chasm between the righteous and the wicked is internecine. Further emphasis should be placed upon the fact that the identification of such groups has to do with each different response to the call to hear the word of God. For example, both chapters show an exhortation to hear the word of Yahweh. In 1:10, which is part of the prophetic Torah of 1:10–17, one group exhorts their opponents who are identical with those who lived in the cities of Sodom and Gomorrah. It is noteworthy that the two Hebrew words, דבר and תורת are in parallel in this verse.

> A. Hear the word of the Lord (דבר),
>   B. you rulers of Sodom;
> A'. Listen to the law of our God (תורת),
>   B'. you people of Gomorrah!

The juxtaposition of "our God" with "you people" indicates that the internal dissension between the survivors referred to as "we" and the opponents called "you" comes to a head. The latter is portrayed as those who are involved in social sins that are "like scarlet" and "red like crimson" (1:18). Though they stretch out their hands with the blood of sacrifice, this practice is abominable to Yahweh since they have the blood of innocent people on their hands. As a result, this wicked group is faced with a call to hear the word of God, a point that suggests that their actions ignore the word and ways of God.

Chapters 65–66, especially 66:1–6 are also dominated by a keen interest in the phrase "hear the word of God." It should be noted in the passages that as was the case in chapter 1 the two opposing groups are at enmity with each other. Some exegetes such as Beuken argue that the opponents portrayed in 66:1–6 are a group outside the community, while several commentators including Conrad contend that they share a common heritage and a common identity as a social group and that there is a division between the two groups in the same community.[84] Given the fact that the opponents are portrayed as "you", the latter seems to be more persuasive. This internal opposition is evident in 66:1–6 by the juxtaposition of "you who trembles at his word" with "your brothers who hate you, and exclude you because of my name." More significantly, the wicked are condemned for rejecting the word of God.

> They have chosen their own ways
> and their souls in delight in their abominations
> so I also will choose harsh treatment for them
> and will bring upon them what they dread
> For when I called, no one answered
> when I spoke no one listened (66:3b–4b).

Divergence between the righteous and the wicked is manifestly found in each different response to the word of God. The former responds to Yahweh's word with trembling since they acknowledge the power of the word to reach fulfilment, while the latter resolutely eschews "hearing the word of God" by being engaged in abominable sacrifices. Though the righteous despair due to their brothers' persecution, they have no doubt that the persecutors will ultimately suffer from divine punishment since what God says about their future will be fulfilled. The way they show their trust is to hear the word of God and look for its fulfilment (66:6). The faithful are asked to hear the word of God in the midst of harsh difficulties. One such example is Hezekiah who repented of his sin, listened to God's word, and finally experienced dramatic deliverance from the Assyrian army. In this sense, the whole book of Isaiah makes it clear that though the faithful meet with great setbacks to their aspirations, it behoves them to trust the

84 For a further discussion on this issue, see Brevard S. Childs, *Isaiah*, 540.

word of God. This point leads us to the conclusion that for the people of God, success or failure only hinges on hearing the word of God.

2.4. Reading Isaiah in a pluralistic Korea

This thesis will concentrate on the major unitary themes found in the book of Isaiah as a whole, especially their particularist and universalist motifs. Isaiah, compared with the remainder of the Old Testament, contains a large number of passages presenting these two seemingly dialectical contradictions. Significantly, the book of Isaiah not only emphases the particularist themes such as the Holy One of Israel, the uniqueness of Yahweh and the Torah as the Word of God, but also the universalist motifs of Zion, the New Israel, and the New Creation.

The Holy One of Israel is not only the major centre of Isaianic theology,[85] but also the most exclusive theme in the book of Isaiah.[86] Yahweh revealed himself as the Holy One of Israel through Isaiah's vision (Isaiah 6), which insinuates a particular relationship between Yahweh and Israel. Yahweh demands that Israel turn away from her ungodliness back to the Holy One so that she can become purified and holy since she made a covenant with Him and has had a special relationship with Him.[87] Regardless of the contrast between Yahweh's holiness and Israel's unholiness, Yahweh's special concentration on his people Israel[88] appears throughout

85 Cf. J. J. M Roberts, "Isaiah in Old Testament Theology", in *Interpreting the Prophets*, (eds.) J. L. Mays & P. J. Achtemeier (Philadelphia: Fortress Press, 1987), 63–64; A. S. Herbert, *The book of the prophet Isaiah 1–39* (London: Cambridge University Press, 1973), 14–15; Elizabeth Achtemeier, "Isaiah of Jerusalem: Themes and Preaching Possibilities" in *Reading and Preaching the Book of Isaiah*, (ed.) Christopher R. Seitz (Philadelphia: Fortress Press, 1988), 27–29; John D. W. Watts, *Isaiah,* WBT (Dallas: Word Publishing, 1989), 38–41; J. Barton, *Isaiah 1–39,* 110–112; Raymond B. Dillard & Tremper Longman III, *An Introduction to The Old Testament* (Grand Rapids: Zondervan Publishing House, 1994), 276–277.

86 John F. Sawyer, *Prophecy and the Prophets of the Old Testament* (New York: Oxford University Press, 1987), 79–80.

87 Pamela A. Foulkes, *God in Isaiah* (NSW: St. Pauls, 1996), 42–47; J. J. Roberts, "Isaiah in Old Testament Theology", 68–69; John F. Sawyer, *Prophecy and the Prophets of the Old Testament,* 79–80.

88 R. E. Clements insists that "the divine election of Israel" is one of the prominent themes in Deutero-Isaiah (R. E. Clements, "Deutero-Isaianic Development." In *The*

the whole book of Isaiah. Indeed, the prophecy is predicated on the positive affirmation that as the Holy One of Israel, Yahweh can create, sustain and redeem His beloved people.

It is widely agreed, likewise, that the notion of monotheism must also be an obvious term referring to particularity and is a foremost motif in the message of Isaiah 40–55.[89] This section of Isaiah justifies God's punishment since Israel has committed idolatry before Him and declares that there are no other gods and that Yahweh is the only God over all the world. The monotheism of Isaiah 40–55 appears to be closely connected with the covenant between Yahweh and Israel. Even though Israel always needs to remain adherent to the only Yahweh as His covenant people, she has violated the divine law and has succumbed to idolatry rather than venerating the one God. Then Israel is urged to turn from worshipping idols and return to Yahweh, since no other god is capable of delivering Israel but the one God.[90]

Moreover, the particular functions of Torah are clearly set forth throughout the entire book of Isaiah. According to the book of Isaiah, it seems that Torah is defined as the "instruction" or "teaching" of Yahweh spoken by the prophet,[91] which was announced to the blind and the deaf

---

Prophets, (ed.) Philip R. Davies [Sheffield: Sheffield Academic Press, 1996], 138–9).

89 For a detailed discussion of monotheism in the book of Isaiah, see Robert Karl Gnuse, *No Other Gods: Emergent Monotheism in Israel*, JSOTsup 241 (Sheffield: Sheffield Academic Press, 1997), 207–208; Norbert Lohfink S.J., *Great Themes from the Old Testament*, trans. Ronald Walls (Edinburgh: T&T CLARK, 1982), 145–147; R. J. Coggins, *Introduction to the Old Testament* (Oxford: Oxford University Press, 1990), 142–144. Claus Westermann, *Handbook to the Old Testament* (Minneapolis: Augsburg Publishing House, 1976), 147. Jonathan Magonet, *A Rabbi's Bible* (London: SCM Press, 1991), 141–42; E. A Turner, *Irony as Ideology Critique in Deutero-Isaiah with Special Reference to the Parody on Idolatry* (Stellenbosch: University of Stellenbosch, 1996), 45–6.

90 For a further discussion of the notion of Yahweh's exclusive prerogative in the book of Isaiah see Ben C. Ollenburger, *Zion, the City of the Great King,* JSOTsup41 (Sheffield: JSOT Press, 1987), 107–29; see also Elmer B. Smick, "Old Testament Cross-Culturalism: Paradigmatic or Enigmatic?" *JETS* 32/1 (1989), 11–6.

91 For a detailed discussion of the etymology and meaning of Torah in the Old Testament, see Joseph Jensen, *The Use of Torah by Isaiah* (Washington, D.C: The Catholic University of America, 1973), 3–27; for a more specific study of the meaning of Torah in the book of Isaiah, see Marvin A. Sweeney's "The Book of Isaiah as Prophetic Torah" in *New Visions of Isaiah,* JSOTsup 214, (eds.) Roy F. Melugin & Marvin A. Sweeney (Sheffield: Sheffield Academic Press, 1996), 50–67; R. E.

but will be audible in a future time when they will see and hear. In this regard, Torah is undoubtedly identified as the divine word and revelation of Yahweh,[92] which is preached by the prophets, through which Israel is able to know Him and understand His will. Yahweh will judge and castigate all nations, including Israel, for their scorning of Torah and turning to the word of other gods; they must not give short shrift to His teaching. In this instance, it comes as little surprise, therefore, that there seems to be the notion of Torah's peculiarity and its particularity to Yahweh in the book of Isaiah.

In contrast to these particularist themes, the Zion motif, which also is a characteristic of the whole book of Isaiah, is made explicit as one of the most central[93] and universal themes.[94] Throughout this book, Zion is clearly identified as Yahweh's dwelling place, the divine mountain, and the city of security and peace for the poor and the weary whose faith is in Yahweh.[95] In addition, this motif is extended to encompass the eschatological features of Zion, which is depicted as the world governmental centre, a New Eden, and the place of pilgrimage at the end of time.[96] In this sense, the book of Isaiah evidently reveals various manifestations of the universal aspect of the Zion theme.

In addition, the New Creation and the New Exodus, which are universal concepts signifying the renewal of the cosmic world and Yahweh's eschatological deliverance for Israel, are highlighted in the book of Isaiah.

Clement, "Deutero-Isaianic Development." In *The Prophets*, (ed.) Philip R. Davies (Sheffield: Sheffield Academic Press, 1996), 141–2; J. M. Myers, *Grace and Torah* (Philadephia: Fortress Press, 1975), 33–8.

92 J. M. Myers, *Grace and Torah* (Philadelphia: Fortress Press, 1975), 33–8; Marvin Sweeney, "The Book of Isaiah as Prophetic Torah.", 62–3; for a further discussion of the word of Yahweh in the book of Isaiah, see Edgar W. Conrad, *Reading Isaiah,* 98–102.

93 John Barton, *Isaiah 1–39,* 117; John D. W. Watts, *Isaiah,* 41–4.

94 William J. Dumbrell, *The Search for Order: Biblical Eschatology in Focus* (Grand Rapids: Baker Books, 1994), 80–95.

95 Isa. 2.2–4; 4.2–6; 11.6–9; 14.32; 24.21–23; 29.1–8; 31.4–9; 49.14–26; 52.7–10; for a specific study of Zion, see Ben C. Ollenburger, *Zion, the City of the Great King*, JSOTsup41 (Sheffield: JSOT Press, 1987); R. E. Clements, *Isaiah and the Deliverance of Jerusalem* (Sheffield: JSOT Press, 1980), 72–89; William J. Dumbrell, *The Search for Order*, 75–95; John D. W. Watts, *Isaiah*, 41–4; For a detail study of 'The New Jerusalem', see Richard J. Mouw, *When the Kings Come Marching In: Isaiah and the New Jerusalem* (Grand Rapids: Eerdmans, 1983).

96 Isa. 60.1–14; 62.1–5.

As Yahweh had saved Israel from oppression and suffering in Egypt, so He would deliver His people from the trouble of the Babylonian exile and bring her into the renewed world. At this time, all nations, including the state of Israel, which turn to Yahweh and have faith in Him, will travel to Zion[97] to participate in Yahweh's redemption with rejoicing and peace in the renewed world.[98] In this sense, Yahweh's deliverance of Israel from the exile in Babylon and the renewed world represented as the New Exodus and the New Creation, seem to constitute a universal aspect in the book of Isaiah.[99] Furthermore, it is evident that "the New Israel" is a remarkable universal aspect. In particular, 19:23–5, which depicts Egypt and Assyria as Yahweh's own people and handiwork, is the most universal passage in the entire Old Testament.[100] The New Israel on no account refers to a nation state; rather she clearly signifies a confessional and universal community, including the Gentiles, who believe in Yahweh.[101]

From the Korean perspective of the ostensibly dialectical concepts, particularism and universalism set forth in the book of Isaiah, this study then will aim to present a critical assessment of the two issues: religious pluralism and iconoclasm. As indicated earlier, since Dr. Pyun, a Protestant theologian, initiated a radical belief system in relation to pluralism in

97 Richtsje Abma, "Travelling from Babylon to Zion: Location and Its Function in Isaiah 49–55," *JSOT* 74 (1997), 3–28.

98 R. E. Clements, *Old Testament Prophecy* (Louisville: Westminster John Knox Press, 1996), 90; Watts, *Isaiah*, 86–87.

99 Walter C. Kaiser Jr., "Promise. " In *The Flowering of Old Testament Theology*, (eds.) Elmer A. Martens, Ben C. Ollenburger and Gerhard F. Hasel (Winona Lake: Eisenbrauns, 1992), 247–8.

100 J. Barton, *Oracles of God: Perceptions of Ancient Prophecy in Israel after the Exile* (London: Darton, Longman & Todd, 1986), 136; Peter D. Miscall, *Isaiah* (Sheffield: JSOT Press, 1993), 58; J. A. Motyer, *The Prophecy of Isaiah* (Leicester: IVP, 1993), 169–70; John D. W. Watts, *Isaiah 1–33,* WBC (Waco: Word Books, 1985), 261–3; For a specific discussion of Isa. 19.25, see John F. A. Sawyer, "Blessed Be My People Egypt" (Isaiah 19.25): "The Context and Meaning of a Remarkable Passage." *JSOT* 42 (1986), 57–71.

101 J. Blenkinsopp, "Second Isaiah – Prophet of Universalism." in *The Prophets*, (ed.) Philip R. Davies (Sheffield: Sheffield Academic Press, 1996), 189–94; John T. Willis, "Exclusivistic and Inclusivistic Aspects of the Concept of 'The People of God' in the Book of Isaiah." *Restoration Quarterly* 40 (1998): 3–12; Rolf. Rendtorff, *Canon and Theology,* trans. Margaret Kohl (Minneapolis: Fortress Press, 1993), 114–24; Walter C. Kaiser, Jr., "Promise." in *The Flowering of Old Testament Theology*, (eds.) Elmer A. Martens, Ben C. Ollenburger and Gerhard F. Hasel (Indiana: Eisenbrauns, 1992), 243–53.

1984, the bulk of Korean conservative theologians have been concerned about a radical position of pluralism's deep inroads within the Korean Churches. On the contrary, religious pluralists have run afoul of the Protestant camps, which uncompromisingly embrace the uniqueness of Yahweh. In recent years, the Korean Protestant Churches have been embroiled in a fiery debate about religious pluralism involving two opposing sides, conservative theologians and their naysayers who espouse religious pluralism.

Interestingly, however, there does seem to be an agreement between them. Both acknowledge the significance of the Bible in confirming their respective position. Almost all Protestant Christians embrace it as the word of God.[102] Until now, yet, there has not been a book that seeks to present a critical assessment of Korean religious pluralism from a biblical perspective, since the debate on religious pluralism has been largely confined to systematic or mission theologians rather than biblical scholars. It is my judgement, in this sense, that the time seems appropriate to propose a way to address the issue of religious pluralism in the light of Isaiah's central key themes, especially their particularist motifs.

Furthermore, special attention will be drawn to another major issue in contemporary Korean Churches, namely, iconoclasm. As noted earlier, the Korean religious societies have been in a predicament due to the illegal annihilation of religious relics in which Christian fanatics, who respond to other religions with intolerance, bigotry, and chauvinism, are actively involved. Also Christian extremists have been engaged in destroying the images of Tangun, the legendary progenitor of the Korean nation, erected at public schools, an iconoclasm that has driven the Korean Churches to impasse. In this sense, this thesis will endeavour to evaluate these acts of vandalism in light of Korean understanding of the notion of universalism embedded in the book of Isaiah, and to show critical but significant implications for such iconoclasm.

102 According to the "1998 Korean Gallup Report," Korean Presbyterians who believe that the Bible is the word of God are more than half of all Protestants. They represent 7, 850, 056 of the total number of 12, 204, 140. It is also assessed that other Protestant Churches besides Presbyterian, such as the Methodist, the Anglican, the Baptist, etc, accept that the Bible is the word of God (*Ministry & Theology*, 1 [1999], 122–3).

Part III

Particularism and Universalism in the Book of Isaiah

The first half of the final part of the thesis (chapters 4–6) will focus on central particularist motifs in Isaiah, such as the Holy One of Israel, monotheism and the distinct role of the Torah, which play crucial roles in evaluating the issue of religious pluralism. It will also present a critical assessment of religious pluralist ideology in light of such exclusive notions predominantly embedded in the book of Isaiah as a whole. Finally, it will be pointed out in this section that a Korean interpretation of the book of Isaiah, especially of its exclusivist themes, has negative implications for and even offers a challenge to Korean pluralist essayists who dilute the mutual contradictions between Korean Christianity and other religions.

The latter half of the final part of the thesis (chapters 7–9), on the other hand, will place particular emphasis on the most universalist themes that are deeply implanted in the book of Isaiah as a whole: Zion, the New Creation and the New Israel. I will also look at how these universalist notions are read in the context of Korean Churches and how they play a central function in assessing an extremist attitude hostile to other religions. As a consequence, this Korean reading of the themes will issue an acute challenge to and offer critical implications for an excessive fundamentalism, which is not concerned with the deep need for the mutual respect between religious communities but seeks antagonistic confrontation with them.

Chapter 4

The Holy One of Israel

It has been commonly agreed that the Holy One of Israel is a central focal point in the book of Isaiah.[1] Given the frequent occurrences of the title "the Holy One of Israel" in Isaianic passages,[2] it is clear that God is revealed as the Holy One of Israel throughout the book of Isaiah. Since the expression, "the Holy One of Israel", occurs only a few times in the remainder of the Old Testament,[3] there can be no doubt that this concept is a primary characteristic of the book of Isaiah. J. J. M. Roberts affirms this observation when he says, "If there is any one concept central to the whole book of Isaiah, it is the vision of Yahweh as the Holy One of Israel".[4]

The Holy One of Israel has an immediate relevance not only to moral themes such as "justice" and "righteousness" that the only God demands for the holy nation, but also to God's unique designations such as "Punisher," "Redeemer," and "Restorer" characterizing the sole sovereignty of Yahweh. Significantly, the phrase makes it obvious that the holy Yahweh is the only living God unlike other gods that are merely idols made by human hands.

This chapter, therefore, will examine several motifs related to the Holy One of Israel: God's holiness and Israel's unholiness, social justice and righteousness, the Holy One of Israel as Redeemer and Restorer.

1 For an excellent summary of the phrase, the Holy One of Israel, see William Sanford Lasor, David Allan Hubbard and Frederic Wm. Bush, *Old Testament Survey* (Grand Rapids: Eerdmans, 1990), 381–383.

2 This phrase is found twenty-five times in the following passages: 1:4; 5:19, 24; 10:20; 12:6; 17:7; 29:19; 30:11ff., 15; 31:1; 37:23; 41:14, 16, 20; 43:3, 14; 45:11; 47:4; 48:17; 49:7; 54:5; 55:5; 60:9, 14; and see Alec Motyer, *Isaiah: An Introduction and Commentary*, 26.

3 The title, "Holy One of Israel" is cited only six times in all the rest of the Old Testament (2 Kgs. 19: 22; Jr. 50:29; 51:5; Ps. 71:22; 78:41; 89:18 [MT 19]).

4 J. J. M. Roberts, "Isaiah in Old Testament Theology", 63.

1. God's Holiness and Israel's unholiness

Isaiah identifies Yahweh as the holy divine. In the inaugural vision of Isaiah, the prophet is overwhelmed by the holiness of God when he is called to his prophetic ministry in the year that King Uzziah died (Isa. 6:1). The prophet Isaiah saw a scene in which Yahweh was seated on a throne, high and exalted, and seraphs were crying "Holy, holy, holy is the Lord Almighty; the whole earth is full of his glory".[5] Having seen this awesome vision in the temple of the holy and exalted Yahweh, the prophet Isaiah responds:

> Woe is me! I am lost, for I am a man of unclean lips, and I live among a people of unclean lips; yet my eyes have seen the King, the LORD of hosts! (Isa. 6:5)

When the prophet Isaiah encounters the divine presence of God in the temple of the Holy Yahweh, this overwhelming experience leads him to look at his own and his people's iniquity. In this sense, the heavenly vision of Isaiah obviously echoes the account of Moses' call in which Moses feels no more worthy to serve than Isaiah does when he encounters Yahweh as the Holy One.

> When the LORD saw that he had turned aside to see,
> God called to him out of the bush,
> 'Moses, Moses!'
> And he said, 'Here I am.'
> Then he said, 'Come no closer! Remove the sandals from your feet, for the place on which you are standing is holy ground.' (Ex. 3:4–5).

It is noteworthy, in particular, that God's holiness forms a striking contrast to Israel's uncleanness in the scene. In other words, the holiness of Yahweh denotes that God is as set apart from iniquity as the chosen people are set apart from the other nations who adore other gods incapable of delivering them. Since God requires Israel to be holy at Mount Sinai surrounded by divine holiness (cf. Ex. 19:56), Israel as the holy chosen nation, which must only worship Yahweh as their holy God, ought to take the responsibility for putting moral commandments into practice according to God's statutes.

5 Isa 6:1–3.

Despite the crucial commission to be clean as a holy people, however, Israel has repeatedly transgressed the divine decrees and refused to venerate Yahweh as their only God who commands her to be holy. Having considered the fact that Israel as the holy nation has committed immoral sins and profaned God's law, the prophet Isaiah from the beginning of the book defines her as a defiler. Particularly, Isaiah 1:4 forcefully indicts Israel for committing a breach of faith in Yahweh, which results in immoral misdeeds[6]:

> Ah, sinful nation,
>   people laden with iniquity,
> offspring who do evil,
>   children who deal corruptly,
> who have forsaken the LORD,
>   who have despised the Holy One of Israel,
>   who are utterly estranged! (Isa. 1:4)

In other words, it is the prophet Isaiah's poignant criticism that the chosen nation has not only failed to place the divine standards in the heart of their life but also engaged in wrongdoing which is detestable to the Holy One of Israel. Since Israel has committed nefarious sins and thereby broken the revealed word of God, the Holy One of Israel blames the chosen people, who were called to be holy at Mount Sinai, for desecrating their holiness. Moreover, for Israel, social and legal justice is the fundamental way by which Israel's cleanness must be kept in the faith community. Far from keeping the divine statute, Israel has stained her holiness with immoral outrages before Yahweh's eyes. Though Isaiah's contemporaries publicly appear to offer up regular sacrifices to God and to keep national festivals and periodic feasts according to God's law (Isa. 1:13–14), their ethical behaviour presents a striking contrast to exterior ritual practices. Thus, the prophet firmly indicts Israel for their unjust conduct:

> Your hands are full of blood.
>   Wash yourselves;

6 Walter Brueggemann observes that "verse 4 follows the general indictment of verses 2b–3 with a massive, comprehensive catalogue of the full Old Testament inventory of vocabulary for sin. The people is said to be 'sinful,' 'with iniquity.' These two terms, together with 'rebel' in verse 2, form the primary triad for sin in the Old Testament" (Walter Brueggemann, *Isaiah 1–39,* WMBC [Louisville: Westminster John Knox Press, 1998], 15).

> make yourselves clean;
> remove the evil of your doings from before my eyes;
> cease to do evil,
> learn to do good;
> seek justice,
> rescue the oppressed,
> defend the orphan,
> plead for the widow. (Isa. 1:15b–17)

Here the Holy One of Israel declares that the chosen people, who are to be purified from social injustice, have sullied their holiness. This is because Israel has forsaken justice for immorality. Thus Yahweh urges Israel to forsake their hypocritical rites and calls upon her to seek justice, so that she will be restored to her holiness.

2. Israel's obligations: Justice and Righteousness

Likewise, it is important to observe that it is the holy God who manifests his holiness by justice and righteousness:

> But the LORD of hosts is exalted by justice,
> and the Holy God shows himself holy by righteousness. (Isa. 5:16)

Significantly, this verse makes it evident that God's pivotal attribute of holiness is intricately linked with his other characteristics of justice and righteousness. In other words, the phrase intimates that just as it is Yahweh who uncovers his holiness by righteousness, Israel is to exhibit her holiness by putting social ethics such as justice and righteousness into practice. John G. Gammie notes, "God manifests the divine holiness by moving human beings to perform righteous acts. The ultimate source of human righteousness is thus not the human being but rather the supreme and holy ruler who brings justice and righteousness to pass in their midst".[7] Having observed Israel's ethical trespass, the eighth-century prophet strongly warns the nation that the chosen people are under im-

7 John G. Gammie, *Holiness in Israel,* OBT (Minneapolis: Fortress Press, 1989), 85.

pending punishment of Yahweh due to their immoral depravity.[8] In particular, the prophet sets forth several metaphors in relation to agricultural images such as plants and trees in which the divine judgment of the holy God is signified as a consuming fire to purify their sins. It is important here to consider Isa. 5:24, where while the Holy One of Israel is portrayed as a flaming fire, the unclean people are described in agricultural metaphors such as roots and flowers, which will be decayed and burnt.

> Therefore, as the tongue of fire devours the stubble,
> and as dry grass sinks down in the flame,
> so their root will become rotten,
> and their blossom go up like dust;
> for they have rejected the instruction of the LORD of hosts,
> and have despised the word of the Holy One of Israel. (5:24)

These agricultural images indicate that the Holy One of Israel will punish Israel for her immoral transgression as a racing fire, a fact that denotes her infidelity to His word. As the bulk of O.T. writers declare,[9] the fate of Israel virtually depends upon the commitment to the divine laws, which inspire her to put morality into practice. In other words, as a holy nation Israel must unfold her distinctiveness by performing the great commission to be holy among the Nations who not only commit immoral sins but also are infatuated with polytheism. Still, like non-Israelites, the chosen people have ethical vice and thereby profane the holiness of Yahweh. That is why the people will be under the unquenchable wrath of God and be unable to evade the judgment of the Holy One of Israel. Regrettably, the prophet's prediction that a formidable calamity would befall Israel because of her immorality has come true. The section of 2 Chronicles 36 gives us details of how the nation goes to wreck and ruin, and eventually falls to the empire of Babylon.

However, the Holy One of Israel is not willing to abandon his chosen people in exile forever. His punishment was meant to purge Israel from impure sins so that she will be able to consider her excessive injustice and

8 John Barton observes, thus, that "though Isaiah shared many of the concerns of the other eighth-century prophets, such as the imperative of 'social justice,' he had his own preferred topics for condemnation". (John Barton, "Ethics in the Book of Isaiah," in *Writing and Reading the Scroll of Isaiah: Studies of an Interpretive Tradition*, (eds.) Craig C. Broyles & Craig A. Evans [Leiden: Brill, 1997], 69).

9 In particular, the presentation of blessings or curses in Deuteronomy 28 makes it clear that Israel's bright future lies only in her fidelity to Yahweh's law.

thereby restore her great commission to be holy among the Gentiles.[10] That is why the prophet Isaiah calls our attention from the divine punishment to Israel's restoration to a holy nation. The only God who reveals himself as the Holy One of Israel has by no means discarded them utterly and still longs for his chosen people to be re-established as a holy nation. In this regard, the renewal remains available to the exiles.

3. The Holy One of Israel as Redeemer

It is commonly agreed that the portrayal of the Holy One of Israel as Redeemer is brought into prominence in Isaiah 40–55.[11] The Holy One of Israel identifies Himself as Redeemer, a designation that has immediate relevance to deliverance from captivity in Isaiah 40–55.[12] Having prognosticated the downfall of Israel in chs. 1–39, the prophet Isaiah now, at the outset of Isaiah 40, conveys God's consolation, a fact which connotes that God's action for Israel's salvation is about to transpire, and that her return to her homeland from exile is near at hand. Having been depicted as a raging fire signifying divine punishment in Isaiah 1–39, the Holy One of Israel is now portrayed in Isaiah 40–55 as a Redeemer who will deliver the exiles from under the hands of Babylon's power and thereby bring them back to the Promised Land. Given the fact that Israel has undergone severe torment under the might of Babylon due to her failure to keep her allegiance to Yahweh and His revealed word, it is of great consequence that the Holy One of Israel is explicitly depicted as Redeemer to His undelivered people in Isaiah 40–55.

Above all, the representation of Isa. 43:14 makes it unequivocal that the Holy One of Israel will commence with his redemptive action for the sake of Israel to set her free from the coercion of mighty Babylon:

> Thus says the LORD,
> your Redeemer, the Holy One of Israel:

10 John G. Gammie, *Holiness in Israel*, 89–90.

11 Cf. Isa. 43:14; 47:4; 48:17; 49:7; 54:5.

12 William Sanford Lasor, David Allan Hubbard and Frederic Wm. Bush, *Old Testament Survey: The Message, Form, and Background of the Old Testament*, 385.

> For your sake I will send to Babylon
> and break down all the bars,
> and the shouting of the Chaldeans will be turned to lamentation. (43:14)

Likewise, it is important to note in this connection, the initial reference to Babylon in Isaiah 40–55. This reference further portends the impending overthrow of Babylon that is to be followed by the restoration of Israel.[13] R. N. Whybray affirms, "Despite the obscurity of its language it is clearly a promise of the downfall of the Babylonians."[14] Having reigned over the people of Yahweh in exile, the empire of Babylon will not retain its prosperity and splendour, but will eventually go to wreck and ruin. This is because the wickedness of Babylon has aroused the fierce rage of the Holy One of Israel and thereby receives a dreadful chastisement from Him.[15]

> Our Redeemer – the LORD of hosts is his name –
> is the Holy One of Israel.
> Sit in silence, and go into darkness,
> daughter Chaldea!
> For you shall no more be called the mistress of kingdoms. (47:4–5)

Having driven His disobedient nation to despair under the distressful conditions of exile, the Holy One of Israel will now listen to the lamentation of His people who are in agony and pain. Just as Yahweh had heard the groaning of the early captives who were under insurmountable trials in Egypt, He will now listen to those in Babylonian exile. This is because the Holy One of Israel keeps His unswerving fidelity to Israel and will open up a monumental avenue of salvation for her.

> The Israelites groaned under their slavery, and cried out. Out of the slavery their cry for help rose up to God. God heard their groaning, and God remembered his covenant with Abraham, Isaac, and Jacob. (Ex. 2:23b–25)

As Redeemer, the Holy One of Israel will never lose sight of the anguished nation while inaugurating a remarkable new era for their redemption. Having responded to the groaning of His afflicted nation in Egypt in

13 Barry Webb, *The Message of Isaiah: On Eagles' Wings,* BST (Leicester: IVP, 1996), 177; Walter Brueggemann, *Isaiah 40–66* (Louisville: Westminster John Knox Press, 1998), 58.

14 R. N. Whybray, *Isaiah 40–66,* NCBC (Grand Rapids: Eerdmans, 1981), 86.

15 Cf. Isa. 13, concentrated on the Babylonians' sins and their consequences.

the past, Yahweh will continue, in this new time, to cling to His unalterable commitment to the exilic community, which is still in unsympathized despondency. The following passage, which bears a special reference to the description of the Holy One of Israel as Redeemer, clearly points to the coming redemption for His covenant people who yearn in captivity to see their motherland again.

> Go out from Babylon,
> flee from Chaldea,
> declare this with a shout of joy,
> proclaim it, send it forth to the end of the earth;
> say, "The LORD has redeemed his servant Jacob!"
> They did not thirst when he led them through the deserts;
> he made water flow for them from the rock;
> he split open the rock and the water gushed out. (48:20–21)

Having reminded us of Yahweh's miraculous actions for Israel in the past in the sterile wilderness, this poetry is concerned with eschatological renewal for Babylonian captivity. Significantly, the initial verb, "Leave" palpably echoes the awesome drama of the Exodus because "the departure from Babylon now to happen is likened to the Exodus from Egypt."[16] Indeed, during the period of sojourn in the barren desert, Israel was able to sustain life due to various spectacular miracles of Yahweh who supplied Israel with what she lacked. In other words, regardless of the harsh surroundings, Israelites suffered no lack of daily needs including water.

Similarly, the exilic community, craving God's mercy, is now about to behold the day of their dramatic salvation and announce the gospel of their redemption; i.e., that "the LORD has redeemed his people." God's people will no longer be seen as discarded since "Israel is a fortunate by-product of Yahweh's honour. Yahweh's self-regard produces miracles for Israel, because Israel is Yahweh's best visible credential in the eyes of the nations."[17] Accordingly, "God is marching with his people through the desert toward his land as he did before."[18] The following imagery sets forth a full and superlative blueprint of Israel's bright future.

> Thus says the LORD,
> the Redeemer of Israel and his Holy One,

16 Walter Brueggemann, *Isaiah 40–66*, 107.

17 Ibid., 108.

18 John D. W. Watts, *Isaiah 34–66,* WBC Vol. 25 (Waco: Word Books, 1987), 179.

to one deeply despised,
    abhorred by the nations, the slave of rulers,
"Kings shall see and stand up, princes,
    and they shall prostrate themselves,
because of the LORD, who is faithful, the Holy One of Israel,
    who has chosen you."
Thus says the LORD:
    In a time of favor I have answered you,
on a day of salvation I have helped you;
    I have kept you and given you as a covenant to the people,
to establish the land, to apportion the desolate heritages;
    saying to the prisoners, "Come out,"
to those who are in darkness, "Show yourselves."
    They shall feed along the ways,
on all the bare heights shall be their pasture;
    they shall not hunger or thirst,
neither scorching wind nor sun shall strike them down,
    for he who has pity on them will lead them,
and by springs of water will guide them.
    And I will turn all my mountains into a road,
    and my highways shall be raised up. (49:7–11)

This optimistic poem initially paints a gloomy scene in which the captives were loathed by nations and rulers. However, the poetry immediately looks at the bright side of the future for these lamenters who remain tortured in exile. It is the prophet Isaiah's emphatic conviction that, as Deliverer, the Holy One of Israel will not forsake His own people: He is Yahweh, who remains faithful to His own covenant and has a great regard for them as His chosen nation.

Unlike their previous wayward lifestyle against Yahweh who expected His chosen people to obey His statutes, the exiles will no longer mar Yahweh's honour. It is the poet's unshakeable affirmation that, despite the thorny tribulation in Babylon, the unrelieved captives will be replaced in the Promised Land, which was one of the most valuable inheritances given to the early tribes. This is because the Holy One of Israel will prepare a superb and redemptive avenue for the sorrowful exiles by transforming uneven hills and rough mountains into plain highways through which the captives will return to their native land with unutterable pleasure. As Paul D. Hanson remarks, "Since the provider of the new generation of exiles remains the same one who guided the early tribes through the wilderness, this section appropriately ends with a hymn in which earth and heavens are invited to join in praising the Lord who shows compassion on 'his suffering ones'."[19]

4. The unique relationship of the Holy One to Israel

It goes without saying that the reference to the Holy One of Israel in the book of Isaiah suggests the exclusive relationship between Yahweh explicitly identified as the Holy One of Israel, and his own people referred to as Israel in the Old Testament. In fact, "this relation of God to Israel is... neither one of blood nor of tribal relation. It is formed by the covenant and thus is at least as strong a bond and obligation as that formed by kinship."[20] In other words, though Yahweh is the Almighty and Supreme God who reigns over all the world including all the nations, He has intimately dealt with his chosen people by making a covenantal pledge to them. Indeed, it is only Israel who is in a unique alliance with God who keeps His interminable faithfulness to His chosen nation. The following poetry undoubtedly sets forth an indication of a distinct relation of Yahweh to Israel based on His covenantal vows.

> Do not fear, you worm Jacob,
> you insect Israel!
> I will help you, says the LORD;
> your Redeemer is the Holy One of Israel. (41:14)

Having reminded us of a peculiar fellowship of Yahweh with Israel, this inspiring poem makes it obvious that it is as the Holy One of Israel that the Almighty God will protect Jacob from great predicament and quandary, and will shield him from various ferocious assaults. This is because it is as Covenanter that the Holy One of Israel remains steadfast to His chosen nation. As R. N. Whybray notes, "The prophet... suggests that Yahweh considers himself under an obligation to help them, an obligation which he will not break; and also, more startlingly, that Yahweh's rela-

19 Paul D. Hanson, *Isaiah 40–66: Interpretation: A Bible Commentary for Teaching and Preaching* (Louisville: John Knox Press, 1995), 133.

20 John D. W. Watts, *Isaiah 34–66,*105–106.

tionship with them [the exiles] is so intimate that he can be described (even though metaphorically) as a 'near kinsman'."[21]

Given the binding relationship of Yahweh to His covenant nation, the term "Jacob" appears to refer neither to an individual patriarch nor to a specific tribe of Israel; rather it seems to point to a whole nation with which God has made an intimate and covenantal relationship. To be sure, as Redeemer, the Holy One of Israel will inspire Jacob depicted as a despicable worm because He will keep evoking His covenantal vows made to him. More interestingly, the following promissory poem, which contains another reference to Jacob, points to the unique alliance of the Holy One, the sole Yahweh, not only to Jacob but also to Abraham who made a primary pledge with Him.

> Therefore thus says the LORD,
>   who redeemed Abraham, concerning the house of Jacob:
> No longer shall Jacob be ashamed,
>   no longer shall his face grow pale.
> For when he sees his children,
>   the work of my hands, in his midst,
> they will sanctify my name;
>   they will sanctify the Holy One of Jacob,
> and will stand in awe of the God of Israel.
>   And those who err in spirit will come to understanding,
> and those who grumble will accept instruction. (29:22–24)

As indicated in the early patriarchal narratives of Genesis, no matter when Abraham, the father of Israelites, encountered some urgent crises, Yahweh fulfilled His redemptive actions by delivering the patriarch due to His fidelity to His abiding promise (cf. Gen. 12:10–20; 20:1–7).

It is the poet's staunch confidence that the Holy One will rescue Jacob from calamitous circumstances as He did earlier since He is the same God who never failed to abide by His covenant. What Israel ought to believe is that she is about to behold the fulfilment of what is promised by God and thereby will partake in a new redemptive era. As Walter Brueggemann observes, "The response of grateful, reassured Israel is to embrace Yahweh's holy name and to accept a holy identity as its own, that is, to reembrace identity as Yahweh's own people in the World."[22]

21 R. N. Whybray, *Isaiah 40–66,* 65.

22 Walter Brueggemann, *Isaiah 1–39*, 239.

5. The Holy One of Israel as Restorer who renews all the earth

Though Yahweh had a covenantal fellowship with Israel, He also made an everlasting covenant with Noah after the Flood. As expressed in the Noachic covenant narrative (Gen. 9:1–5), God granted Noah and his sons control over all creatures. He also commanded them to subdue all the earth as Adam, the first created man, did earlier, a permission that is concerned with ecological ethics.

Likewise all people are allowed to eat meat, but prohibited to kill human life. This prohibition is because all human beings bear the image of God. Significantly, this covenant has immediate relevance to global regulations that all humans must put into practice. The Noachic covenant is not exclusively confined to Israel, but embraces all human beings, a fact that indicates that all people are intricately bound with this universal covenant. Bernhard W. Anderson observes:

> the Noachic covenant is a universal covenant that embraces all human beings-the descendants of Noah and his wife. This covenant is not made exclusively with Israel, the people of God, but with 'all peoples that on earth do dwell,' as we sing in a well-known doxology. Further, it is an ecological covenant that includes the whole nonhuman creation ('every living creature of all flesh,' Gen. 9:15) and the earth itself (9:13). This universal covenant, which demands reverence for life, both animal and human, has tremendous implications for global ethics today.[23]

For this reason, all nations including God's chosen nation must take responsibility for putting these ethical obligations into practice.[24] Sadly, the following vision of a cosmic catastrophe on all of the earth connotes that all human beings including Israel were unwilling to perform the proviso of the covenant. They showed disregard for God's decree, a failure to embrace the everlasting covenant that subsequently infuriated Yahweh' anger.

> The earth shall be utterly laid waste
> and utterly despoiled;

23 Bernhard W. Anderson, *Contours of Old Testament Theology* (Minneapolis: Fortress Press, 1999), 81–82.

24 Barry Webb, *The Message of Isaiah*, 106.

> for the LORD has spoken this word.
> The earth dries up and withers,
> the world languishes and withers;
> the heavens languish together with the earth.
> The earth lies polluted under its inhabitants;
> for they have transgressed laws, violated the statutes,
> broken the everlasting covenant.
> Therefore a curse devours the earth,
> and its inhabitants suffer for their guilt. (24:3–6b)

Particularly, since the nations were never willing to preserve their integrity to Yahweh, whom they must acknowledge as their sovereign Creator, Yahweh excluded them from an ongoing relationship with His own people. In fact, their idolatrous behaviour not only rankled God's heart but also spurred Israel to plunge herself into idolatrous syncretism, ungodly deeds that fuelled His wrath and eventually resulted in tremendous woes. For God's people who infringe His divine laws and even non-Israelites, none are virtually immune from God's judgement. As indicated above, all nations including God's chosen one shall face His wide-ranging punishment on all of the earth, on which all nations utterly contravened the Noachic covenant by their atrocious behaviours.

However, this dreary doom would be neither God's ultimate goal for all nations nor His total purpose for all creation. While it is as Punisher that the Holy One of Israel drives those who break the ecological covenant, as Restorer He will also bring stupendous blessings to those who would cease their brutal misdeeds, and keep unfeigned faith in Yahweh who is their Maker. The following two visionary poems lead us to a vivid expectation on the day of the cosmic restoration when all of the earth and heavens will be transformed anew.

> This is like the days of Noah to me:
> Just as I swore that the waters of Noah
> would never again go over the earth,
> so I have sworn that I will not be angry with you
> and will not rebuke you. (54:9)

> For I am about to create
> new heavens and a new earth;
> the former things shall not be remembered
> or come to mind.
> But be glad and rejoice forever in what I am creating;
> for I am about to create Jerusalem as a joy,
> and its people as a delight. (65:17–18)

Indeed, the Holy One of Israel will no longer drive His own people to invincible disasters like the Flood of Noah because He will keep His fidelity to them and remain steadfast to His everlasting covenant. As Restorer, Yahweh will renew all creation and reshape all the defiled earth into a paradise, which would be unlike the former things.

Still, these eschatological imageries lead the suffering ones to the unshakable conviction that the time will come when Yahweh will usher in an epochal era culminating in His redemptive activity. In time, the exiles will march into the Promised Land through the new highway with irresistible gladness and inexpressible appreciation. Motyer, "The new creation will be observed and enjoyed by new, fresh minds. All *(I will create)* is the work of God, a work of such greatness and newness that no other agent could account for it. It will be eternal and without anything to disturb its joy."[25]

6. Implications

So far it has been shown that the description of Yahweh as the Holy One of Israel is dominantly set forth throughout the book of Isaiah, a fact that indicates that the subject of the Holy One of Israel is one of the most central topics in the book. By censuring Israel for immoral outrage and hypocritical practices exterior to heartfelt faith, the prophet draws a striking distinction between Yahweh's holiness and Israel's unholiness. The holy God is not an onlooker who allows His own nation to remain unethical.

Rather, it is as an Indictor that the Holy One of Israel condemns His chosen people for the infraction of the covenant incurred by their iniquitous trespasses. Subsequently, as Judge, the Holy One of Israel brings His own nation to a relentless devastation, namely the crushing attack of the empire of Babylon, which is merely a rod under the control of God. What Yahweh intends to do ultimately is to urge Israel to turn away from her obscene lifestyle and return to the one God who is portrayed as the Holy One of Israel.

25 Alec Motyer, *Isaiah: An Introduction and Commentary*, 389.

Significantly, while Yahweh is an Accuser who spurs the wicked nation into the downfall, as Redeemer He also pays attention to the lament of the remorseful exiles who have a great longing for the deliverance from the might of Babylon. This is because, as Covenanter, the Holy One of Israel bears in mind His promissory vows to His own people, a covenantal pledge that indicates the unique fellowship of the Holy One to Israel. To be sure, the Holy One of Israel, Yahweh himself, will no longer throw His own nation into despair; rather He will usher them into a new dramatic epoch of redemption. Therefore the future of Israel practically depends on her loyalty to the living God who is identified as the Holy One of Israel.

More strikingly, the book of Isaiah has immense theological importance for the Korean Churches who embrace it as the word of God. It is of vital consequence that Isaiah's message, especially its key expression, "the Holy One of Israel," is not confined to the world of ancient Israel but remains relevant to contemporary Korean Christians. It is remarkable that the great majority of the Korean Churches wholeheartedly worship Yahweh as the holy Lord in Sunday service.

> The God of Abraham praise,
>   Who reigns enthroned above,
> Ancient of everlasting days,
>   and God of love.
> Jehovah, great I AM,
>   by earth and heav'n confessed;
> I bow and bless the sacred Name,
>   Forever blest.[26]
>
> Holy, holy, holy, Lord,
>   God of hosts when heav'n and earth,
> out of darkness, at Thy word
>   issued into glorious birth,
> All Thy works before Thee stood,
>   and Thine eye beheld them good,
> While they sang with sweet accord,
>   "Holy, holy, holy Lord!"[27]

In the context of the Korean Churches who are deeply committed to the holiness of God, the notion of the Holy One of Israel is so central that it plays a crucial role in evaluating liberal pluralist ideology. It is true that

26 No. 30 in *Korean Hymnal* (Seoul: Korean Hymnal Society, 1984).
27 No. 10 in *Korean Hymnal* (Seoul: Korean Hymnal Society, 1984).

the bulk of Korean Christian readers express the identification of themselves with a holy people who have an exclusive relationship with the Holy God who expects and commands their holiness in a Korean pluralistic world. Chul-Soo Park states:

> Recently, the Korean Churches are so corrupt that they are actively involved in social injustice. Despite their involvement in social depravities, we believe that the Korean Churches are the glorious and holy church of God. We realise that God acts on behalf of the remnant in the history of the Old and New Testaments as well as in the history of the church in the world... Therefore, we need to be the remnant in the midst of these corrupted churches... The priority of what contemporary Korean Churches ought to do is to be holy people found in the Bible.[28]

It is significant to observe, here, that the largest proportion of Korean Christian people are entirely devoted to the three-fold image of the Holy One of Israel: Promisor, Punisher and Saviour. To begin with, the Korean Christians believe that as Promisor the holy God alone can solely make a covenantal promise to them and continue to be in exclusive allegiance to the covenant. A systematic theologian, Young-Bae Chah claims, "He [the Christian God] creates the whole world and continues to make a covenant to his people. The God of covenant is not seen in the midst of other religions. No god can make a covenant to mankind besides the God who creates heavens and the earth."[29]

For the Korean reader, furthermore, the holy God is exhibited as Punisher who blames the ungodly for committing amoral injustice. This characteristic holiness of God urges the Korean reader to take into account that a series of sin not be allowed to remain unchecked but be purged.

Finally, and most important of all, the Korean Churches have no doubt that it is as Saviour that the holy God alone is capable of delivering them from the bondage of sin. For the Korean Christians, the Holy One of Israel, who redeemed Israel from Egyptian slavery, can also become the God whose saving action for the sake of the chosen, including the Korean Christian people, will bring freedom from bondage. Indeed, this point leads the Korean reader to the conclusion that because Yahweh alone is the holy God who operates as Saviour whose saving activity remains on-

28 Chul-Soo Park, "The Model and Nature of the Church" in *How Should the Contemporary Church be Born-Again?* (Seoul: DaeJangKan, 1991), 80.

29 Young-Bae Chah, "Uniqueness of Christianity" in *Bible and Theology*, vol. 11, (eds.) Sung-Soo Kwon et al. (Seoul: Christian Wisdom Press, 1992), 142.

going in Korea, the worship of other gods is sheerest folly. This Korean theological reflection on Isaiah's central motif, "the Holy One of Israel," issues a challenge to pluralist writers who belong to the Korean Churches.

Recently, several Korean liberal theologians are not reluctant to espouse religious pluralism in order to foster dialogue between Korean Christianity and other religions. In a pluralistic Korea, contemporary pluralists, such as Sun-Whan Pyun and Kyung-Jae Kim, pose fundamental objection to the uniqueness of Christianity. Their pluralist claim is adamant that all religious cultures and traditions are little more than different but equally valid responses to the one ultimate divine reality. Sun-Whan Pyun asserts:

> Since God wishes that all people shall be saved and prepares various routes to a common salvation, Christianity is merely one of religions that lead to the ultimate truth and love.[30]

He maintains:

> When one is immune to the colonial understanding of God implanted by missionaries, it can be seen that God has acted for the sake of all the people in the history of humanity. Though many names standing for the Ultimate internally seem to refer to different gods, they point to the same one God.[31]

Yet the attempt to enhance pluralist ideology results in the neglect of the Korean Churches' deep commitment to Yahweh who is portrayed as the Holy One of Israel in the book of Isaiah. The more Korean liberal writers claim religious pluralism, the more a deep and long-standing wedge between pluralists and the Korean Churches is driven. Commenting on the situation confronted by the Korean Churches, Tae-Soo Yim affirms:

> Israelites never identified Eyptian or Babylonian deities with Yahweh. They claimed that Yahweh is entirely distinguished from other gods and worshiped Him as the only God... We thank our faithful ancestors for not identifying Yahweh with

30 Sun-Whan Pyun, "Dialogue between Buddhism and Christianity", "Dialogue between Buddhism and Christianity," in *Encounter Between Buddhism and Christianity: Sun-Whan Pyun Collection II*, (ed.) Sun-Whan Pyun Archive (Chunan: The Korean Theological Study Institute, 1997), 128.

31 Sun-Whan Pyun, "Other religions and theology" in *Dialogue between religions and Asian theology: Pyun Sun-Whan Collection I*, (ed.) Sun-Whan Pyun Archive (Chunan: The Korean Theological Study Institute, 1996), 192.

> other gods. We need to follow in their footsteps and transmit their faith in Yahweh to posterity.[32]

This Korean understanding of the uniqueness of the holy God has negative implications for a pluralist worldview that seeks to treat all religious teachings and traditions as different but equal routes to a common salvation. It should be pointed out that if liberal pluralists are members of the Korean Churches who are deeply committed to the exclusive divinity of the holy God, they should take the adoption of Yahweh as the one living God. This is because, for Korean Christians, there is no other god who is holy besides Yahweh.

No god can redeem the broken-hearted from the hands of fatal forces but Yahweh who is revealed as a holy God. In this sense, one comes to the position that Korean pluralist theologians must not only negate their dismissal of Yahweh's unique holiness but also have great regard for the Korean reader's assertion of the absolute efficacy of the holy God's saving power.

32 Tae-Soo Yim, "Religious Pluralism and Indigenisation from the Perspective of Old Testament" in *Christian Thought*, Vol. 465 (1997): 124.

Chapter 5

The monotheistic manifesto of Isaiah

There is not the slightest doubt that monotheism is brought into prominence in the book of Isaiah, especially in Isaiah 40–55. Isaiah strongly proclaims God's exclusive claim to divinity set forth in the core notions such as 'no other gods', 'Yahweh's incomparability', 'the hollowness of idols' and 'God's sole existence'. Significantly, Isaiah's emphatic announcement of monotheism is more militant than that of other passages in the Old Testament. Robert Karl Gnuse states:

> Second Isaiah, however, provides us with what is the revolutionary breakthrough to monotheism, and most scholars acknowledge that his is an absolute and universalistic monotheism developed well beyond the thought of his predecessors. Second Isaiah not only denies the existence of other gods, he ridicules the idol statuary and the craftspersons who make the idols... The extent of such criticism indicates that in this prophet we have an aggressive monotheist with strident rhetoric.[1]

Though several O. T. passages such as Deut. 4:35; 6:4; 32:39 and 1 Kings 8:60 have striking monotheistic overtones, the section of Isaiah 40-55 reaches the singular conviction that Yahweh remains unique and is the sole living God.[2] He is unlike the false gods, which are merely products of human hands. Isaiah 40-55 clearly points to the fact that Yahweh deserves to be exalted as the one supreme God while idols representing pseudo gods, which in fact are unreal, are futile and delusive. It is as a resolute monotheist that the prophet affirms that no god is able to equate with the supreme God. Since it is as Creator that Yahweh rules over all creatures as well as over all the cosmic world, there is nothing with which He can be

1 Robert Karl Gnuse, *No Other Gods: Emergent Monotheism in Israel* (Sheffield: Sheffield Academic Press, 1997), 206–7.

2 Ronald E. Clements also points oust that "eventually this sense of uniqueness finds its fullest and firmest expression in the Old Testament in the monotheism of Isaiah 40–55 (cf. esp. Isa. 40.18, 25; 41. 21–4; 43.11; 44.6–8). Here with this exilic prophet the ultimate consequence is clearly drawn that Yahweh alone is God, and the other gods that men seek to worship do not in reality exist." (*Old Testament Theology: A Fresh Approach*, [Louisville: John Knox Press], 1979).

likened, a monotheistic view that demonstrates Yahweh's incomparability. This chapter, therefore, will not only be concerned with several underlying motifs crystallizing the prophet's monotheistic promulgation, but also outline prior monotheistic movements since they appear to lie at the root of phenomenal assertions referring to monotheism in Isaiah.

1. Recent scholarship on the origin of monotheism in ancient Israel

Over the past decades, both biblical scholars and archaeologists have actively embarked on quests for the origin of monotheism.[3] Traditionally, the view of ancient Israelite religion as monotheistic has long been espoused by Judaism or Christianity. Practitioners in both faiths were adamant that the origin of Israel's religion and belief in Yahweh is based on the manifestation of religion of ancient Israel described in the Old Testament. According to this view, it should be taken for granted that Yahweh is the only God who created the whole cosmos and revealed his will to Moses, a point that indicates that monotheism is a very early development. It is still found in circles of Orthodox Judaism and conservative Christian churches and accepted as historical fact. However, the rise of historical criticism, which was influenced deeply by the new scientific theory of evolution, led to the radical thesis that monotheism is nothing more than a late development. For instance, a pioneer of historical-critical approach to ancient Israel, A. Kuenen claimed:

> The religion of Israel was initially polytheism. During the 8th Century the majority of the people still acknowledged the existence of many deities and, moreover, worshipped them. We may add that during the 7th Century and until the beginning of the Babylonian Captivity (586 BCE) this situation did not change. Without fear to be refuted Jeremiah could address to his contemporaries: 'as the number of your

3 For a detailed discussion of the origin of monotheism in ancient Israel, see *Only One God: Monotheism in Ancient Israel and the Veneration of the Goddess Asherah*, (eds.) Bob Becking, et al. (Sheffield: Sheffield Academic Press, 2001); Robert Karl Gnuse, *No Other Gods*, 62–128; Bill T. Arnold, "Religion in Ancient Israel" in *The Face of Old Testament: A Survey of Contemporary Approaches*, (eds.) David W. Baker & Bill T. Arnold (Grand Rapids: BakerBooks, 1999), 391–420.

> cities, are your gods, O Judah!' [Jer. 11:13]. This polytheism cannot be taken exception to as a later thing crept into it; on the contrary, everything suggests its originality.[4]

Julius Wellhausen also undertook a study of Pentateuchal sources based on the JEDP theory that is intimately interwoven with this evolutionary assumption. This biblical critical scholarship reaches to the conclusion that Israelite monotheism is nothing more than the product of the Israelite prophetic movement of the eighth to sixth century B.C., a point that indicates that the order of law and prophets should be reversed. Though the last decades have seen the proliferation of publications on various theories of the origin of monotheism in ancient Israel, many comes to the consensus that the sheer monotheistic practice of faith and cult was in fact developed in and after the Babylonian Exile.[5]

Interestingly, this critical approach to the history of ancient Israel is bound up with current debates on the origin of monotheism in Israel. For instance, Morton Smith avers that the "Yahweh alone" movement grew out of a prior polytheistic religious milieu. His thesis is that though there a "Yahweh alone" party existed as a minority religio-political movement in the pre-exilic period, it was peripheral in society and that the majority of ancient Israel adhered to syncretistic worships. According to Mortan Smith, it is true that the movement from polytheism to monotheism emerged in the ninth century and the "Yahweh alone" movement was widely spread during the postexilic period.[6] Having built upon the work of Morton Smith, Bernhard Lang advocates a new model for understanding the development of monotheism in ancient Israel. His attention is much more given to political factors in the development of monotheism. He argues that the emergence of "Yahweh-alone" ideology took place after

4 The quotation is from A. Kuenen's book, *Godsdienst van Israël I* (Haarlem: A. C. Kruseman, 1869), cited in Meindert Dijkstra, "EL, the God of Israel – Israel, the People of YHWH: On the Origins of Ancient Israelite Yahwism," 90.

5 In the face of such skepticism about the substantial historicity of ancient Israel described in the Old Testament, William Foxwell Albright and his followers were adamant that the Old Testament serves as a historical source for Israel's history. For a detail discussion, see Robert Karl Gnuse, *No Other Gods*, 62–128.

6 See Morton Smith, *Palestinian Parties and Politics That Shaped the Old Testament* (London: SCM, 1971).

the fall of Jerusalem in 586 B.C. to explain the reason for the destruction and to give hope to people who were in despair.[7]

Though this evolutionary theory has been maintained by others such as Rainer Albertz, Mark Smith, and H. W. F. Saggs,[8] voices espousing an alternative view have begun to be heard. These scholars focus on the revolutionary nature of Israelite monotheism and are reluctant to accommodate evolutionary explanations. Such a revolutionary approach has been advocated by J. H. Tigay, Othmar Keel, Christopher Uehlinger, and Johannes C. de Moor. Recently, de Moor has proposed an intriguing theory of monotheism, which he sets forth in his book, *The Rise of Yahwism: The Roots of Israelite Monotheism*. His focal point is that the appearance of Yahwism took place during the Late Bronze Age (1550–1200 B.C.) in which the conflict between deities in Canaan made their worshipers feel a certain indisposition to polytheistic practices. He refers to this period as "a crisis of polytheism" that led ancient people to embrace a new deity such as Yahweh.[9] As a result, Baal was revered in the north of Palestine, while Yahweh was worshiped in the south. Indeed, Yahweh eventually became a single deity who was jealous of other gods, especially Baal in the north. With the entrance of nomads into Palestine in the fourteenth century B.C, who were called the *'apiru*, Yahwism increasingly made inroads into the south and came to fruition. His position, then, is a challenge to an evolutionary theory that understands monotheism to have evolved in the preexilic period and to be at its zenith in the exilic period. His alternative view about the emergence of that monotheism maintains that monotheism was an earlier phenomenon that was well established even before the emergence of the monarchy.

More recently, a number of critical interpreters, called "revisionists" by their opponents, have emerged.[10] They have also been accused of being committed to post-modern ideology, most notably by Iain Provan[11] or

7 Bernhard Lang, *Monotheism and the Prophetic Minority: An Essay in Biblical History and Sociology* (Sheffiled: Almond, 1983), 13–56.

8 For a concise discussion of their ideas, see Robert Karl Gnuse, *No Other God*, 73–109.

9 J. C. de Moor, *The Rise of Yahwism: The Roots of Israelite Monotheism* (Leuven: Leuven University Press, 1990), 97–100.

10 Currently this revisionist position is advocated by minimalists such as Philip R. Davis, Thomas L. Thompson, Niels Pieter Lemche, Keith W. Whitelam and so on.

11 Iain W. Provan, "Ideologies, Literary and Critical: Reflections on Recent Writing on the History of Israel," *JBL* 114/4 (1995), 585–606.

William Dever.[12] These so-called revisionists have argued that the scrolls that later became the Old Testament did not originate until the Persian or, according to some the Hellenistic era or even as late as the first-second century B.C.[13] For that reason, these revisionist historians advocate the view that the biblical books do not present an outline of an actual historical Israel united as a common monarchy at the time of David and Solomon but a literary construct of the community that produced the scrolls of the Old Testament in Persian times or later. The shift has been to move away from reconstructing the history of Israel to read the Old Testament as an ideological creation of later communities largely devoid of any historical fact. They argue that because the biblical literature is an exilic or post-exilic creation, the biblical narratives are better understood as akin to fiction rather than a record of events. To argue that the biblical texts do not give us as easy an access to history as scholars traditionally assumed means that they are intensely resistant to the traditional historical criticism that has dominated for more than a century and dismisses it as passé. These critics, who dismiss the Old Testament books as providing us with historical fact, maintain that scholars should concentrate on the ideologies of later writers (or editors) that created the biblical narratives.

These revisionists, then, disagree with the evolutionary view of a gradual move from polytheism to monotheism propounded by traditional historical critics because they do not believe that the texts appeared over a long period of time. They also disagree with those scholars who advocate that the roots of monotheism are to be found in a Late Bronze Age crisis with polytheism because they do not understand this period as an actual period in Israelite history. For the revisionists monotheism appeared in the Persian period or later, that is, at the time when the texts themselves were formed.

12 William G. Dever, "Archaeology, Ideology and the Quest for an 'Ancient' or 'Biblical' Israel," *Near Eastern Archaeology* 61:1 (1998), 39–52.

13 See P. R. Davies, *In Search of 'Ancient Israel'* (Sheffield: JSOT Press, 1992); N. P. Lemche, *The Canaanites and Their Land* (Sheffield: Sheffield Academic Press, 1991); idem, "The Origin of the Israelite State – A Copenhagen Perspective on the Emergence of Critical Historical Studies of Ancient Israel in Recent Time," *JSOT* 12/1 (1998), 44–63; T. L. Thompson, *Early History of the Israelite People from the Written and Archaeological Sources* (Leiden: Brill, 1992); idem, *The Bible in History: How Writers Create a Past* (London: Jonathan Cape, 1999); K. W. Whitelam, *The Invention of Ancient Israel: The Silencing of Palestinian History* (London: Routledge, 1996).

I have offered a concise overview of current debates on the origin of monotheism in ancient Israel in order to indicate that no consensus position about the emergence of monotheism exists among scholars. The opposing views reflect the impasse that has been reached in attempts to reconstruct the development of monotheism in ancient Israel. Because all historians are inevitably influenced by their own strategies for reconstructing history, it should not be surprising that arguments about origin lead to different conclusions.

As discussed earlier, the last two decades have seen a dramatic shift in biblical interpretation. With the rise of current literary criticism, including reader response approaches, a growing number of scholars have sought to bring their academic interest to bear on the role of the reader in interpretation.[14] It is increasingly realized that when texts are read, the reader is involved in the construction of meaning. This point leads us to the recognition that the historical critical reconstruction of ancient Israel is not so much a *reconstruction* as a *construction* of ancient Israel in the image of the historical critics themselves. Indeed, it needs to be asserted that historical critics are also readers actively engaged in creating a "history of ancient of Israel." It is also true that revisionists are readers actively involved in constructing the ideologies of later communities who shaped the biblical narratives about Israel's past. Fewell and Gunn are right when they contend that "readers not only bring their own ideologies to bear on the interpretations of texts, but they use texts to push their ideologies on to others."[15] It needs to be pointed out, therefore, that what the ideology of a text means can now be seen to be a product of what they as readers say it means. Though both historical critics and revisionists are readers subjectively involved in reconstructive work, they sometimes present themselves as detached as if they are basing their arguments on evidence while ignoring their own input.[16] Yet Iain W. Provan correctly points out:

14 For a detail discussion of reader response criticism, see chapter 3.

15 Dana Nolan Fewell & David M. Gunn, *Narrtive in the Hebrew Bible* (Oxford: Oxford University Press), 193.

16 James Barr remarks that "it[the revisionist picture] rests very little upon evidence, very largely on the conceptions and methods of those who have constructed it. It forms rather a *reductio ad absurdum* of the way in which the narrative traditions referring to earlier times have been handled." See his *History and Ideology in the Old Testament: Biblical Studies at the End of a Millennium* (Oxford: Oxford University Press, 2000), 101.

> Testimony, story-telling if you like, is central to our quest to know the past; and therefore interpretation is unavoidable as well. All testimony about the past is also interpretation of the past. It has its ideology or theology; it has its presuppositions and its point of view; it has narrative structure; and (if at all interesting to listen to or to read) it has its narrative art, its rhetoric. We cannot avoid testimony, and we cannot avoid interpretation. We also cannot avoid faith.[17]

Though the historian of Israel's religion should not be divorced from historical research to avoid beguiling preconceptions,[18] it is misguided to believe himself/herself to be independent of all metaphysical or theoretical presuppositions. For this reason, I think that it is inappropriate to privilege historical reconstruction in interpretation. Rather attention must be given to the present text as it is. When I deal with monotheism in Israel here, my interest is neither in analyzing the biblical narratives as if they were data for writing a history of ancient Israel nor in debunking ideologies of the later communities that led to the birth of the Hebrew Bible. Rather my focus is on reading the biblical text as a whole in its present form. Emphasis is placed upon its literary context in front of the eyes of every reader, needing no construction whatsoever.

2. Monotheistic precursors

2.1. Jacob

It is narrated in the book of Genesis, especially in Gen. 35 that Jacob, the father of the tribes of Israel, appears as one of the distinguished monotheists in the Old Testament. Having escaped from the intimidation of Esau who plotted the murder of his twin brother, Jacob had a fabulous dream at Bethel in which "he saw a stairway resting on the earth, with its top reach-

17 Iain W. Provan, "In the Stable with the Dwarves: Testimony, Interpretation, Faith, and the History of Israel," in *Window into Old Testament History*, (eds.) V. Philips Long, David W. Baker & Gordon J. Wenham (Grand Rapids: Eerdmans, 2002), 168.

18 Robert Karl Gnuse mounts an acute attack against revisionists. His judgment is that "the models of Lemche, Thompson, Garbini and Davies too easily surrender the biblical text as a source in reconstructing the history and religion of Israel in the opinion of many, and thus throw away the baby with the bath water." See his *No Other God*, 115.

ing to heaven, and the angels of God were ascending and descending on it."[19] After awakening from the dream, he became aware that Yahweh was in that place. Then he made a pledge that if Yahweh would protect him from the scarcity of both food and clothing He would be his God. However the crafty man had not kept this vow until he was abruptly in turmoil due to the ill-fated incident of his daughter, Dinah, who was raped by Shechem, son of Hamor. Having recalled the earlier promise made to Yahweh at Bethel, the contrite ancestor urged his family to get rid of images of foreign gods, while opting for an unfeigned monotheism:

> So Jacob said to his household and to all who were with him, 'Put away the foreign gods that are among you, and purify yourselves, and change your clothes; then come, let us go up to Bethel, that I may make an altar there to the God who answered me in the day of my distress and has been with me wherever I have gone.' (Gen. 35:2–3)

Given the fact that all his families were in the midst of a polytheistic milieu, it is thought provoking here that Jacob vehemently expresses a positive affirmation of monotheism at the outset of the patriarchal period.

2.2. *Moses*

The plague narratives, focused on Israel's deliverance from the relentless tribulation in Egypt, draw attention not only to Yahweh's tremendous power to baffle all of the Egyptian king's resistance but also to His uniqueness. In ancient times the Egyptians worshiped indigenous sects and animals or even rivers as their gods since they presumably believed that those objects would bring affluence and fecundity to them. In the context of these polytheistic settings, the puissant Yahweh, who was the God of Abraham, Isaac and Jacob, obviously unfolds His divine omnipotence by performing spectacular miracles that lead the Egyptians to insurmountable pain. According to Yahweh's command, Moses uncompromisingly makes distinct statements of monotheism:

> And he said, 'Tomorrow.' Moses said, 'As you say! So that you may know that there is no one like the LORD our God.' (Ex. 8:10)

19 Gen. 28:12.

> But on that day I will set apart the land of Goshen, where my people live, so that no swarms of flies shall be there, that you may know that I the LORD am in this land. (Ex. 8:22)

> For this time I will send all my plagues upon you yourself, and upon your officials, and upon your people, so that you may know that there is no one like me in all the earth. (Ex. 9:14)

In addition to these proclamations of Yahweh's uniqueness, the songs of both Moses and Miriam in which Yahweh is acclaimed as warrior extol God's victory over the Egyptian army, a wholehearted eulogy that certainly conveys the expression of monotheistic confession:

> 'Who is like you,
> O LORD, among the gods?
> Who is like you,
> majestic in holiness,
> awesome in splendor,
> doing wonders? (Ex. 15:11)

Likewise the Ten Commandments in the earlier section of Ex. 20, which is the locus of the Divine Law, sets forth the most exclusive presentation of Yahweh's uniqueness. Above all, it must be noted that the first half of the Decalogue, especially both the first and the second commandments, articulates prominent decrees referring to Yahweh's distinctiveness. Having rescued His own nation from the pernicious force of the Egyptian army and brought them to Mount Sinai, Yahweh firmly incites His people to venerate Him as the one and only God while alerting them that ruinous misbeliefs such as polytheism and idolatry must be followed by His harsh punishment:

> I am the LORD your God, who brought you out of the land of Egypt, out of the house of slavery; you shall have no other gods before me. You shall not make for yourself an idol, whether in the form of anything that is in heaven above, or that is on the earth beneath, or that is in the water under the earth. You shall not bow down to them or worship them; for I the LORD your God am a jealous God, punishing children for the iniquity of parents, to the third and the fourth generation of those who reject me, but showing steadfast love to the thousandth generation of those who love me and keep my commandments. (Ex. 20:2–6)

Indeed, it is noteworthy that Moses insists on the fact that Yahweh is exalted not merely as the sole God but as the Supreme Being whose ascendancy is unparalleled at the outset of a new covenantal epoch of the community at Mount Sinai.

2.3. Gideon

The book of Judges makes it evident that God's chosen people were not strictly obedient to God's statutes, especially to the Ten Commandments. Instead, they were so enamoured by polytheistic cults worshiping Canaanite gods such as Baal and the goddess Asherah. Having kept His eye on Israel's idolatrous and unlawful behaviour, Yahweh is unwilling to sustain them. His intolerance of the worship of other gods indicates that He in no way makes a compromise with idolatry. Given the fact that the jealous Yahweh will by no means put up with polytheistic rites, it comes as little surprise that the one living God would coerce His chosen nation into insuperable anguish by stirring up several foreign nations to assault on Israel. It is in the context of these chaotic settings that Gideon, son of Joash who is a man of the clan of Abiezer, is called to release his nation from the hand of the Midianites. Having listened to the groaning of the people of Israel under the sway of the Midianites, Yahweh appears to Gideon in order to address a vital message in which he is urged to raze the images of foreign gods that Israel ardently idolizes:

> That night the LORD said to him, "Take your father's bull, the second bull seven years old, and pull down the altar of Baal that belongs to your father, and cut down the sacred pole that is beside it; and build an altar to the LORD your God on the top of the stronghold here, in proper order; then take the second bull, and offer it as a burnt offering with the wood of the sacred pole that you shall cut down." (Judg. 6:25–26)

It is remarkable that Gideon immediately responds to Yahweh's urgent mandate by obliterating the images of other gods in a time when fervid idolatry reaches its acme, a revolutionary action that marks a crucial conviction of monotheism.

2.4. Elijah

The second half of 1 Kings centres on breathtaking and unique ministries of the prophet Elijah, who lived in the midst of a gloomy era in which foreign religious cults are ardently rampant in the Northern Kingdom. Sadly most of the northern monarchs fail to embrace monotheistic faith while being enchanted with polytheistic rites as ancestors did earlier. In this context, it is the appearance of Elijah that makes a dramatic shift by which God's exclusive power is at its zenith in contrast with the feebleness of other gods. As a robust Yahwist the prophet Elijah, who has looked at Israel's absorption in the adoration of Baal and the goddess Asherah, raises his voice against her erroneous conduct. His rigid commitment to the uniqueness of Yahweh leads him not only to scold those idolatrous worshipers but also to call upon them to abandon their disorderly syncretism clinging to both Yahweh and Baal. It is on Mount Carmel where the monotheist offers a proposal to verify who the living and unique God is. In other words, it is the only God who is capable of replying by fire as both Elijah and the prophets of Baal call on the name of their god. Then the prophet Elijah craves Yahweh's answer accompanied by the divine fire.

> At the time of the offering of the oblation, the prophet Elijah came near and said, "O LORD, God of Abraham, Isaac, and Israel, let it be known this day that you are God in Israel, that I am your servant, and that I have done all these things at your bidding." (1 Kings 18:36)

In addition to this resolute affirmation of Yahweh's peculiarity, it is radically monotheistic that without hesitation the prophet Elijah urges Israel to put the prophets of Baal to death as soon as he beholds flaming fire from the heavens. To be sure, this awful spectacle eventually leads the people of Israel to the recognition that Yahweh is their only God.

2.5. The monotheistic monarchs of Judah

While a large proportion of the monarchs of the Northern Kingdom seldom remained faithful to Yahweh, several monarchs of Judah seek to adhere to the confident faith of monotheism. Succeeding to the spirit of prior monotheists including the great king David who made an unswerving commitment to Yahweh, they uncompromisingly refuse to walk in prior idolaters' footsteps. These monotheistic traditions are evident in reformatory comportments of the following figures. To begin with, king Jehoshapat's mandatory administration oriented to Yahwism comes to the fore. Unlike monarchical predecessors such as Rehoboam Jehoshaphat on his own initiative takes the lead in a revolutionary reform by which he relentlessly demolishes foreign images and exterminates idolatrous rituals in Judah.

> The LORD was with Jehoshaphat, because he walked in the earlier ways of his father; he did not seek the Baals, but sought the God of his father and walked in his commandments, and not according to the ways of Israel. Therefore the LORD established the kingdom in his hand. All Judah brought tribute to Jehoshaphat, and he had great riches and honor. His heart was courageous in the ways of the LORD; and furthermore he removed the high places and the sacred poles from Judah. (2 Ch. 17:3–6)

What is more, unlike his father, Ahaz, who built sacrificial places to burn incense to false gods and made Yahweh furious, one of the eminent kings of Judah, Hezekiah, earnestly agitates for a radical religious movement. This drastic religious revolution results not only in the wide-ranging recovery of religious observances including the Passover but also in the whole restoration of the crucial function of the house of the LORD. Significantly the Yahwist's epoch-making reformation provokes the people of Judah to eliminate the statues of the Cannanite gods without reserve.

> Now when all this was finished, all Israel who were present went out to the cities of Judah and broke down the pillars, hewed down the sacred poles, and pulled down the high places and the altars throughout all Judah and Benjamin, and in Ephraim and Manasseh, until they had destroyed them all. Then all the people of Israel returned to their cities, all to their individual properties. (2 Ch. 31:1)

It is plain that such decisive action is derived from the wish for a rejuvenation of the monotheistic faith. In other words, Hezekiah's bona fide commitment to the unique Yahweh leads him to take up the position that since other gods must be delusive and illusive, it is inescapable to demolish entirely all images of them. Besides, Josiah, perhaps the last solid monotheistic monarch of Judah, who mounted the throne at the age of eight, is keen to subvert the statues of foreign gods in order to purge away idolatrous syncretism. Being disgusted at the syncretistic belief system of his progenitors, Josiah no longer remains an onlooker of idolatrous practices. Indeed, his focus on the uncleanness of idols representing false gods results in a prodigious and wide-ranging revival of Yahwism.

> For in the eighth year of his reign, while he was still a boy, he began to seek the God of his ancestor David, and in the twelfth year he began to purge Judah and Jerusalem of the high places, the sacred poles, and the carved and the cast images. In his presence they pulled down the altars of the Baals; he demolished the incense altars that stood above them. He broke down the sacred poles and the carved and the cast images; he made dust of them and scattered it over the graves of those who had sacrificed to them. He also burned the bones of the priests on their altars, and purged Judah and Jerusalem. In the towns of Manasseh, Ephraim, and Simeon, and as far as Naphtali, in their ruins all around, he broke down the altars, beat the sacred poles and the images into powder, and demolished all the incense altars throughout all the land of Israel. Then he returned to Jerusalem. (2 Ch. 34:3–7)

In short, as indicated above, despite the struggle with a polytheistic environment in which the bulk of Israel is engaged in idolatrous rites, some influential Yahwists by no means hesitate to take up the conviction that Yahweh is the one God while other gods are false and nonexistent. Significantly, it is thought provoking here that there is a corresponding and crucial point; that is, prior monotheistic traditions arise in the heyday of fervent idolatry. In other words, it is of vital importance that this point leads us to anticipate the fact that since earlier monumental affirmations of Yahwism were given to their forefathers, an unprecedented statement of monotheism would be addressed to the Babylonian exiles who were in the midst of a polytheistic milieu. Indeed, the sterling worth of monotheistic faith eventually culminates in Isaiah's confirmation of Yahweh's exclusive prerogative.

3. Isaiah's monotheistic promulgation

In the book of Isaiah, particularly in the section of Isa. 40–55, Yahweh, whose power is unrivalled, repeatedly insists on His exclusivity. These claims are described in passages such as 40:18, 25; 41:21–24; 43:11–121 44:6–8; 45:5–6, 45:18; 45:21–22; 46:9 and 47:10. Exiles in Babylon surrounded by idolatrous cults might have questioned whether Yahweh remained Lord not only of Judah but also of the nations including Babylon, where Bel was revered. This is because ancient people who were immersed in polytheistic rites believed that the strength of territorial gods was proved by that of their worshipers.

Given the common worldview of this era that gods were territorially bound and would yield fecundity and affluence to their worshipers, the exilic community may have doubted whether Yahweh remained the unique God whose dominion was unrivalled. Regardless of the forlorn impasse, the prophet stressed the uniqueness of Yahweh who is the one living God, a conspicuous monotheism that forms a striking contrast to the ardent polytheism of the Babylonians. It is significant here to look closely at pivotal passages in association with the exclusive features of the sole God.

3.1. Yahweh's incomparability

For an exilic community who might have raised the question whether Yahweh remained unique during a time when enthusiastic polytheism may have been under way, or presumably reached its consummation, the prophet makes monotheistic claims about the peerlessness of Yahweh with whom no-one or no thing can be matched. Above all, the poet presents the essential notion of Yahweh's incomparability in several passages that makes it possible to label the prophet as the most unbending monotheist. Walter Breuggemann observes that "because the statement of incomparability comes early and yet is a most sweeping generalisation, we may regard it as the most poignant spine and leitmotif of all of Israel's testimony concerning Yahweh."[20]

With regard to Yahweh's unequalness, the language of Isa. 40:12–31 comes to the forefront. These verses are part of a larger unit that includes a rhetorical frame on which the five sets of both questions and answers are based, rhetorical exchanges that play a crucial role in demonstrating the inevitability of the LORD's plan.[21] Particularly 40:18 functions as the

20 Walter Brueggemann, *Theology of The Old Testament: Testimony, Dispute, Advocacy* (Minneapolis: Fortress Press, 1997), 139.

21 Edgar W. Conrad shows these sets in 40:12–31 as below:

Questions	*Answers*
40:12–14	40:15–17
40:18	40:19–20
40:21	40:22–24
40:25	40:26
40:27–28a	40:28b–31

(*Reading Isaiah*, 65).

pivotal key of this passage (Isa. 40:12–31) by stressing the point of Yahweh's matchlessness.[22]

> To whom then will you
> liken God,
> or what likeness
> compare with him?

As soon as God's consolation is addressed to the captives, who are perhaps starving for His salvation, at the outset of the second half of the book of Isaiah, the poet begins to focus on the unrivalled claim of Yahweh to unique divine status to whom the exilic community pays homage as the Sovereign LORD. It was during a time when idolatries became predominantly influential in Babylon that the exiles might have succumbed to the temptation to worship the Babylonian gods. It is important to observe here that the prophet does not describe God as *Elohim,* which is the most common term for Him,[23] but as *El,* which "apart from being a common Semitic word for 'god', was also the personal name of the king of the gods in the Canaanite religion."[24] Indeed, the intentional use of the term, *El,* indicates that as the prime God Yahweh is unconditionally superior over the Babylonian idols. In other words, the prophet makes it clear that

22 John D. W. Watts describes the verses 18–20 as the keystone in an arch pattern based on the literary structure:
A See, Lord Yahweh comes with power
He tends his flock like a shepherd (vv. 10–11)
B Who can gauge Yahweh's spirit or teach him? (vv. 12–14)
C Surely nations are like a drop from a bucket (v. 15)
D Lebanon is not enough (vv. 16–17)
Keystone To whom or what will you liken God?
An idol made by human hands? (vv. 18–20)
D' To the One on the rim of the universe,
People are like grasshoppers (vv. 21–22)
C' He appoints and dissmisses princes and judges (vv. 23–24)
B' Look at the stars! Israel, why do you think
Yahweh has failed you? (vv. 25–27)
A' Yaweh is a God of the long view; he does not faint.
One cannot probe his thinking; but he gives power to the faint, to those who wait (vv. 28–31)
(John D. W. Watts, *Isaiah 34-66* [Waco: Word Books, 1987], 88–89).

23 John N. Oswalt, *The Book of Isaiah: Chapters 40–66* (Grand Rapids: Eerdmans, 1998), 62.

24 R. N. Whybray, *Isaiah 40–66*, 55.

the captives need to remain steadfast in their loyalty to Yahweh, with whom no one in the syncretistic religious context is able to compare him.

In addition to Isa. 40:18, Isa. 40:25–26 also takes up the point that the matchless God is supreme in all the universe including the stars, to which the Baylonians bowed down in idol worship. According to the prophet they are simply something made by His hands.

> To whom then will you compare me,
>   or who is my equal? says the Holy One.
> Lift up your eyes on high and see:
>   Who created these?
> He who brings out their host
>   and numbers them, calling them all by name;
> because he is great in strength, mighty in power,
>   not one is missing.

Given the fact that the hosts of heaven are merely the products of God's hand, they are unable to be objects deserving of worship. Accordingly it is totally absurd to pay homage to the stars as gods. In other words, since the heavenly hosts belong to all the universe created by God in the beginning, the stars fervently idolised by the Babylonians can never be equal to the sole God. It is the poet's affirmation, therefore, that Yahweh is the paramount and sovereign God with whom nothing can be compared.

Likewise Isa. 46:5, echoing the prior statements of Yahweh's incomparability,[25] reiterates the view that since the Babylonian gods are simply sculptures produced by the hands of humans such as carpenters and goldsmiths, there can be no attempt to make a comparison between the Creator and His creation. That is to say, while "they [idol-gods] are the creation of humans and are subject to all the limitations of time and space, He [the Lord] is the Creator of humans – and all else – and is limited by nothing."[26]

> To whom will you liken me
> and make me equal,
> and compare me,
> as though we were alike?

25 Walter Brueggemann, *Isaiah 40–66*, 89; John N. Oswalt, *Isaiah 40–66*, 231.

26 John N. Oswalt, *Isaiah 40–66*, 231.

3.2. No other god

There is no doubt that the prophet's monotheistic manifesto of single-minded devotion to Yahweh clearly culminates in the core expression of monotheism, "There is no god besides Yahweh," described in several passages in Isa. 40–55. The expression points to the bedrock fact that Yahweh is the unique God while all other gods are nothing.

To begin with, Isa. 44:6–8 takes up the position that Yahweh is the sole living God who is capable of disclosing His divine presence to the exiles who are often faithless in the idolatrous environment.

> Do not fear, or be afraid;
> have I not told you from of old and declared it?
> You are my witnesses!
> Is there any god besides me?
> There is no other rock. (44:8)

What is more, the sections Isa. 45:1–7 and 45:21–22, which are intimately related to the expression ("There is no god besides Yahweh"), catch the eye. Having been represented as Yahweh's shepherd (44:28) Cyrus is appointed as "the anointed" who would save Israel from the hands of Babylon (Isa. 45:1–7). The choice of Cyrus as "the anointed" to achieve God's long-term plans for the sake of the exiles indicates that Yahweh fulfils His purpose in history by using even a Gentile as one of His historical instruments.

Thus the exilic nation would behold the effulgent day when the sole God would punish their oppressor, Babylon, by using the Gentile emperor, Cyrus, as an executor who would accomplish what God has intended for Israel who is craving God's mercy in the exilic setting. Thus no one is able to thwart God's divine providence on behalf of His chosen people's redemption. Here the mighty Yahweh makes explicit the point that there is no other god capable of saving God's nation from the Babylonian exile.

> I am the LORD, and there is no other;
> besides me there is no god.
> I arm you, though you do not know me,
> so that they may know,
> from the rising of the sun
> and from the west,

> that there is no one besides me;
> I am the LORD, and there is no other. (Isa. 45:5–6)
>
> Turn to me and be saved,
> all the ends of the earth!
> For I am God, and there is no other. (Isa. 45:22)

Particularly, the prophet emphasises that Yahweh not only yields gracious deliverance to His chosen nation who is under the arduous tribulation, but sustains the whole cosmic world that He created.

> For thus says the LORD,
>   who created the heavens (he is God!),
> who formed the earth and made it
>   (he established it; he did not create it a chaos,
> he formed it to be inhabited!):
>   I am the LORD
> and there is no other. (Isa. 45:18)

Here Yahweh identifies Himself as the Divine Maker who produced the cosmic universe that is under the supervision of His precise control. Without His concern for the entire creation, all nature is unable to exist or remain even for a moment. To be sure, no one else is competent to sustain the whole world. Instead, only Yahweh can sustain the cosmic world. It is Yahweh's divine supervision that draws our attention to His sole existence. As Donald E. Gowan remarks, "the prophet had the audacity to claim that his God was in control of everything, and in fact was the only God there is."[27]

3.3. The hollowness of idols

Being mindful of the fact that Yahweh as both Creator and Saviour sustains all the cosmic world and keeps His eye on the exiles, the prophet delivers full-scale assaults on the scandalous idol worship of the exilic community. These diatribes against cultic idols spread throughout Babylon are made explicit in Isa. 44:9–20, while several Isaianic passages charge the idols with impotence (e.g., Isa. 41:21–24).

27 Donald E. Gowan, *Theology of the Prophetic Books: The Death and Resurrection of Israel* (Louisville: Westminster John Knox Press, 1998), 151.

> All who make idols are nothing,
> and the things they delight in do not profit. (Isa. 44:9a)

The opening statement of this long presentation of idols (Isa. 44:9–20) offers a diatribe against the idol-makers by referring to them as "nothing". The Hebrew term for "nothing" implies "elemental chaos."[28] In the Babylonian myth of creation, the Enuma Elish, the chaos monster, Tiamat, is tamed by the warrior god, Marduk, to whom the Babylonians pay homage as their god. Given this ancient Near Eastern cosmology, the idol-producers clearly expect their gods not only to bring to an end the unruly and chaotic environment but also to bring cosmic order into the world. It is ironic here, however, that the makers of idols are referred to as "embodiments of disorder and practitioners of disorder."[29] Specifically, "far from finding order, those who choose the gods not only find chaos but they themselves become part of it!"[30]

Then the prophet turns to a description of how idols are manufactured by artisans such as the blacksmith and the carpenter. In particular, the language of verses 16–17 presents a satirical picture in which the fatuousness of those who shape images with their tools is manifested.

> Half of it he burns in the fire;
> over this half he roasts meat,
> eats it and is satisfied.
> He also warms himself and says,
> "Ah, I am warm, I can feel the fire!"
> The rest of it he makes into a god, his idol,
> bows down to it and worships it;
> he prays to it and says,
> "Save me, for you are my god!"

How can objects consumed by fire for human needs be objects deserving of worship? From the monotheistic perspective of the prophet, it is a tremendous mistake to make an image out of wood and adore it as his/her god by expecting it to save him/her. In other words, as John N. Oswalt comments, "The obvious conclusion from recognising that the god and

28 See John N. Oswalt, *Isaiah 40–66*, 176.
29 Walter Brueggemann, *Isaiah 40–66*, 68.
30 John N. Oswalt, *Isaiah 40–66*, 176.

these ashes came from the same source is that this is not a god, and therefore it is an abomination."[31]

Having recognised that idols are nothing but carved wood the prophet moves his acrid critique to the foolishness of idolaters. The monotheist seeks to explain why heathen worshipers remain adherents of idols. It is the prophet's understanding that the reason idol worshipers are 'hooked on' idolatry is that "they know nothing, they understand nothing; their eyes are plastered over so that they cannot see, and their minds closed so that they cannot understand (44:18)." Judging that idol-worshipers are out of their senses, the prophet concludes that the fundamental problem of idolatrous cults comes from a lack of awareness of their true situation before Yahweh.

4. Implications

So far it has been noted that Isaiah's monotheistic manifesto has no doubt not only that Yahweh is the matchless God, but that there is no god besides Him. Further, it gives short shrift to idol worship by expressing a radical presentation of idol statuary: that is, an idol is a mere piece of wood disappearing as a handful of dust. In this sense, a Yahweh-centred view exhorts the captives to remain faithful to the one God who can save His people, create and sustain the entire universe, and who will punish idol worshipers who are ignorant of venerating Yahweh. In a gloomy period when zealous syncretism was at its zenith, and single-minded loyalty to the sole God presumably shrank due to the exiles' idolatrous environment, the oft-faithless captives are urged to vitalise singular commitment to Yahweh who gives comfort to them and will bring them back to their homeland. Having had no choice but to repudiate polytheistic rites, the exilic community must take to heart the core essence of the monotheistic manifesto of the prophet: that is, there is no god but Yahweh!

Furthermore, the monotheistic assertion of Isaiah has notable theological implications for the Korean Churches. In a murky period when the worship of the Shintō shrine was the acme of the Japanese imperialistic colo-

31 Ibid., 185.

nialism, the early Korean Churches suffered persecution. While the Japanese colonial policy imposed the expression of their adoration of the emperor of Japan on the early Christians, many godly people labelled it idolatry and were not reluctant to fight against what they considered to be idol worship. Having espoused the monotheistic faith that there is no god but Yahweh, which is set forth in the Ten Commandments and culminates in Isaiah's monotheistic assertion, many early Korean Christians refused to recant their faith in Yahweh as the unique Lord. James Huntley Grayson describes:

> A group of Korean Protestant Christians who during the last eight years of Japanese colonial domination were killed or died as the result of torture for their Christian faith, for their refusal to participate in State shintō rites because these rites were perceived to be idolatrous, in contravention of the first three commandments of the Ten Commandments not to worship any god but God.[32]

As a consequence, a number of Korean Christians were executed for their Christian faith; others died as a result of their treatment during incarceration in prison. According to Korean historians, including Nam-Shik Kim, during the period 1938 to 1945, over 200 Korean Protestants were tortured due to their refusal to adopt Shinto shrine rites and 50 Korean Christians referred to as martyrs were killed as the result of torture for their Christian faith.[33] Though this Japanese imperialism centred on Shintō shrine rites led them to be tortured and to die as martyrs, they did not shrink from declaring their singular allegiance to Yahweh during this colonial era. Rev. Ki-Chul Ju, one of the most influential Shintō shrine martyrs, claimed:

> I cannot bow down to other gods except my Lord. I choose to be a martyr rather than an apostate so that I can keep my singular commitment to my Lord. It is my wish that I am able to die for my Lord. I am only prepared for death.[34]

32 James Huntley Grayson, "The Shintō shrine Conflict and Protestant Martyrs in Korea, 1938–1945," in *Missiology: An International Review*, Vol. XXIX, July (2001), 288. Also see Nam-Shik Kim, *Shinto Nationalism and The Korean Churches* (Seoul: SaeSoon Press, 1990), 167.

33 See Nam-Shik Kim, *Shinto Nationalism and The Korean Churches*, 146–74.

34 Sang-Gyoo Lee, "Rev. Kichul Ju's Resistance against Shinto Shrine Worship," in *Journal of Christian Thought*. 4 (1997), 232.

Since the 1945 Liberation of Korea, this monotheistic confession of the early Christians has been the most central heritage of the Korean Churches. It is not too much to say, therefore, that the existing Churches would not flourish without unreservedly embracing the Yahweh-centred view that underlies the Korean Christian faith. Considering how the effect of the persecution of the church continues to influence the religious context of modern Korea, James Huntley Grayson states:

> The Korean Christians' reaction to the pressure to conform to ritual observances at Shintō shrines in colonial Korea is seen to be one of the principal sources of the conservative and fissionable tendency of contemporary Korean Protestant churches.[35]

Indeed, the Korean reader has been adamant that Yahweh is the unique God who cannot be confused or identified with any other deity and intensely focused on the vigorous defence of the spirit of biblical writers' monotheistic manifesto. This Korean reading of their monotheistic proclamation has negative implications for the contemporary liberal scholars who are not inclined to express the avowal of the traditional Yahweh's centred view but pose the approval of a radical pluralist position.

Given that the Korean Churches are rigorously grounded in a set of coherent assertions concerned with the uniqueness of Yahweh, it is inappropriate to defend a pluralist worldview that treats all religions as superficially different but equally valid responses to the one ultimate divine reality. In this respect, one finds it of passionate importance to realise that there is no other god but Yahweh in a pluralistic Korea. Yahweh is the one God in Korea!

35 Ibid., 287.

Chapter 6

The unique role of Torah in Isaiah

There can be no doubt that the Hebrew term תורה comes to prominence in the Pentateuch as well as in the rest of the Old Testament including prophetic texts such as the book of Isaiah. Though there are several eminent figures such as Moses who play a vital role in mediating between Yahweh and His chosen people they are mere messengers to direct God's instruction,[1] תורה, to Israel, who is to keep it. This is because the Torah is the only agent to instruct Israel in what she ought to do as God's chosen people in the midst of a pagan world. In this regard, it can be recognised that it is as the divine revelation of God that the Torah has direct relevance to the notion of monotheism. Walter Brueggemann comments that "the mediation of Yahweh by Moses in the Torah of Sinai is monotheistic... The Torah centres in the incomparability of Yahweh, which mediates the incomparability of Israel."[2]

Particularly in the book of Isaiah, the Torah is clearly understood to be what is spoken by the prophet who holds the view that Israel must take the divine statutes into consideration in order to live as Yahweh's holy nation. Given the fact that the future of Judah lies in embracing the Torah, it is clear that the term plays a pivotal role in delivering the will of the sovereign God in the book of Isaiah. In addition to this point, the Hebrew term תורה sets forth a range of manifestations such as the teaching of Yahweh, the divine decrees in eschaton, the canon to evaluate moral behaviours, the everlasting word for a future time and Yahweh's justice. In this instance, this chapter will be initially concerned with the definition of Torah[3] and then will focus on the examination of several passages in which the unique role of Torah is explicit.

1 Marvin A. Sweeney defines the Hebrew term תורה as 'instruction.' See his "The Book of Isaiah as Prophetic Torah," in *New Visions of Isaiah*, 51.

2 See Walter Brueggemann, *Theology of the Old Testament*, 580–581.

3 For a summary of various definitions of the Torah, see Elmer A. Martens, "Embracing the Law: A Biblical Perspective," in *BBR* 2 (1992), 3.

1. What is the Torah?

Prior to the investigation of the understanding of Torah, it is important to elucidate how Torah should be defined in the context of the Old Testament. It is in the Greek Septuagint that תורה was rendered as *nomos*, a translation that is employed as a technical term contrasted with the gospel. This law-gospel polarity is seemingly predominant throughout the New Testament, especially in the Pauline writings. "Historically as well as theologically, however, such opposition can only give us a distorted picture of the biblical concept of Torah."[4] Walter C. Kaiser, Jr. points out:

> When the Hebrew word תורה was rendered in the Greek Septuagint as *nomos*, an incorrect (or at least as overly restrictive, narrow, and inadequate) translation arose. This, in turn, gave rise to the English rendering "law," the French *loi*, and the German *Gesetz*. Unfortunately, each of these translations continues to give credence to the notion that this portion of Scripture denotes merely formal regulations, often with ritual associations, to which those in the community who wished to attain redemption were subjected. This incorrect conclusion has led to the misguided inference that the Pentateuch must now be replaced in the life of the believing community, since legal instructions have now been exchanged for gracious acceptance and the material emphasis of the Torah has now been replaced with the spiritual tone of the New Testament.[5]

In fact, it is widely agreed among scholars that such translation is inaccurate and the Hebrew term תורה should be rendered with a more precise wording. To be sure, תורה means much more than 'law.' It is argued that the Hebrew word תורה should be translated as 'instruction', and several scholars such as Marvin A. Sweeney insist that "the Hebrew word תורה is more properly translated as 'instruction' (cf. TDNT IV: 1046), as indicated by its derivation from the *hiphil* form of the root *yrh* which means 'to guide' or 'to instruct".[6] My point is that the meaning of the term is not to be confined to a definite phrase; rather the word has broader senses and multiple implications. Having sympathised with the point, the German

4 Frank Crüsemann, *The Torah: Theology and Social History of Old Testament Law*, translated by Allan W. Mahnke (Minneapolis: Fortress Press, 1998), 1.

5 Walter C. Kaiser Jr, "Images for Today: The Torah Speaks Today," in *Studies in Old Testament Theology*, (eds.) Robert L. Hubbard Jr., Robert K. Johnston and Robert P. Meye (Dallas: Word Publishing, 1992), 117–118.

6 Marvin A. Sweeny, "The Book of Isaiah as Prophetic Torah", 51.

Old Testament theologian, Frank Crüsemann offers various clues to the understanding of Torah:

> The word Torah in the everyday speech of Old Testament times meant to their children to instruct them in matters of living and to warn them about mortally dangerous situations. In that early function as well as all later uses, the word implies information, advice, instruction, the establishment of norms, demand as well as encouragement, the command but also the benefits included. The concept of Torah became a technical term for priestly instruction to the laity (Jer 18:18; Ez 7:26), but it also designates speech of the wisdom teachers (Prov 7:2; 13:14) or the prophets (Isa 8:16, 20; 30:9) to pupils. Finally, in Deuteronomy Torah became the most important concept for the comprehensive written will of God (e.g. Deut 4:44f.; 30:10; 31:19). Already here "Torah" contained narrative (especially Deut 1:5) and laws (see especially also Ps 78:1, 5, 10). This deuteronomic concept was a later designation for the Ezra law (e. g. Neh 8:1), the entire Pentateuch, but also the prophetically proclaimed eschatological word of God (Isa. 2:3 and its paralled Mi 4:2, and also Isa. 42:4).[7]

In sum, the meaning of תורה is so wide-ranging that it is inappropriate to label תורה unconditionally as the Pentateuch or law in opposition to the gospel. Instead, as Frank Crüsemann comments, we ought to consider the word תורה in all its aspects in order to define what the Torah means since it appears to vary with each different context. For instance, the use of Torah as wisdom teaching is evident in wisdom literature including the book of Proverbs[8], while in prophetic books such as the book of Isaiah, the Torah is intimately linked with the eschatological vision of Isa. 2:2–4, which is one of the best known passages in the book. It is my conclusive suggestion, therefore, that the Torah should be understood to be the revelation of God[9] which teaches His people, guides them to His ways, provides them with wisdom instructions, and presents prophetic teachings in which eschatological expectations are set forth.

7 Frank Crüsemann, *The Torah: Theology and Social Historical of Old Testament Law*, 1–2.

8 For a concise study of the Torah as a source of wisdom, see Bernhard W. Anderson, *Contours of Old Testament Theology,* 257–8.

9 Elmer A. Martens remarks that "law is the revelation of the divine will. Torah is an expression of God's intent." See his "Embracing the Law: A Biblical Perspective," 5.

2. The distinct role of Torah in the book of Isaiah

2.1. The Torah as the teaching of God

The Hebrew term תורה occurs twelve times in the book of Isaiah,[10] and plays a central role in understanding the prophetic message of the book. The initial reference to תורה is found in Isa. 1:10 that is part of the larger unit (Isa. 1:10–17) centred on a diatribe against the hypocrisy of the sacrificial system of the temple.

> Hear the word of the LORD,
>   you rulers of Sodom!
> Listen to the teaching (תורה) of our God.
>   you people of Gomorrah! (Isa. 1:10)

In the language of verse 10, which serves as the opening phrase of the section Isa. 1:10–17, the poet offers a portentous picture in which Jerusalem, the centre of worship, is portrayed as Sodom and Gomorrah, the vilest cities, while Judah is identified with atrocious men in those cities. The prophet stresses here that Judah has defiled the temple of the city of God with false offerings, resulting in the failure to please the holy God who yearns for inner loyalty to Him rather than external sacrifices. The wide-ranging corruption of the cults of the temple, which makes it possible to reconcile offenders to Yahweh, indicates that the intimate relationship between Yahweh and Israel has come to an end.

Significantly, by forming a striking contrast between the word of Yahweh/the Torah of God and Judah/Sodom and Gomorrah, the parallel structure of the phrase points to the fact that Israel is under obligation to turn from false worship back to the word of Yahweh so that she can hold communion with Him.

> A. Hear the word of the LORD,
>   B. you rulers of Sodom!
> A'. Listen to the teaching (תורה) of our God.
>   B'. you people of Gomorrah! (Isa. 1:10)

10 The Hebrew word תורה is found in the following passages: 1:10; 2:3; 5:24; 8:16, 20; 24:5; 30:9; 42:4, 21, 24; and 51:4, 7.

It is not too much to say that the future of Israel deserving of punishment depends on her adherence to the Torah. The only way of passing this religious crisis is to embrace the teaching of God without reluctance. Indeed, there is no escape from this demise, but the Torah as the word of Yahweh[11] is essential for a revitalisation of Judah.

2.2. *The Torah as the divine decrees to effect the eschatological peace*

It is widely agreed that the oracle in Isaiah 2:2–4 sets forth one of the most significant eschatological pictures in the Old Testament in which Zion is identified and elevated not only as the world governmental centre but also as God's dwelling place to which the nations would go on a pilgrimage in the latter days.

> Many peoples shall come and say,
> "Come, let us go up to
> the mountain of the LORD,
> to the house of the God of Jacob;
> that he may teach us his ways
> and that we may walk in his paths."
> For out of Zion shall go forth instruction,
> and the word of the LORD from Jerusalem. (Isa. 2:3)

Interestingly, the poet offers a sublime presentation in which the Torah will emanate from Zion so that the pilgrims who long to learn it will gain an insight into God's ways and walk in them. As a consequence, the nations will partake in an epoch-making era in which military equipment such as swords and spears are to be turned into life-yielding utensils, a dramatic era that is followed by the worldwide peace.

> they shall beat their swords into plowshares,
> and their spears into pruning hooks;

11 According to Brevard S. Childs, "this [word of Yahweh] is also torah, not in the strict sense of Mosaic formulation, but as imperatives commensurate with everything that Israel had learned from its long historical experience with its God. These are not universal ethical teachings, but a highly existential application of the divine will that has long since been revealed to Israel, and now delivered with a fresh poignancy to a corrupt, complacent, and self-righteous population" (See his *Isaiah* [Louisville: Westminster John Knox Press, 2001], 20).

> nation shall not lift up sword against nation,
> neither shall they learn war any more. (Isa. 2:4b)

Indeed, in this unimaginable description, the poet envisions the glorious Zion, from which emanates the divine decrees that will lead the nations to cease aggressive battles. It is the poet's conviction that due to their enthusiastic commitment to the Torah in the latter days all the nations will participate in a peaceful epoch with one accord. Marvin A. Sweeney states:

> The term, Torah, again parallel to 'the word of Yahweh', apparently refers to Yahweh's instruction on the proper way to conduct international relations. It appears in the context of the legal resolution of disputes between the nations, in which Yahweh is portrayed as the typical ancient near eastern monarch who employs his 'Torah' as a means to settle disagreements among his subjects. In this sense, Torah signifies a means to effect world-wide order.[12]

Though there have been various efforts to lead people into a peaceful society, humans have never been inseparable from antagonism causing numerous wars. We have faced the danger of fatal weapons such as nuclear missiles and atomic bombs being used in wars. Until recently we have been alarmed at rumours of wars including bloody battles in Yugoslavia and the Middle East crisis, which have resulted in many deaths, and even angry outbursts have been a constant part of our lives. It is plain that humans are incapable of establishing a peaceful world. In other words, it seems that intense combat will not cease.

From the visionary perspective of the prophet, however, in the latter days those who shall receive Yahweh's Torah, which will go out from Zion, will not engage themselves in hostilities but enjoy a transformed life in a new era. Indeed, in the last day the Torah will play an exclusive role in causing the nations to eliminate all dissension. In this regard, there is no power or organization to establish an eschatological peace, but only the Torah makes it possible to fulfil what is anticipated in the superb vision of Isa. 2:2–4.

12 Marvin A. Sweeney, "The Book of Isaiah as Prophetic Torah," 60.

2.3. *The Torah as the criterion of God's judgment on immoral Judah*

The Hebrew term תורה occurs in Isa. 5:24 related to the context of a series of woes (Isa. 5:8–23) focused on social depravities of the people of Judah including a failure of leadership. This verse is concerned with the indictment that the people are involved in a range of unethical conduct, abhorrent misdeeds inevitably followed by catastrophes that Judah shall undergo.

> Therefore, as the tongue of fire devours the stubble,
> and as dry grass sinks down in the flame,
> so their root will become rotten,
> and their blossom go up like dust;
> for they have rejected the instruction of the LORD of hosts,
> and have despised the word of the Holy One of Israel. (Isa. 5:24)

The depressing language of the verse addresses a gloomy outlook on Judah's impending future by using a series of images in which God's punishment is depicted as fire while Judah is portrayed as what disappeared in dust or ash. Substantially and ultimately this imminent destruction derives from the repudiation of the Torah. Judah's immoral iniquities, which are strictly forbidden in the Torah, show a disdain for the divine ordinances in the Torah. As John D. Watts observes, "Social crimes and degradation are symbols of their 'lack of knowledge' (v. 13) and their 'rejection of the instruction of Yahweh of Hosts' (v. 24)."[13]

It is not too much to say, therefore, that success and failure depends on embracing the Torah, a point reminiscent of a series of blessings or curses described in Deuteronomy 27–28 in which Moses urges Israel to keep the divine statutes by warning her not to break them. In other words, "Israel can only merit punishment by rejecting Mosaic law, in future years, the prophetic and wisdom writings based on that law."[14] In this sense, it is noteworthy that in the passage of Isa. 5:24, the Torah plays a significant role as the norm or guide to assess Judah's unethical crime, as it also did in Deuteronomy. Indeed, it seems to be the prophet's deep-seated conviction that there is no criterion for social order except the Torah, which serves as the canon to evaluate the transgression of God's people.

13 John D. Watts, *Isaiah 1–33*, 63.

14 Paul R. House, *Old Testament Theology*, 192.

2.4. The Torah as the everlasting word for a future time

The Torah not only is used in relation to a series of legal terms such as "testimony" and "witness", but it also refers to the everlasting word of God spoken by the prophet. To begin with, the word of Isa. 8:16 identifies the Torah with what is to be bound up as a "testimony". Having had a look at the failure to hear what Isaiah has spoken to his contemporaries, Yahweh decides to withdraw it from them and then commands Isaiah seal up the Torah, which parallels "testimony", in order to preserve it as legal written words till a future time when it will be audible. Having been aware that there is no hope that Isaiah's community would pay attention to his words, Isaiah longs for a latertime when his vision will be read and is relevant to a community who will see and hear.

> Bind up the testimony,
> seal the teaching among my disciples.
> I will wait for the LORD,
> who is hiding his face from the house of Jacob,
> and I will hope in him. (Isa. 8:16–17)

Then another description of the command to Isaiah echoing 8:16 is also reflected in the passage of 30:8. Here the vision of Isaiah is depicted as what is to be inscribed on a scroll by Isaiah according to Yahweh's command.

> Go now, write it before them on a tablet,
> and inscribe it in a book,
> so that it may be for the time
> to come as a witness forever. (Isa. 30:8).

Here the vision of Isaiah, referred to as what is to be written on a tablet in 30:8, parallels the Torah. Therefore the Torah has immediate relevance to the vision of Isaiah which will be audible to later generations. Thus Edgar W. Conrad argues:

> Notice that what was "inscribed-written" in a "tablet-book" in 30:8 is "teaching" in 30:9 and "word" in 30:12. These passages in which "teaching" and "word" are used as synonyms for that which is contained in Isaiah's vision lend weight to my

argument that what the reader is to read in 40:8 is the vision of Isaiah, containing the "teaching-word" of the LORD.[15]

Though the Torah is sealed and thereby is not available for a time while the community is blind and deaf, a future audience is to read the Torah as Yahweh's word spoken in the past vision of the prophet Isaiah. In this respect, the Torah as the word of God will not shrink like mortal humans or their ephemeral words, but will be everlasting.

> The grass withers, the flower fades,
>   when the breath of the LORD blows upon it;
> surely the people are grass.
>   The grass withers, the flower fades;
> but the word of our God will stand forever. (Isa. 40: 7–8)

Though earlier generations in the age of Isaiah, whose community became blind and deaf, had to face the withdrawal of Torah, a future descendant who will be apart from their spiritual obstacles, blindness and deafness, shall behold a time when the Torah as the word of God will stand for ever. Indeed, the Torah shall not be confined to a space-time continuum. As the only and everlasting word, the Torah will eternally remain available for a later time when the blind will see and the deaf will hear, an infinite principle that forms a singular contrast to the transience of the word of man, which will fade in a time.

2.5. *The Torah as Yahweh's justice*

It is significant that several passages such as 42:4 and 51:4, 7 parallel Torah to Yahweh's justice.[16] This parallelism suggests that the Torah can be understood to be Yahweh's justice that the Servant will bring to the nations to establish the restoration of the earth. The use of Torah as Yahweh's justice occurs this way in 42:1–4.

> Here is my servant, whom I uphold,
>   my chosen, in whom my soul delights;

15 Edgar W. Conrad, *Reading Isaiah*, 140.

16 H. G. M. Williamson, *Variations on a Theme: King, Messiah and Servant in the Book of Isaiah* (Carlisle: Paternoster Press, 1998), 136–7.

> I have put my spirit upon him;
> he will bring forth justice to the nations.
> He will not cry or lift up his voice,
> or make it heard in the street;
> a bruised reed he will not break,
> and a dimly burning wick he will not quench;
> he will faithfully bring forth justice.
> He will not grow faint or be crushed
> until he has established justice in the earth;
> and the coastlands wait for his teaching.

Sadly, so far human designed laws have failed to guide us to an epoch in which there is no more chaos. Rather, a number of disorderly phases including violation, defiance and infraction have been so much a part of our lives that we have no hope to see an orderly era realised. As Paul D. Hanson comments,

> Throughout biblical history and the history of the religions that fell heir to the legacy – Judaism, Christianity, and Islam – Holy War has appealed to many as the most expedient means of bearing witness to God's universal reign. The Hasmoneans in their dedication to the principle of the *herem*, the ban of all captives and booty, those followers of the Prophet Mohammed who interpreted one of the Pillars of Islam, *jihad*, in martial terms, and medieval Christians who sought to advance God's kingdom through the Crusades, each in turn set out to bring forth God's justice to the nation. In each the result was bloodshed and a legacy of hatred that maintained the grip of war and terror on large segments of humanity.[17]

Yet, some day, the Servant of Yahweh will actively accomplish his mission to bring forth Yahweh's justice that will generate a life-giving order that is beyond the reach of human efforts. While chaotic human systems in the world shall come to an end, a lasting orderliness will be given to the nations which long for a future time when the Servant will make it possible for the righteousness of Yahweh to reign over the earth. More significantly, the two Hebrew terms, משפט (justice) and תורה (Torah), are in parallel with each other in 42:4, a fact that implies that they are employed as synonyms. In this sense, it goes without saying that Yahweh's justice in the verse apparently refers to the Torah that will undergird a divine orderly system on the earth. Another description of Torah as God's justice is also shown in the context of Isaiah 51:4–8, centred on the salvation of

17 Paul D. Hanson, *Isaiah 40–66*, 45.

Yahweh for the sake of His nation that yearns, in Babylon, to return to her motherland.

> Listen to me, my people,
> and give heed to me, my nation;
> for a teaching will go out from me,
> and my justice for a light to the peoples.
> I will bring near my deliverance swiftly,
> my salvation has gone out
> and my arms will rule the peoples;
> the coastlands wait for me,
> and for my arm they hope. (Isa. 51:4–5)

This passage is unequivocally reminiscent of the Servant's task to bring forth justice on the earth as expressed in 42:1–4. Despite no description of the Servant's mission in the passage (51:4–5), it is generally agreed that both passages (42:1–4 and 51:4–5) are directly linked with each other since the two terms, משפט (justice) and תורה (Torah), are in parallel in those texts. R. N. Whybray points out:

> The similarity of this passage [Isa. 51:4–6] to the first 'Servant Song' (42:1–4) has often been remarked: the universal rule of Yahweh (משפט [justice]) and his law (תורה [justice]) which it is the Servant's task according to 42:1–4 to 'bring forth' to the nations will, according to 51: 4–6, go forth directly from Yahweh. According to both passages the coastlands will wait for Yahweh or for his law.[18]

It is noteworthy, however, that Isa. 51:4–6 is more linked with the salvation for the captives than is 42:1–4, a point that indicates the certainty of a future renewal of the glorious Zion. In this poem, Yahweh promises that His people will behold an epoch-making time when the Torah will emanate from Him and His justice will be a light to the nations, and thereby God's deliverance for the suffering people in Babylon will come to pass. Furthermore, according to 51:7, in a later era in which all chaotic systems of human government will vanish, no longer will the Torah be written on a scroll, but it will be put into the hearts of the peoples. Indeed, those who have the Torah in their hearts will reach the realisation that, while Yahweh's justice will permeate the whole world, the unrighteous ultimately will go to wreck and ruin.

18 R. N. Whybray, *Isaiah 40–66*, 155–6.

3. Implications

As discussed earlier, various uses of Torah are evident in the book of Isaiah. While the Hebrew word תורה is identified with the teaching of Yahweh the term is portrayed as the eschatological divine statutes to generate a worldwide peace. Besides these descriptions of the Torah in the book, the word serves not only as the everlasting word announced by the prophet to address the intention of the sovereign God but also as the norm by which Judah's immoral iniquities are assessed. Finally, the Hebrew word תורה clearly refers to משפט that will pervade the earth when Zion, embracing the Torah, is restored. In this sense, it needs to be pointed out that the Torah in the book of Isaiah plays a unique role in serving as Yahweh's instruction, the abiding word for a future time, the clue for social order and the universal justice of God.

On the other hand, there is no doubt that this prophetic understanding of Torah has immense implications for the Korean Churches. Significantly, a number of Korean readers believe that the teaching of Torah set forth in the Old Testament is on a par with the word of God and is at its zenith in the teaching of Jesus Christ articulated in the New Testament. For Korean Christians, no Scripture can play a crucial role in delivering the teaching of Yahweh besides the biblical Scriptures. The Korean Churches refuse to identify the biblical teachings with other religious traditions such as the Buddhist Scriptures or the Analects of Confucius.

Instead, they are not reluctant to view the Bible and its divine teachings, not simply as one of the classical or mythical teachings, but as the unique medium to disclose the divine revelation in words. It is not surprising, therefore, that the Korean Churches have become preoccupied with a high view of the Bible and dealt with its teaching as the locus of God's instructions to contemporary Christians. It is not too much to say, indeed, that the Korean Churches cannot exist and flourish without unreservedly embracing the Bible. Considering the relationship of the Korean Churches, especially the Protestant Church, to the authority of the Bible, Yong-Kyu Park asserts:

> The rise and development of the Korean Protestant Church is intimately tied to the issue of biblical authority. For Korean Christianity, failure or success depends on the issue of biblical authority.[19]

Even pluralist theologian Kyung-Jae Kim agrees:

> The fundamental reason why in 120 years Korean Protestant Churches can have 1,000 Christians is that they yearn to love the biblical Scriptures... Though profound thoughts in relation to wisdom that leads us to attain spiritual enlightenment are found in the Confucius teachings or the Buddhist Scriptures, they lack spiritual influences and activities that create spirituality. Therefore, Korean people loved the biblical Scriptures, and continue to love them more than other nations.[20]

According to the Korean Christian, it is inconceivable to treat the biblical teachings like Torah as something that has receded into the past, unavailable for contemporary readers. For instance, the Korean Churches embrace, Deuteronomy 6:5,[21] which serves as the nub of Torah, as the most central bedrock of Christian faith. According to a leading pluralist writer, Kyung-Jae Kim, one of the considerable reasons for religious conflicts in Korea is that the Korean Churches have failed to embrace the teaching of Torah centred on the passage of Deut. 6:5 but degenerated its core spirit. He points out:

> Korean Protestant Christians have marred the true faith... This is because they have violated our Lord's command, "Love the Lord your God with all your heart and with all your soul and with all your mind and love your neighbour as yourself," but focused on inferior matters.[22]

In this regard, the teaching of Yahweh, Torah, is not restricted to the past world, but teaching through which the knowledge of what Yahweh wants them to do is not only accessible to ancient Israel, but also continuously available for today's Korea.

As indicated earlier, several Korean pluralists firmly insist that no religion has a monopoly on how to know what the teaching of God is;

19 Yong-Kyu Park, *A History of Presbyterian Theological Thought in Korea: Korean Protestantism and Biblical Authority* (Seoul: Chongshin Publishing Company, 1992), 17.

20 Kyung-Jae Kim, "Can Christianity and Buddhism Exist Together Harmoniously?" *Christian Though.* 479 (1998), 12–3.

21 "Love the Lord your God with all your heart and with all your soul and with all your strength."

22 Ibid.

rather, all religious teachings can be a medium to conceive and experience God. This radical worldview is the basis for their severe criticism of the Korean Christian whose particular attention is drawn to Torah's exclusive role in shedding light on God's ways. Having walked in the footsteps of the writer who exhorts us to turn our attention to the One God and His teaching in Deuteronomy 6:5, however, Korean readers are committed to the scrupulous teaching of Torah that helps them keep exclusive adherence to Yahweh in a pluralistic Korea. Indeed, Korean Christians have no other religious principle or instruction to stimulate them to recall what God desires them to do and who urges them to put it into practice.

This Korean understanding of the teaching of God, Torah, set forth in the Bible, is problematic for the pluralist position that all religious traditions, cultures and teachings are nothing less than equally valid manifestations of the same God or the ultimate divine reality. A serious difficulty arising from a liberal pluralist worldview lies in the dismissal of mutual differences between all religions.

It should be pointed out, however, that one finds it improper to suppress such differences in terms of an *a priori* belief that each individual religion equally has access to truth. In the modern Korean world, it is common belief that, for the most part, Christians never identify the scriptures of other religious teachings, such as Qur'an of Islam or the Buddhist and Sanskrit scriptures, with the teaching of God.

Rather, what is emphasised for contemporary Korean Christians, especially those who are bitterly disillusioned by the frustrations and disappointments of life, is that only the teaching of Yahweh enables them to feel the satisfaction of the realisation of the overcoming of futility and the giving of meaning to life. Considering the exclusive role of the biblical scriptures in the Korean Churches, Sung-Soo Kwon asserts:

> The Bible is a mirror of the pure soul. It is a mirror that reflects our soul and its blemish. It is the pillar of salvation that enables us to remain in the midst of the storm of tribulation. It is not only the disserting knife to heal the illness of soul but the perfume that is used to cure a wounded soul. It is the standard for education that shows how to teach in God's way.[23]

This Korean Christian perspective leaves no doubt that since the fundamental structure of a pluralist approach that all religions and their teach-

23 Sung-Soo Kwon, *Biblical Hermeneutics*, Vol. 1 (Seoul: Chongshin Publishing Company, 1991), 26.

ings are innately the same is called into question as an untenable, the Korean Christians must beware of taking up such an imperialist position. No other religious teachings can play as a central role in delivering what God wants Korean readers to do. Only the biblical Scriptures serve as the single canon to reveal God's teaching in a pluralistic Korea.

Chapter 7

Mount Zion as the Cosmic Centre

It is widely agreed that the concept of Jerusalem/Zion is a central focal point in the Old Testament, especially in prophetic books including the book of Isaiah.[1] As John F. A. Sawyer remarks, "The Zion traditions, including beliefs about the Davidic royal family, constitute the most highly developed and influential theme in biblical prophecy."[2] Indeed, the book of Isaiah as a whole draws special attention to the Jerusalem/Zion motif.[3] This is because "the thesis of Jerusalem as the integrating factor in the book finds support not only from the initial emphasis placed upon Jerusalem in Isaiah 1 and then again in conclusion in chapter 66, but also in the internal structuring of the various subsections of the book (chaps. 1–12, 13–23, 24–27, 28–33, 34–35, 36–39, 40–55, and 56–66)".[4] Indeed, the book of Isaiah is concerned not only with the demise of Jerusalem which has been in bondage to sin resulting in the Babylonian invasions but also

1 The term Jerusalem is found 49 times while the word Zion occurs 47 times in the book of Isaiah according to the following lists:
Jerusalem: 1:1; 2:1, 3; 3:1, 8; 4:3, 4; 5:3; 7:1; 8:14; 10:10, 11, 12, 32; 22:10, 21; 24:23; 27:13; 28:14; 30:19; 31:5, 9; 33:20; 36:2, 7, 20; 37:10, 22, 32; 40:2, 9; 41:27; 44:26, 28; 51:17; 52:1, 2, 9; 62:1, 6, 7; 64:9; 65:18, 19; 66:10, 13, 20.
Zion: 1:8, 27; 2:3; 3:16, 17; 4:3, 4, 5; 8:18; 10:12, 24, 32; 12:6; 14:32; 16:1; 18:7; 24:23; 28:16; 29:8; 30:19; 31:4, 9; 33:5, 14, 20; 34:8; 35:10; 37:22, 32; 40:9; 41:27; 46:13; 49:14; 51:3, 11, 16; 52:1, 2, 7, 8; 59:20; 60:14; 61:3; 62:1, 11; 64:9; 66:8.

2 John F. A. Sawyer, *Prophecy and the Prophets of the Old Testament*, 51.

3 For a considerable outline of Zion theology in Isaiah 1–39, consult Donald E. Gowan, *Theology of Prophetic Books: The Death and Resurrection of Israel*, 65–68; see also J. Barton, *Isaiah 1–39*, 115–17. For a discussion of the Zion/Jerusalem motif in Isaiah 40–55, see Klaus Baltzer, *Deutero-Isaiah: A Commentary on Isaiah 40–55*, (trs.) Margaret Kohl (Minneapolis: Fortress Press, 2001), 32–33. For a survey of the Zion tradition in Isaiah, see Bernhard W. Anderson, *Contours of Old Testament Theology*, 224–236.

4 William J. Dumbrell, *The Faith of Israel: Its Expression in the Books of the Old Testament* (Leicester: APOLLOS, 1993), 99.

with the glorification of Zion[5], which shall be reinstated as God's abode to which all the nations will go on a pilgrimage from the four quarters of the earth. William J. Dumbrell maintains:

> Thus chapters 1–39 move from the prospect of judgement upon Jerusalem to certainty of it; chapters 40–66 move from the prospect of the exiles' return to the city of the emergence of the New Jerusalem, which is to arise as the centrepiece of the new creation (chapters 65–66). Jerusalem is the key to the movement in the book. And it is the notion of the centrality of Jerusalem and its role as the city of God, the centre of the world, that binds the total prophecy of Isaiah together.[6]

Strikingly, the theme of Jerusalem/Zion is inextricably bound up with universal concepts set forth in the book of Isaiah as a whole.[7] Though Jerusalem has been occupied by the nation of Israel as her capital, eventually this city shall be devastated and live in dishonour. In the book of Isaiah, however, the prophet paints universal scenes of a far-reaching redemptive era in which the glorious Zion will be elevated as the cosmic centre where all the nations will be gathered to worship Yahweh. The purpose of this chapter is therefore to treat the universal manifestations of Zion that are widespread throughout the book of Isaiah: the world governmental centre, the universal refuge for the faithful, the new Garden of Eden and the cosmic sanctuary of eschatological worship.

1. Mount Zion as the world governmental centre

A universal depiction of Zion as the cosmic mountain is characteristically set forth in the eschatological vision of Isa. 2:2. The language of the verse makes it clear that in the latter days Jerusalem will be raised up as the cosmic mountain above all hills of the world, a mountain that functions as

5 Barry G. Webb argues that "the transformation of Zion is the key to both the formal and the thematic structure of the book as a whole." See his "Zion in Transformation: A Literary Approach to Isaiah", 65–84.

6 William J. Dumbrell, *The Search for Order: Biblical Eschatology in Focus*, 81.

7 For an analysis of universalism of Zion from an ideological perspective, see Antti Laato, *The Book of Isaiah as an Ideological Unity: "About Zion I will not be silent"*, 152–55.

a world governmental centre where God will dwell and govern the entire universe.

> In days to come
> the mountain of the Lord's house
> shall be established as
> the highest of the mountains,
> and shall be raised above the hills;
> all the nations shall stream to it. (Isa. 2:2)

According to Richard J. Clifford, who finds parallels between the biblical references to Mount Zion and the myths of the ancient Near East, the cosmic mountain is characterised by four aspects in Ugarit: the meeting place of the gods, the battleground of conflicting natural forces, the meeting place of heaven and earth, and the place where effective decrees are issued.[8] In fact the cosmic mountain of Ugarit is understood to be the place where Baal, the Canaanite god, dwells in Canaan while it serves as the locus of the universal reign of the great king.[9] Similarly the cosmic King, the sovereign Yahweh, will rule over the entire world when He will abide in Zion, which will emerge as the cosmic mountain at the end time.

It is important to note, furthermore, that Zion shall act as a magnet that draws all the nations into itself from everywhere. In this respect, no longer will Jerusalem exist as only the state of Israel, but will serve as a core location of the universal dominion of Yahweh which shall reach to the nations whose faith is in the cosmic King, Yahweh. To be sure, the prophet emphatically asserts that the exclusion of the Nations, who are willing to worship Yahweh as their Lord, from Mount Zion will come to an end in the latter days. John Calvin points out:

> The word רבים, *(rabbim,)* many, implies a contrast; for it means that there will not be, as formerly, but one nation which devotes itself to the worship of the true God, but that those who formerly were strangers and foreigners (Epp. Ii. 19) will come into the same agreement with them about religion.[10]

8 Jon D. Levenson, *Sinai and Zion: An Entry into the Jewish Bible* (Minneapolis: Winston Press, 1985), 111–112.

9 Ibid., 111; See also William J. Dumbrell, *The Search for Order*, 82.

10 John Calvin, *Commentary on the Book of the Prophet Isaiah: Chapters 1–32*, translated by William Pringle (Grand Rapids: Baker Book House, 1984), 93.

In this sense, there is no doubt that Mount Zion shall not serve as the capital of a specific state; rather it will function as the centre of the divine universal reign over all nations that "would flow to it as if the rivers were overflowing through the great abundance of waters."[11]

2. Zion as a cosmic refuge for the faithful

The image of Zion as a safe haven for the God-fearers is made explicit in several passages in the book of Isaiah. To begin with, Isaiah 14:32, which is part of the larger unit, 14:28–32, concerned with an oracle about the fate of the Philistines, calls our attention to the motif of Zion as the location of security for God's people.

> What will one answer
> the messengers of the nation?
> "The LORD has founded Zion,
> and the needy among his people
> will find refuge in her." (14:32)

In the section 14:28–32, while the city of the Philistines is doomed to ruin, the city of God, Zion, is destined to be transformed as a safe refuge for the poor and weary. In other words, "their [the poor] assured protection by Yahweh contrasts with the wretched future of the Philistines."[12] Judah's neighbouring nations, including the Philistines, seek to secure their own defence through military means, a self-centred scheme that drives them into a severe devastation caused by Yahweh. However, the people of God shall have a safe refuge in Yahweh who has founded Zion as the place of security for the afflicted whose faith is in Him.

In this sense, as David Stacey expresses, "Zion represents total security in a terrifying world. Zion is not for the great and predatory nations; it is for the afflicted among Yahweh's people. This reversal of fortune is a recurring theme throughout the book [the book of Isaiah], and, indeed, throughout the whole Bible."[13]

11 Ibid.
12 Walter Brueggemann, *Isaiah 1–39*, 136.
13 David Stacey, *Isaiah: Chapter 1–39* (London: Epworth Press, 1993), 110.

> See, I am laying in Zion
> a foundation stone, a tested stone,
> a precious cornerstone,
> a sure foundation:
> "One who trusts will not panic." (28:16b)

In this verse, Zion is depicted as a sure stone to defend God's people from an overwhelming scourge including military assault. In fact, in the myths of the ancient Near East, a foundation stone of the cosmic mountain is understood to be a spot of communication between the two spheres, namely the netherworld called Sheol, and the heavens. In this way, as Jon D. Levenson states, "Zion would also be perceived as reaching into the highest heavens, above the clouds and the stars. But the other side of this dizzying height is the depth of the base of the mountain in the chaotic abyss here called Sheol."[14]

Moreover, in the view of the ancient Near East, a stone as the base of the cosmic mountain plays a pivotal role in hindering Sheol from sweeping away those who are in the cosmic mountain.[15] Similarly in 28:16 Zion is portrayed as a new capstone of the solid foundation in which the godly shall be secure and immune from the formidable calamity.

The point made in the verse is, therefore, that unlike the inhabitants of Jerusalem expelled from the city, in the future all residents of Zion will enjoy rest and repose in the presence of Yahweh. Indeed, the benefit of the eschatological peace, which is granted to Zion as a new cornerstone, shall be given to all who will have a safe refuge in Yahweh. More significantly, the poet dramatically paints a prodigious picture of the ideal Zion, in which all the nations will gain access to the city, an epoch-making era that marks the climax of universalism in Zion.

> And the foreigners who join themselves to the LORD,
> to minister to him, to love the name of the LORD,
> and to be his servants, all who keep the sabbath,
> and do not profane it, and hold fast my covenant
> these I will bring to my holy mountain,
> and make them joyful in my house of prayer;
> their burnt offerings and their sacrifices will be accepted on my altar;
> for my house shall be called a house of prayer for all peoples.
> Thus says the Lord GOD, who gathers the outcasts of Israel,
> I will gather others to them besides those already gathered. (Isa. 56:6–8)

14 Jon D. Levenson, *Sinai and Zion*, 124.

15 William J. Dumbrell, *The Search for Order*, 82.

It must be noted here that some day the Sovereign Yahweh will lead the outcasts into His residence called Zion, and that Zion will be accessible to all nations willing to pay homage to Yahweh with their sacrifices. Whoever seeks shelter in Yahweh shall not be barred from citizenship in Zion. Even non-Israelites will be incorporated as members of Zion's cosmic community. In this regard, no longer will Zion be unapproachable to aliens; it is, instead, as the universal refuge, that the glorious Zion will stand as a safe sanctuary unblocked to all international people including the poor and weary whose faith is in Yahweh. As Donald E. Gowan observes:

> The glorification of Zion will be a necessary part of that final restoration, as in the other prophets. . . . Third Isaiah moves beyond the resident alien [*ger*] to claim that the "foreigner" [*ben nannekar*] and the eunuch, who are faithful to Yahweh, are not to excluded from the worshiping community in Jerusalem. Like other prophets, he also looks forward to the day when all peoples and nations will worship the one God [Isa. 66:18–21].[16]

3. Zion as the universal paradise

It is noteworthy that the depiction of Zion as the universal paradise is evident in the book of Isaiah, an image that is reminiscent of the Garden of Eden, which is the central location of the creation, described in the narrative of Gen 2:10–14.[17]

> A river watering the garden flowed from Eden; from there it was separated into four headwaters. The name of the first is the Pishon; it winds through the entire land of Havilah, where there is gold. (The gold of that land is good; aromatic resin and onyx are also there.) The name of the second river is the Gihon; it winds through the entire land of Cush. The name of the third river is the Tigris; it runs along the east side of Asshur. And the fourth river is the Euphrates.

16 Donal E. Gowan, *Theology of the Prophetic Books: The Death and Resurrection of Israel*, 173.

17 For an analysis of the similarity between Zion and Eden, see Jon D. Levenson, *Sinai and Zion*, 129–31.

As expressed in this narrative, a primordial river streams from Eden and then is separated into four great branches serving as the fountain of life of many lands. Since the four streams proceed from Eden, it is plain that the Garden of Eden stands for the source of abundance and fertility on the earth. Given the fact that the Hebrew term for "Eden" denotes "luxury" or "delight",[18] it is assumed that all humanity finds gratification in dwelling in an exuberant place called Eden and enjoys the affluence of paradise. In similar but more striking manner, Zion is portrayed as a new Eden in some Isaianic passages, especially in the section 33:21–24 concerned with a new cosmic river surrounding Zion.

> But there the LORD in majesty
> will be for us a place of broad rivers and streams,
> where no galley with oars can go,
> nor stately ship can pass. (Isa. 33:21)

Being mindful of the Garden of Eden functioning as a place of sufficient fresh water, abundance and fruitfulness, this visionary poem of the cosmic streams leads us to envisage an opulent era of eschaton in which Zion's people will have sufficiency and reach to ultimate satisfaction. Just as the primal paradise called the Garden of Eden, from which four streams flowed, served as the fountain of life of the creation, Zion will become the new Garden of Eden in which its stupendous waterworks supplied by the cosmic rivers will fertilise the face of the entire world. Another magisterial image of Zion as the new Garden of Eden is set forth in 11:6–9 centred on peaceful coexistence between the mighty and the vulnerable in both the human and the zoological realms.

> The wolf shall live with the lamb,
> the leopard shall lie down with the kid,
> the calf and the lion and the fatling together,
> and a little child shall lead them.
> The cow and the bear shall graze,
> their young shall lie down together;
> and the lion shall eat straw like the ox.
> The nursing child shall play over the hole of the asp,
> and the weaned child shall put its hand on the adder's den.
> They will not hurt or destroy on all my holy mountain;
> for the earth will be full of the knowledge of the LORD
> as the waters cover the sea.

18 Ibid., 128.

Realistically, this splendid vision of worldwide peace is in contrast to a chaotic phase of the present world in which the weak still suffer from great assault and the strong remain dominant over the helpless. It comes as little surprise, therefore, that there is no country or city that is utterly immune from harm and that every human society is under uneasiness in the face of danger. It is undeniable that even Israel, the chosen nation of God, has engaged in assaults on Palestine, which appears to be merely a fragile country in comparison with Israel. It is the poet's unshakeable conviction that in the future, universal peace in Zion will be at its zenith and all human life and values shall be transformed.

To be sure, no longer will Jerusalem/Zion be an exclusive space, but a universal place called the new Garden of Eden, as Barry Webb points out, "The entire earth, not just Jerusalem/Zion, will be the LORD's *holy mountain* (9, cf. 2:2; 4:5). In other words, he will be known, and his rule will be experienced, everywhere."[19] Indeed, it is as the cosmic paradise that Zion will usher the whole creation into an era of universal peace.

4. Zion as the cosmic sanctuary of eschatological worship

The crucial role of the ideal Zion as the cosmic centre of eschatological pilgrimage and worship is manifest in the book of Isaiah. As described in several passages in the book of Isaiah, it is evident that a dramatic reversal of worship in the Temple in Jerusalem, of which Israel has taken sole possession, will mark an era of cosmic restoration. Authorisation to worship will be granted not only to Israel; rather it shall be available to all the nations, once regarded as idolaters, who will remain loyal to Him. In addition to the superb vision of Isa. 2:2–4 in which Zion is portrayed as a magnet to draw pilgrims into the cosmic worship centre, Isa. 18:7 (part of the larger unit, 18:1–7, associated with an oracle against Cush) comes to the fore.

> At that time gifts will be brought to
> the LORD of hosts from a people tall and smooth,

19 Barry Webb, *The Message of Isaiah*, 75.

> from a people feared near and far,
> a nation mighty and conquering,
> whose land the rivers divide, to Mount Zion,
> the place of the name of the LORD of hosts.

Echoing an ancient context in which the inferior pays tribute to the superior according to the suzerainty-vassal treaty, this verse points to a day when all the nations will come in submission to their Great King called Yahweh whose lordship will reach to all the cosmic world. It is anticipated, as a consequence, that they will be invited to go to the cosmic mountain in order to offer gifts to Him. This universal manifestation of bringing gifts from the people of the world to Zion is diametrically opposed to a Jerusalem-centred sacrificial system. In other words, no longer will Zion become an exclusive place in which worship at the Temple is available only to Israelites. It is expected, instead, that the ideal Zion will be transformed as a cosmic sanctuary to which a myriad of gifts from all international peoples will be sent. It is not surprising, furthermore, that the eschatological vision of Zion as the site of cosmic worship is at its zenith in Isa. 66:20–21, which appears at the end of the book of Isaiah as a whole.

> "And they will bring all your brothers, from all the nations, to my holy mountain in Jerusalem as an offering to the LORD – on horses, in chariots and wagons, and on mules and camels," says the LORD. "They will bring them, as the Israelites bring their grain offerings, to the temple of the LORD in ceremonially clean vessels. And I will select some of them also to be priests and Levites," says the LORD.

In these prose verses, the prophet offers an eschatological presentation of the future Zion to which all nations and tongues will make their pilgrimage at the end time. It is striking, likewise, that even non-Israelites whose faith is in Yahweh shall be invited to Zion to bring a variety of gifts of homage to the sole God deserving of worship. As indicated in these verses, the emergence of a new cosmic community that shall encompass aliens will result in the disintegration of conventional institutions such as priesthood. No nationalism nor sole possession of institutions shall remain in the future Zion because "the openness will keep nothing reserved for special groups."[20] More radically, the prophet envisages a future time when foreigners will be chosen as priests and Levites, a universal priest-

20 John D. W. Watts, *Isaiah 34–66*, 365.

hood available to a new community that makes it evident that the ideal Zion will appear not as the national sacrificial rite but as the cosmic worship centre. To be sure, Zion will remain as the eschatological worship centre to which pilgrims, once regarded as pagan, from all the nations will seek to go on a journey to bring special gifts to the Almighty God.

5. Implications

As discussed earlier, the universal manifestations of the Zion motif are embedded in the book of Isaiah. It is plain that this magisterial book as a whole identifies Zion as the cosmic mountain where Yahweh as the Great King will perform His universal reign over all the world. It is visualised, then, that in the book of Isaiah Zion will function as the cosmic refuge for the gathering of God's people. The glorious Zion shall be transformed as the new Garden of Eden and then the special streams proceeding from it will fertilise the surface of all lands on the earth. It is as the source of life that Zion will become the cosmic sanctuary of fecundity and perfection, which its habitants will share.

More significantly, it is prognosticated that Zion shall be identified as the cosmic centre to which all the nations will be invited to participate in a universal celebration of cosmic worship. In this sense, it is concluded that Zion as the universal sanctuary will function as the world governmental centre, as the cosmic refuge for the people of God, as the new Paradise, and as the centre of eschatological worship.

In addition, the Zion theology, infused into the book of Isaiah as a whole, has great influence on the Korean Churches, who take the position that Zion is spiritually transformed into the church. It is understood that the eschatological vision set forth in Isaiah 2:2–4, in which all the nations go on a pilgrimage to Zion at the end time, is in part fulfilled in the universal mission of the church based upon the work of Jesus Christ. It is interesting that the bulk of Korean Churches are not reluctant to express their identification with a glorified Zion that shines its light on nations as they sing in their services the hymn:

> O Zion, haste, thy mission high fulfilling,
> To tell to all the world that God is light

> That He who made all nations is not willing
> One soul should perish, lost in shades of night.
> Publish glad tidings, tidings of peace,
> Tidings of Jesus, redemption and release. Amen.[21]

More significantly, the Korean Christian affirmation is that access to Zion is neither bounded by any geographical, physical, cultural or social factor, nor even confined to a Christian denomination. It should be said quite firmly that it is not physical Israel but the church that is the agent to serve as a whole new way of approach to God on behalf of humankind. It is pointed out, therefore, that worshiping God is available not only for a denomination but for all of Korean people who have put their faith in Yahweh and that even non-Christians, including other religionists, are invited to partake in the celebration of God's redemptive action.

This Korean theological reflection on Zion mounts a powerful criticism of extremists who abhor other religious groups and strongly dislike their relics. Until recently, as indicated earlier, the Korean Churches have been in a predicament due to Christian fanatics who in secret have demolished and burnt Buddhist statues in the temple, an unfortunate incident that has been a major social issue in Korea. Unfortunately, these extreme fundamentalists fail to recognise that it is within the bounds of possibility that non-Christians, including other religionists, participate in going on a pilgrimage to worship Yahweh. It is pointed out, however, that even other religious people have a right to receive an invitation to membership in an eschatological Zion. Moon-Jang Lee claims:

> It is non-Christian behaviours to justify this vandalistic attempt to destroy Buddhist statues in the light of Christian faith... It is intolerable to justify such vandalism from a Christian perspective. The Korean Churches also should avoid concentrating on this iconoclasm for their mission. The Korean Churches need to focus on humble attitudes toward other religions. It should be remembered that vandalism of Buddhist images is not only inconsistent with Christian faith but makes mission ineffective.[22]

Yung-Han Kim also points out:

> Christians need to proclaim the living God by showing their sacrificial love toward people of different religious traditions. Christians ought to focus on honest words

21 No. 255 in *Korean Hymnal* (Seoul: Korean Hymnal Society, 1984).

22 Moon-Jang Lee, "A Religious pluralistic context and Christian faith" *Ministry & Theology,* 2 (1999), 52.

> and righteous acts that lead to a spontaneous conversion of them. This approach is entirely divorced from an attempt to convert them into Christianity with violence as the crusades did in the Middle Ages.[23]

Indeed, no longer can a nation, a denomination, or a community have a monopoly on the access to Zion. No one can take sole possession of the way God's saving will is universally available through the church. This point leads us to the realisation that non-Christians, including other religionists, are targets, not for condemnation or curse, but for sacrificial service.

23 Young-Han Kim, *The 21st Century and Reformed Theology, Vol. 2: The Postmodernism and Reformed Theology* (Seoul: The Presbyterian Church of Korean Publishing House, 1998), 41.

Chapter 8

The New Creation

Given frequent occurrences of the Hebrew terms associated with creation such as ברא, תהו, שמים, הארץ, השה, and יצר,[1] the book of Isaiah places particular emphasis on the fundamental key doctrine of a New Creation[2] heralding the dawn of the new heavens and the new earth that the Creator Yahweh will bring into being. As insinuated in the theology of New Exodus earlier, God will usher His people to a new age in which they will sufficiently experience an efficacious outcome of Yahweh's miraculous

1 These words predominantly appear in the book of Isaiah according to the following lists:

ברא – 4:5; 40:26, 28; 41:20; 42:5; 43:1, 7, 15; 54:7, 8, 12, 18; 54:16.

תהו – 24:10; 29:21; 34:11; 40:17, 23; 41:29; 44:9; 45:18; 45:19; 49:4; 59:4.

שמים – 1:2; 13:5, 10, 13; 14:12, 13; 34:4, 5; 37:16; 40:12; 40:22; 42:5; 44:23, 24; 45:8, 12, 18; 47:13; 48:13; 49:13; 50:3; 51:6, 13, 16; 55:9, 10; 63:15; 64:1; 65:17; 66:1, 22.

הארץ – 1:2, 7, 19; 2:7, 8, 19, 21; 3:26; 4:2; 5:8, 26, 30; 6:3, 12; 7:18, 22, 24; 8:8, 9, 22; 9:1, 2; 10:14, 23; 11:4, 9, 12, 16; 12:5; 13:5, 9, 14; 14:7, 9, 12, 16, 20, 21, 25, 26; 16:1, 4; 18:1, 2, 6, 7; 19:18, 19, 20, 24; 21:1, 9, 14; 22:18; 23:1, 8, 9, 10, 13, 17; 24:1, 3, 4, 5,. 6, 11, 13, 16, 17, 19, 20; 25:8, 12; 26:1, 5, 9, 10, 15, 18, 19, 21; 27: 13; 28:2, 22; 29:4; 30:6; 32:2; 33:9, 7; 34:1, 6, 7, 9; 36:10, 17, 18, 20; 37:7, 11, 16, 18, 20, 38; 38:11; 39:3; 40:12, 21, 22, 23, 24, 28; 41:5, 9, 18; 42:4, 5, 10; 43:6; 44:23, 24; 45:8, 12, 18, 19, 22; 46:11; 47:1; 48:13, 20; 49:6, 8, 12, 13, 19, 23; 51:6, 13, 16, 23; 52:10; 53:2, 8; 54:5, 9; 55:9, 10; 57:13; 58:14; 60:2, 18, 21; 61:7, 11; 62:4, 7, 11; 63:6; 65:16, 17; 66:8, 22.

השה – 2:8, 20; 3:11; 5:2, 4, 5, 10; 7:22; 9:7; 10:11, 13, 23; 12:5; 15:7; 16:3; 7:7, 8; 19:10, 15; 20:2; 22:11; 25:1, 6; 27:5, 11; 28:15, 21; 29:16; 30:1; 31:7; 32:6; 33:13; 36:16; 37:11, 16, 26, 31, 32; 38:3, 7, 15; 40:23; 41:4, 20; 42:16; 43:7, 19; 44:2, 13, 15, 17, 19, 23, 24; 45:7, 9, 12, 18; 46:4, 6, 10, 11; 48: 3, 5, 11, 14; 51:13; 53:9; 54:5; 55:11; 56:1, 2; 57:16; 58:2, 13; 63:12, 14; 64:3, 4, 5; 65:8, 12; 66:2, 4, 22.

יצר – 22:11; 27:11; 29:16; 30:14; 37:26; 41:25; 43:1, 7, 10, 21; 44:2, 9, 10, 12, 21, 24; 45:7, 9, 11, 18; 46:11; 49:5; 54:17; 64:8.

2 Bernhard W. Anderson argues that "the theme of the new creation dominates the message of Second Isaiah, who grasps profoundly the interrelation of creation and history." See his *From Creation To New Creation: OBT* (Minneapolis: Fortress Press, 1994), 37.

action, the New Creation. It is noteworthy likewise that a host of its universal manifestations are explicitly articulated in several Isaianic passages. The broken hearted people of God are to partake in a new epoch in which they will witness the consummation of the whole course of human history and enjoy total redemption. Werner H. Schmidt states:

> God 'forms' the individual (Jer. 1:5; Isa. 49:5; cf. Ps. 139:16) and the nation (Isa. 44:2; 27:11 et al.), and as creator achieves new history: 'Behold, I am doing a new thing' (43:19; 48:7; Jer. 31:22 etc.). Thus not only what is never changing, but also what is new and event-filled is drawn into the belief in a creator. Creation becomes eschatology, because eschatology is God's creation; creation is not only the remembered past, but also the expected future (esp. Isa. 65:17; 66:22 etc.). The Old Testament expresses this conceptually by the double expression 'heaven and earth' or occasionally by the single world 'all' (Isa. 44:24 etc.). So the worship of Yahweh as creator implies a confession of the God of the world.[3]

Indeed, Yahweh will inaugurate a prodigious era of the new creation that fulfils every biblical expectation, a phenomenal cosmic event that in an unimaginable manner supplements and completes the old creation.[4] Moreover, the advent of the New Creation will makes it possible to reveal Yahweh's universal Creatorship. This chapter therefore will seek to explicate the universal properties of this theme that dominates the message of the book of Isaiah as a whole.

1. The newness of Israel as a New Creation

It is difficult to avoid the observation that the recovery of future Israel is inextricably woven with the creation motif in the book of Isaiah, especially in chapters 40–66, a blending of both themes that marks the universal governance of Yahweh. Intriguingly the writer considers Yahweh's capacity to create in relation to Israel's redemption, a point that leads us to the realisation that the redemption of Israel is inseparable from a new

3 Werner H. Schmidt, *The Faith of the Old Testament: A History*, tr. John Sturdy (Philadelphia: The Westminster Press, 1983), 177.

4 John I. Durham, "Isaiah 40–55: A New Creation, A New Exodus, A New Messiah," in *Yahweh/Baal Confrontation and Other Studies in Biblical Literature and Archaeology* (New York: Edwin Mellen Press, 1995), 49.

creative action of Yahweh. In the book of Isaiah, the prophet firmly claims that the sovereign Yahweh will renew His people, who have sinned sliding away from their Creator, by resecuring them from the bondage of the power of chaos represented by empires like Assyria or Babylon.

The prophet makes it evident, then, that given the unique creatorship of Yahweh who has fashioned His people as the chosen ones, the God of a New Creation will recreate Israel as the renewed one. In other words, "confidence in Yahweh, the cosmic creator and king, leads the prophet to announce that the new beginning in Israel's history will be God's new act of creation."[5] It goes without saying, in this sense, that the renewal of a disheartened people plays a crucial role as a New Creation in the book of Isaiah, especially in 40–66 throughout which the notion of a New Creation is described. The following passages will present how the newness of God's people as a New Creation is dramatically characterised.

1.1. 43:1–7

In this poetry, Yahweh promises that His beloved people will be immune to flood or flame typical of a series of inflictions due to the divine presence in the midst of Israel whom Yahweh has brought into existence and chosen as His people.

> Because you are precious in my sight,
>   and honored, and I love you,
> I give people in return for you,
>   nations in exchange for your life.
> Do not fear, for I am with you;
>   I will bring your offspring from the east,
> and from the west I will gather you;
>   I will say to the north, "Give them up,"
> and to the south, "Do not withhold;
>   bring my sons from far away
> and my daughters from the end of the earth
>   everyone who is called by my name,
> whom I created for my glory,
>   whom I formed and made." (43:4–7)

5 Bernhard W. Anderson, *From Creation To New Creation*, 37.

It is clearly seen here that "'you are mine' and 'I am with you' [v. 5] are central expressions of the intimate relationship between God and people that flows from his creation and continued support of them."[6] If Yahweh shall perform His saving activity by dealing kindly with Israel, she can be set free from harsh affliction. This is because it is as a God of a New Creation that Yahweh remains steadfast to His people who will be remade. It is patent, therefore, that the future deliverance of Israel depends on the creative activity of Yahweh who will be concerned with the renewal of His people which will completely outshine anything experienced in the past. Paul D. Hanson states:

> It [43:1–7] highlights the constancy of divine compassion as evidenced in the creation of Israel. As alpha and omega, God remains Creator "in the beginning" as well as "at the end of time." Simultaneously, 43:1–7 also develops along a temporal plane, thereby delineating how the Creator God is at the same time the God who declares, "I have redeemed you... and called you by name" (v. 1). Because the Creator God is the God who enters history to establish a relationship with human beings and to heal their brokenness, the return to the theme of God as creator in verse 7 goes beyond the formulation of 1 by identifying the ultimate goal reached in the creative-redemptive activity of God.[7]

What is made explicit here is that God's people will by no means be an outcast from the redeemed ones, a renewal that originates from the unique creatorship of the mighty God. It is clear, in this prophetic vision, that such creatorship is the ground for the motivation for anticipating what Yahweh is on the verge of doing for the revival of the downhearted. It is evident that "by speaking of what were normally thought of as redemptive acts in terms of creation, he [Isaiah] was making it possible for the new redemptive acts of which he was about to speak to be regarded as nothing less than a new creation."[8] In the prophetic imagination, therefore, the creative-redemptive acts of Yahweh in the past lead the prophet to the anticipation that a new saving activity of God will generate the newness of the redeemed ones marking a New Creation.

6 Peter D. Miscall, *Isaiah*, 106.
7 Paul D. Hanson, *Isaiah 40–66*, 61.
8 R. N. Whybray, *Isaiah 40–66*, 82.

1.2. 44:1–4

Given the manifestation of the cardinal image of Yahweh as Creator who has made and will renew Israel, the language of 44:1–4 deserves consideration.

> But now hear, O Jacob my servant,
> Israel whom I have chosen!
> Thus says the LORD who made you,
> who formed you in the womb and will help you:
> Do not fear, O Jacob my servant,
> Jeshurun whom I have chosen.
> For I will pour water on the thirsty land,
> and streams on the dry ground;
> I will pour my spirit upon your descendants,
> and my blessing on your offspring.
> They shall spring up like a green tamarisk,
> like willows by flowing streams.

The crucial point made here is that no matter what forces terrify Israel, she will need not fear and surrender to such intimidations since she will be cherished by Yahweh as His chosen one whom He brought into being. This visionary poem holds the view that the future restoration of Israel is laid on what Yahweh has done in her experience. It is significant to observe, in particular, that the two verbs, "made" and "will help" are in parallel with each other. The point evidently alludes to the fact that Yahweh's unfailing care for the sake of His chosen people will not cease but remain since He has brought them into existence. It is obviously inferred, here, that the portrayal of Yahweh as Creator is intimately bound up with Yahweh as Helper who will lead her to the ultimate abundance that will be entirely experienced in an age of the New Creation in which God's life-saving activity will be at its zenith. It is the prophet's positive affirmation, in this regard, that an indescribable era of Israel's newness will by all means be instigated by Yahweh who is willing to take responsibility for recreating His people anew.

1.3. 51:9–11

It can be recognised that the interrelation of creation and redemption is obviously manifest in the poetry of 51:9–11 since Yahweh is depicted not only as Creator who will bring the powers of chaos into debacle and then establish a well-ordered world, but also as Redeemer who will produce the restoration of Israel.

> Awake, awake, put on strength,
> O arm of the LORD!
> Awake, as in days of old, the generations of long ago!
> Was it not you who cut Rahab in pieces,
> who pierced the dragon?
> Was it not you who dried up the sea,
> the waters of the great deep;
> who made the depths of the sea a way
> for the redeemed to cross over?
> So the ransomed of the LORD shall return,
> and come to Zion with singing;
> everlasting joy shall be upon their heads;
> they shall obtain joy and gladness,
> and sorrow and sighing shall flee away.

The elucidation of what this significant poetry means appears to be awkward since it may allude to the myths of ancient Near East such as the Enuma Elish, the Babylonian myth of creation in which Marduk, a warrior god, triumphs over the sea monster, Tiamat who causes the unruly and chaotic sea. At the same time, it is assumed that the imagery of the poem is closely connected with the Canaanite story found in the Ugaritic texts in which a great warrior god, Baal, defeats his adversary, Yam, the god of the sea. Echoing these creation myths of the ancient Near East, the poem portrays Yahweh as a sea monster slayer who overthrows Rahab, the sea dragon, typical of the chaotic power, reminding us of a miraculous event (Exodus) followed by creation of a people who were immune from the inundation of the overwhelming water.

Given this fact, it can be anticipated that just as Yahweh did earlier, He will subdue the fatal powers of chaos embodied in the secular empires such as Babylon and then will be concerned with a new creation of His people. No longer will God's people be driven to exile. The ultimate vindication will be given to the lamenters who have yearned for emancipation from oppression, suffering, and the bondage of sins in a disorderly world. Then the redeemed people will see Yahweh's final conquest of the powers of evil and chaos, a cosmic victory of the Divine Warrior that culminates in a New Creation. There will be no opponent or adversary that can obstruct Yahweh's new redemptive action that will inaugurate an epoch making era in which the God of a New Creation will be enthroned as cosmic King. Thus, the redeemed will on no account be placed under the baneful forces of chaos. They shall appear not as the suffering ones but as the restored ones whose newness will be instigated by Yahweh who will act in a new creation.

As Paul D. Hanson asserts, "God has not changed! God will act as God acted in creation and the exodus! God's power is sufficient to defeat the pernicious forces of chaos! God's love reaches out to the people even in their bondage, even most emphatically in their bondage!"[9] As expressed in 51:9–11, thus, the poet has no doubt about an eschatological age of the New Creation in which the vindication and exaltation of the future Israel will reach its culmination.

2. A new heaven and a new earth as a New Creation

It can be recognised that the birth of a new heaven and a new earth dominates in the latter half of the book of Isaiah, especially in 65–66 concerned with Yahweh's new creative action. The New Creation will also cause a sharp break from the past that one has kept in mind since this spectacle is so epochal that it cannot compare with the former things. The most extreme manifestation of what is referred to the rehabilitation of creation is plainly set forth in 65:17–25 that is "perhaps the most sweeping resolve of Yahweh in all of Israel's testimony."[10]

> For I am about to create new heavens and a new earth;
> the former things shall not be remembered
> or come to mind. (65:17)

9 Paul D. Hanson, *Isaiah 40–66*, 146–7.
10 Walter Brueggemann, *Theology of the Old Testament*, 548.

In this wondrous prophetic imagination, interestingly, a conspicuous discontinuity between the former things and what is to take place in a new era is articulated. It is understood here that the phrase, "the former things" seems to refer to the former saving acts of God[11] or the whole-created order,[12] while some argue that it has intimate relevance to all troubles deriving from the initial creation.[13] No matter what the term indicates, there is little doubt that the dramatic emergence of a new heaven and a new earth will play a central role as a radical reversal of the cosmic order of the initial creation in which every human is seldom immune to an unruly chaos.

This point could be supported by the connotation of the word "new" that "may mean several different things. It may be temporal in describing something that has never existed before and therefore is unknown to this time. It may distinguish what is different from what has already existed."[14] The whole course of human history in the world has faced a sequence of unsolved problems such as violence, upheaval, antipathy and conflict. No one has found an alternative way of overcoming such disorderly factors characterising the imperfection of the former creation.

However, the new cosmic realm controlled by the creator Yahweh will fulfil all biblical expectations of a new age in which chaotic turmoils will never exist and "all elements of existence are to come under positive, life-yielding aegis of Yahweh."[15] Significantly it is imagined here that the newness of creation culminates in the grandiose transformation of Jerusalem that serves as the locus of the new cosmic world.

> But be glad and rejoice forever in what I am creating;
> for I am about to create Jerusalem as a joy,
> and its people as a delight.
> I will rejoice in Jerusalem,
> and delight in my people;
> no more shall the sound of weeping be heard in it,
> or the cry of distress. (65:18–19)

11 Claus Westermann, *Isaiah 40–66* tr. David M. G. Stalker (London: SCM Press, 1985), 408.
12 Cf. Whybray, *Isaiah 40–66*, 276.
13 See Walter Brueggemann, *Isaiah 40–66*, 245–6.
14 John D. W. Watts, *Isaiah 34–66*, 353.
15 Walter Brueggemann, *Theology of the Old Testament*, 549.

The past fateful history of the city of God, Jerusalem, threatened or colonised by secular empires leads us to a reminder of a gloomy period in the past when the city was in jeopardy without being in the safekeeping of Yahweh. In other words, Jerusalem/Zion has seen a sequence of insuperable miseries such as exile that originates from the failure of God's people to remain faithful to Yahweh and that eventually drives Israel to despair. It is noteworthy, however, that the visionary poem guarantees the renewed Jerusalem all ecstasy of what is to be experienced in the New Creation. The expectation on the future of glorious Jerusalem shall come true because this city will be newly restored when Yahweh commences with His new creative action. The city of God will by no means meet catastrophes followed by sadness and will be invited to enjoy entire gladness.

Interestingly, it seems that the imagery of the miraculous metamorphosis of Jerusalem strikingly forms a singular contrast to Jeremiah's awful message of judgement that the city would be separable from joy and filled with sorrow (Jer. 7:34; 16:9; 25:10). Indeed, "in the new Jerusalem transformed by God's new creation and among its inhabitants there is to be no more making lament or weeping (v. 19b)."[16] Instead the whole exultation of human life will be at its zenith as Jerusalem will be vindicated, restored and elevated as the centre of a new heaven and a new earth.

3. The new lifestyle in a New Creation

The poem goes on to paint an optimistic picture in which the eschatological and radical transformation of human lifestyle in relation to the life span subsequent to a new creation is metaphorically described.

> No more shall there be in it an infant
> that lives but a few days,
> or an old person who does not live out a lifetime;
> for one who dies at a hundred years
> will be considered a youth,
> and one who falls short of a hundred
> will be considered accursed. (65:20)

16 Claus Westermann, *Isaiah 40–66*, 408.

In this metaphorical description of what is transformed in a New Creation, the poet imagines a tremendous new age in which humankind will be a recipient of the extended life span. In the former creation, a number of people have died of disease, of hunger, or of an unexpected accident in the days of their youth. Even the lack of daily needs such as food, potable water, and medical service has put a great deal of babies to death, a miserable tragedy that remains in human life without pause. It is difficult to avoid the fact that mankind who longs for long life has been subject to the terror of death. However, this panoramic scene of the new lifestyle points to a radical reversal of a life span of the old creation. Some interpreters such as John N. Oswalt suggest, "This may be an allusion to the great ages of the antediluvian people, where a life span of hundreds of years was considered normal (Gen. 5)."[17] No matter what it indicates the point made here that the old system of a life span will no longer exist while the untimely death will be absent, a fact that connotes that a very long life will remain in a New Creation. Another stupendous manifestation of the eschatological transformation of the New Creation is found in the following verses.

> They shall build houses and inhabit them;
> they shall plant vineyards and eat their fruit.
> They shall not build and another inhabit;
> they shall not plant and another eat;
> for like the days of a tree shall the days of my people be,
> and my and my chosen shall long enjoy the work of their hands. (65:21–22)

In this prophetic vision of what is to be renewed in a new paradisiacal age, special attention is drawn to the prosperity of the new city. The fruitfulness of the reconstituted city set forth in the verses seems to be inextricably bound up with the image of Jerusalem as a barren/fertile woman, a female city metaphor that is prevalently circulated throughout the book of Isaiah as a whole.[18] In the ancient Israelite world, the social statues of women had intimate connection with their capability of giving birth. It was mainly seen that while prolific women are identified with the blessed, barren ones are devoid of the benevolence of Yahweh who forms life. Even some biblical texts hold the view that infertile women were regarded

17 John N. Oswalt, *Isaiah 40–66*, 658.

18 For a detailed and excellent treatment of female city imagery in the book of Isaiah, see Katheryn Pfisterer Darr, *Isaiah's Vision and the Family of God*, 124–164.

as those who deserve shame (e.g., Gen 20:18; 1 Sam 1:1–11). In other words, it was believed that sterility is signified as Yahweh's curse or punishment while childbirth is an evidence of divine charity.

Interestingly, it is conspicuous that in the book of Isaiah Jerusalem is personified as barren/fertile women in ancient Israelite society. This female city imagery dominates various Isaianic passages. Like an infertile woman, Jerusalem, the personified city, has undergone desolation that made it impossible to be immune from shame (e.g., 1:8, 21–26; 3:25–26 etc). Subsequently such severe fruitlessness has driven the forsaken city to despair, resulting in weeping and lament without any vivid expectation on Jerusalem's future fruitfulness. On the other hand, in the book of Isaiah, especially in 65–66 concerned with Jerusalem/Zion's future exaltation, the spoiled city is urged to anticipate a magisterial era in which Jerusalem will be as productive as a fertile woman.

In particular, 65:21–22 place great emphasis on the productiveness of the reconstituted city, a fertility that indicates that Yahweh turns old curses into blessing. Echoing the benefits of covenant keeping found in Deut. 28:1–14, this optimistic vision of the fertile city presents a deliberate reversal of the former curses for disobeying the covenant expressed in Deut. 28:15–46. No warnings will be given. No longer will the danger of covenant breaking take place. Only the prosperity of the new city as a fertile woman who retains a singular fidelity to Yahweh will exist. In addition to the fruitfulness of the renewed city, the long-term security for the city is promised. No foreign armies will deliver an attack on the city of God. No great empires will occupy or colonise the new Jerusalem. Indeed, it is the poet's emphatic affirmation that the prophetic imagination of what is promised in the verses shall come true when a new heaven and a new earth are brought into existence.

In addition to the fecundity of the new city, another eschatological vision of a New Creation is figuratively delineated in the imagery of 65:23–25, which forms a striking contrast to the gloomy expression in Gen. 3:16 concerned with the curse on the fallen men and the serpent.

> They shall not labor in vain,
>   or bear children for calamity;
> for they shall be offspring blessed by the LORD
>   and their descendants as well.
> Before they call I will answer,
>   while they are yet speaking I will hear.

> The wolf and the lamb shall feed together,
> the lion shall eat straw like the ox;
> but the serpent – its food shall be dust!
> They shall not hurt or destroy
> on all my holy mountain, says the LORD. (65:23–25)

In other words, the visionary poem clearly echoes that the Creator has blessed men created in His image, a reversal of the old curse that will mark a New Creation. Given the fact that "the promise in v. 23 may refer to the disability pronounced in Gen. 3:16," it is obvious that "whatever is amiss in creation will now be restored and made whole, even the most deeply embedded distortions in Yahweh's world."[19]

In fact, the effect of the New Creation will make it possible to return to the blessing of the Eden highlighted in Gen. 1:28. Without question the prophetic imagination in 65:23 leads us to anticipate a new cosmic era in which no women will be barren, no women in childbirth will be at risk and no pregnancies will result in miscarriage or stillbirth. Just as Yahweh enabled mankind to propagate offspring after creating the heavens and the earth, His renewed people shall be abundant in their descendants, a fruitfulness that signifies the return to what was blessed by God before the fall of men.

Moreover the language of 65:25 reminiscent of the earlier eschatological oracle of 11:6–9 shows a new kingdom governed by the sovereign Yahweh who will generate a full peaceful coexistence in a New Creation. It is figuratively described that the vulnerable will no longer become the victim of the strong and the fierce animals will coexist with humans in harmony. In a vivid day when Yahweh's new creation is at its zenith, all creatures will be satisfied with perfect environmental security in a dramatic era in which no longer will violence, brutality, and cruelty exist.

In summary, as spelled out above, Yahweh will inaugurate a fabulous new age in which the former creation of the natural world will be transformed into a New Creation. The prophet anticipates that the "new things" will reverse the negative aspects of the old creation and restore its former and intended perfection. Indeed, it is in a New Creation that all humankind will be immune from chaotic forces bringing about absurdity of life in the present world, and will never suffer heavy losses caused by 'natural' calamities, which have been part of our life.

19 Walter Brueggemann, *Theology of the Old Testament*, 549.

4. Implications

Significantly, from a Korean perspective, the advent of Kingdom of Heaven proclaimed by Jesus Christ, who will bring it to completion in the future, means the partial fulfilment of the metaphorical imagination of what is transformed in a new epoch. John Calvin states:

> The Lord means that everything will be fully restored when Christ reigns... it is the office of Christ to bring back everything to its condition and order, and so the Lord declares that the confusion or ruin that now exists in human affairs will be removed by the coming of Christ. At that time, corruptions having been taken away, the world will return to its original state.[20]

Walking in the footsteps of Calvin, a number of Korean Christians view the Kingdom of Heaven not only as a future reign but also as a present spiritual reign on the earth. Indeed, an efficacious outcome of a New Creation is an experiential reality, which is conceived in the present time, especially in contemporary Korea, though its consummation will reach the climax at the arrival of the New Jerusalem dubbed the heavenly Zion, the centre of a New Creation. That is to say, Korean Christians not only possess the status of "people of God" as an indication of the future age in which God will restore His people but also even now experience the reality of the heavenly arena. It is clear that Christians need to reflect the moral nature of heaven itself that allows others to experience, partially but sensibly, the universal reign of Yahweh who can instigate a new era of New Creation. Se-Yoon Kim comments:

> If the appearance of God's people demonstrates that the kingdom of God is already present, our lives need to reflect the reality of the present kingdom. Since living in the kingdom of God is associated not with self-assertion but with self-sacrifice, the realities of kingdom need to be conceived in our lives.[21]

This Korean perspective takes a pessimistic view of fundamentalists who respond to people of diverse beliefs and practices with criticisms, curses and denunciations. Most recently, vandalistic attempts to obliterate the images of Tangun[22] that are erected in public institutions and schools have

20 John Calvin, *Isaiah* (Wheaton: Crossway Books, 2000), 389.

21 Se-Yoon Kim, *Jesus and Paul* (Seoul: The Chammal Publishing House, 1993), 107.

22 As explained in Chapter 2, Tangun is the legendary father of all Koreans.

been a polemical issue in Korean society. Several Christian fanatics have been engaged in beheading Tangun statues and thereby prosecuted for their damage. While the vast majority of Korean people have responded with resentment to such naïve misconduct, some fundamentalist Christians have spoken in their defence. In this circumstance, greater parts of the Korean Churches have been heavily concerned about this extremist iconoclasm that results in antagonism against Christianity. Jung-Woo Kim correctly points out:

> However, it should be considered that an attempt to behead Tangun statues is an improper way to express our consciousness and point of view because it includes violence. Instead we need to focus on our social persuasion and legal step so that displaying Tangun statues will be annihilated.[23]

David F. Wright also observes:

> In the end of the day, what iconoclasts forget is that God's work has to be done in God's way, by the Spirit and not in the flesh of our impatient zeal, our righteous indignation, our love of a quick victory. A broken idol is a broken idol. The offence lies not in stone or wood or metal, but in the worship men and women give to idols, and this will not be broken so easily. After all, new idols can be made or bought which reminds us of Isaiah's prophesying against the folly of those who hired craftsmen to make a god which they could then fall down and worship (chs. 45–46). Prophetic critique and sharp apologetic are among the weapons God has put into people's hands. The sledgehammer and axe are not.[24]

In other words, it is of decisive importance for Korean Christians to reflect the reality of the Kingdom of Heaven in their lives by kindness, respect and humility to others. There is a significant implication here for Christians who cannot disregard the words of Jesus: "Let your light shine before men, that they may see your good deeds and praise your Father in heaven" (Mt. 5:16). To be sure, it is in a pluralistic Korea that Christians must not show off religious pride or self-righteous chauvinism (or bigotry), but focus on unceasing services to others.

23 Jung-Woo Kim, "The Conflict Between the Mythical Tangun and The Historical Tangun and the Extent of Religious Respect," in *JBS* 9 (1999), 6.

24 David F. Wright, "Down with Idolatry! And Down with Iconoclasm [or Idol-breaking] Too!" in *Ministry & Theology* 2 (1999), 87.

Chapter 9

The New Israel

Without question the book of Isaiah panoramically paints a distinct universalist picture of "the new Israel" that can be little seen in other books in the Old Testament. As clearly set forth in Exodus, Israel is chosen as God's special nation to make a covenant with Yahweh, a holy nation that plays a central role in serving as a priestly kingdom in order to reveal the saving power of Yahweh to the nations (cf. Exod. 19:3–6).

Particularly, like Moses' prediction of God's choosing one single place where Israel must worship (cf. Deut 12:1–14), the worship of Yahweh is exclusively centralised in Jerusalem, and the office of the temple is primarily untaken only by the Levites, especially priests. In the book of Isaiah, however, God's people are no longer bound by racial, geographical, and political confines; rather they are marvellously transformed into universal confessional groups, even including all people of all nations who turn away from idols to Yahweh and seek to worship Him with tributes.

In addition to this point, it is of quite exceptional importance that even the exclusive role of Israel as priest is strikingly universalised with the emergence of worldwide worship even by non-Israelites who will become priests and who are commissioned for service in the Temple. Indeed, the fact that the access to the worship of Yahweh is to be available for all humankind leads us to a new theological understanding of the New Israel. Above all, several remarkable passages such as 19:18–25, 56:6–7 and 66:18–21, concerned with the eschatological vision of God's yearning to include all the nations in His new people, deserve observation.

This chapter will canvass what is envisaged in the prophetic imagination of a universal people who will make a pilgrimage to pay homage to Yahweh with special gifts from every quarter by having a look at these unique texts concerned with the notion of the New Israel. Then a proper implication for the concept will be given in the context of the contemporary Korean Church.

1. Egypt and Assyria as God's people

Compared with other passages in the Old Testament, Isa. 19:19–25 is the most universalist message.[1] Special attention is drawn to a visionary image of God's world-wide people, including Egypt and Assyria historically typical of both Israel's archenemies and fatal oppressors. Strikingly, the prophet paints a universal picture in which these two nations, Egypt and Assyria, are incorporated into a new international people who worship Yahweh as their Lord not in Jerusalem but in their own places. Here one finds it necessary to delve a little deeper into what is set forth in the passage in relation to a new theological concept of the New Israel.

The initial statement of this breathtaking text (Isa. 19:19–25) begins with the prophetic anticipation of the universal worship of Yahweh in a pagan land such as Egypt:

> On that day there will be an altar to the LORD in the center of the land of Egypt, and a pillar to the LORD at its border. It will be a sign and a witness to the LORD of hosts in the land of Egypt; when they cry to the LORD because of oppressors, he will send them a savior, and will defend and deliver them. The LORD will make himself known to the Egyptians; and the Egyptians will know the LORD on that day, and will worship with sacrifice and burnt offering, and they will make vows to the LORD and perform them. The LORD will strike Egypt, striking and healing; they will return to the LORD, and he will listen to their supplications and heal them. (Isa. 19:19–22)

It is in an epoch-making event that a worship centre will be built in the midst of Egypt and access to God's temple will be available for the non-Israelite. No longer will Solomon's temple be the only worship centre where the relationship between the holy God and the sinner is restored. According to the Law, God's forgiveness and mercy on the iniquitous is dependent on the sacrifice only on the altar in the temple.

Thus, the true reconciliation between God and the offender has been achieved through the exclusive function of the temple placed in Jerusalem. Yet such Jerusalem centred worship stands in a wonderful contrast to what is dramatically foreseen in the prophetic imagination of the common worship of Yahweh found in the present passage. It is anticipated that a

1 See John F. A. Sawyer, "'Blessed Be My People Egypt' (Isaiah 19:25): The Context and Meaning of a Remarkable Passage," 57.

new sacrificial system, in which non-Israelites, symbolised here by Egypt, will be actively engaged, will be established. And a new place where Yahweh dwells will be built and serve as "a sign and witness" which "recalls the altar built by the returning Transjordanian tribes (Jos. 22), lest in the future the barrier of the Jordan might separate them from the unity of the people of God. Their altar was a witness (Jos. 22:34) to the reality of their membership of Israel."[2]

In this way, the emergence of an altar or a pillar in Egypt suggests that even non-Jewish people, including Israel's old adversaries, will be devoted to the universal worship of Yahweh and be incorporated into the people of God while recanting their failed religious commitments. In addition, during a time when Egyptians are under oppression and are craving God's deliverance, their prayer will be answered without delay. Having paid attention to the cry of the ancient Hebrew slaves in Moses' days and to the groaning of the Israelites during the Judges period, Yahweh will now listen to the lamentations of the Egyptians who are under the hands of oppressors. He will never show indifference, even to Israel's long-term enemy.

In an unprecedented era in which Yahweh rescues the Egyptians from the hand of a hard master, they will come to acknowledge Yahweh as the one living God, worship Him as their Lord, and be incorporated into the universal community of Yahweh. No longer will Egypt be chastised by Yahweh with plagues as it was during the Exodus period. Rather it is the oppressed Egyptians who will be healed and experience God's divine presence in the altar:

> On that day there will be a highway from Egypt to Assyria, and the Assyrian will come into Egypt, and the Egyptian into Assyria, and the Egyptians will worship with the Assyrians. (19:23)

Verse 23 points to the involvement of Assyria in the worship of Yahweh whose unfailing love and saving power reaches even to the Gentiles. Politically, the two dominant rivals, Egypt and Assyria, are at times in hostility at the ends of the Fertile Crescent. Despite incessant conflict for hegemony, these two empires are inevitably in trade with each other. In this circumstance, a highway leading from Egypt to Assyria plays a central role not only as the great trading route but also as the military road on

2 J. A. Motyer, *The Prophecy of Isaiah,* 169.

which troops march. Yet no longer will the highway be intended for the military procession. Indeed, it will be used not to carry out domination but for the common worship of Yahweh that eventually leads to reconciliation and intimate relationship instead of endless antipathies.

> On that day Israel will be the third with Egypt and Assyria, a blessing in the midst of the earth, whom the LORD of hosts has blessed, saying, "Blessed be Egypt my people, and Assyria the work of my hands, and Israel my heritage." (19:24–25)

Then the eschatological anticipation of the incorporation of foreign nations into a new Israel culminates in one of the most remarkable and superb expressions found in the Old Testament. Breathtakingly, it is expected that Yahweh will identify Israel's long-standing adversaries with "His people" and "His hands". The Lord of hosts will never be reluctant to announce that they are on a par with the Israelites before Him. No longer will the access to God's saving grace be blocked by a series of physical boundaries. To be sure, all the foreign nations that are single minded to the true God will be welcome and Yahweh's aspiration to reconstitute a universal people of God, including the Gentiles, will be realised.

2. A new people of God and a universal worship

The prophet here presents another manifestation of what is oriented toward the appearance of God's new reconstituted community in which aliens are united with Israel.

> And the foreigners who join themselves to the LORD,
> to minister to him, to love the name of the LORD,
> and to be his servants, all who keep the sabbath,
> and do not profane it, and hold fast my covenant
> these I will bring to my holy mountain,
> and make them joyful in my house of prayer;
> their burnt offerings and their sacrifices
> will be accepted on my altar;
> for my house shall be called a house of prayer for all peoples.
> Thus says the Lord GOD, who gathers the outcasts of Israel,
> I will gather others to them besides those already gathered. (56:6–8)

Though Israel has undeniably had a monopoly on God's elect and the office of a single worship centre, it will come true that the active involvement of the foreigners in the worship of Yahweh will be taken for granted. It is not Yahweh's intention that they will be dealt with as His collateral people who are originally different from the Israelites. Indeed, any attempt to discriminate between the Israelites and the proselytes is totally divorced from what is designed to facilitate the emergence of a new Israel. In other words, "the status of proselytes is to be exactly the same as that of native-born Jews, including the right to present acceptable sacrifices to Yahweh at the Temple."[3] Whoever remains loyal to God and keeps His commands with their full and whole heart will not be excluded from but actively engaged in a new sacrificial worship system.

What is more, privileges will be given to the non-Israelites. Amazingly, the instant access to the house of God in prayer will be available for them. It is promised that "their burnt offerings and sacrifices" will lead to the peaceable reconciliation between God and man, which has been marred by sins. As Forgiver, Yahweh will be pleased to hear the prayer not only of His chosen people Israel, but also of foreigners who convert to Him and benevolently forgive what they have sinned. Then, as Gatherer, God will be devoted to His entire program for a universal expansion of His gathering work so that all people can join in the common worship of Yahweh.

3. The priesthood of the non-Israelites

One of the most emphatic and grandest announcements of what emerges as a New Israel in the Old Testament is explicitly stated in the final section of the book of Isaiah (66:18–21).

> For I know their works and their thoughts, and I am coming to gather all nations and tongues; and they shall come and shall see my glory, and I will set a sign among them. From them I will send survivors to the nations, to Tarshish, Put, and Lud – which draw the bow – to Tubal and Javan, to the coastlands far away that have not heard of my fame or seen my glory; and they shall declare my glory among the nations. They shall bring all your kindred from all the nations as an of-

3 R. N. Whybray, *Isaiah 40–66,* 199.

> fering to the LORD, on horses, and in chariots, and in litters, and on mules, and on dromedaries, to my holy mountain Jerusalem, says the LORD, just as the Israelites bring a grain offering in a clean vessel to the house of the LORD. And I will also take some of them as priests and as Levites, says the LORD.

The opening statement of the passage begins with a visionary manifestation of the eschatological gathering of all the nations from the ends of the world. It is envisaged that Yahweh who reinstates the outcasts of Israel will not forsake but invite even "all nations and tongues" to a new age in which they will behold God's glory. This visionary expression is "apparently a great inclusive, universal reach of Yahweh to claim sovereignty over all peoples and to include all nations in the protected, blessed, covenanted community."[4]

In addition, a new remarkable understanding of the priestly office is radically introduced in Isa. 66:20–21. The prophet paints a magisterial and overwhelming picture in which all the nations are incorporated into a New Israel and called 'brothers' who, like the Israelites, have the equal privilege of having instant access to the house of Yahweh with special gifts. In other words, "the Gentiles will not only be adopted by God but will also be elevated by him to the highest honor. Already it was a great honour that unclean and polluted nations were reckoned a holy people; but now here is something far more wonderful – they are elevated to the highest rank."[5] Surprisingly, Yahweh will also be pleased to allow some of the foreigners to be involved in the ministry of the sacrificial worship like Israelite Levites and priests who have had a monopoly on the office of Jerusalem's temple. Indeed, there will be no fearful restraint to bar the non-Israelites from membership of Levites.

Rather, they will be actively involved in reconciliation between God and sinners like Israelite priests who have been authorised to minister the ceremonies on the Day of Atonement or a particular sacrifice such as the Passover. In that day, the qualification of the priesthood will not be confined to physical Israel but be commissioned to all people who retain an exclusive loyalty to Yahweh.

In summary, an eschatological vision of an unimaginable transformation of the Nations into God's new people, dubbed a New Israel, is clearly set forth throughout the book of Isaiah. The section of Isa. 19:19–25

4 Walter Brueggeman, *Isaiah 40–66*, 258.

5 John Calvin, *Isaiah* (Wheaton: Crossway Books, 2000), 398.

makes it evident that Israel's foreign oppressors such as Egyptians and Assyrians will be incorporated into a New Israel and called "God's people". Then the two major enemies of Israel will astonishingly be reckoned God's cherished people who are substantially on a par with native-born Jews before Yahweh. As a result, the long-term hostility between Israel and the Gentiles, especially her adversaries will be eradicated. Furthermore, a wondrous speculation on the universal worship of Yahweh is influentially spelled out in Isa. 56:6–8.

It is visualised that the foreign nations will partake in the worship of God, keep a festival and offer a special gift to Yahweh on whom they are dependent. While Jerusalem centred worship will be annihilated, a worldwide sacrificial system, in which all people are actively involved, will mark a new epoch-making age in which as Yahweh's people, the foreigners are not absorbed in idols but embrace the one living God. Finally, the Gentiles will be qualified for the priesthood, on which Levitical priests of Israel have had a monopoly. It is within the bounds of possibility that even non-Israelites will be engaged loyally in the office of sacrificial practices that lead to reconciliation between Yahweh and His people, including the non-Israelites.

4. Implications

Over the last decade, deep-seated hostility toward other religions has been a major issue in the Korean religious societies. The Korean Churches are heavily concerned that several Christian fanatics have been actively involved in the destruction of Buddha statues. Most recently, an extremist, Soo-Jin Kim demolished 750 Buddha images in a temple in JeJu-Do, the biggest island in Korea, and thereby inflicted a great loss for the temple.[6] As a consequence, many Buddhist leaders immediately responded with rage to this appalling misconduct and labelled it barbarism. They convened a special committee to investigate meticulously what had been spoiled in the temple and were not reluctant to make this disastrous affair

6 See *Christian Though* 479 (1998), 56–64.

known in major newspapers and magazines. A Buddhist priest, Ma-Kun Suk, strongly comments:

> Hostile destruction of Buddhist relics or vestiges because of their different faith is regrettable... If Buddhists do this, how would Christians respond? ... Buddhist relics are nothing less then footprints and traces of our ancestors. They are not solely Buddhist possessions or religious symbols. They are not only cultural artefacts that all [Korean] people should preserve; they are our national spirit and soul.[7]

Having faced fervent challenges by Buddhists, many Christian leaders have become aware that lack of mutual respect between Christianity and Buddhism is worse than ever and that the antagonism between them is coming to a head. They have sought to criticise acutely this fanatical attitude toward other religions, expressing regret to the Korean Buddhists. In spite of this, such religious fervour is not decreasing, but is becoming still more intense.

In this circumstance, a remarkable understanding of the New Israel found in the book of Isaiah has a considerable theological implication for the Korean Churches, who clearly reckon themselves not only as the spiritual seeds of Abraham but also the new Israel. The bulk of the Korean Churches are not resistant to the interpretation that the prophetic vision of what is reconstituted as a new people of God in the book of Isaiah as a whole is universally fulfilled with the emergence of the church. They have come to the realisation that no one can have a monopoly on access to Yahweh. From a Korean perspective, every attempt to limit and exclude a part of humankind from the benefit of experiencing God's saving activity has no place in our world. It is taken for granted that whoever embraces Yahweh as their Lord is already incorporated into the renewed people of God. It comes as little surprise, therefore, that even non-Israelites who put their faith in Yahweh are invited to join in celebration of Yahweh's redemptive action on behalf of His reconstituted community. This Korean universal perspective on the New Israel has a radical and negative implication for naïve fundamentalists who give short shrift to other religionists, and are at enmity with them.

Given that Yahweh remains actively involved with mankind so that people might seek and worship Him, one finds it improper to approach diverse religious beliefs with a superior air in a global society like Korea.

7 Ma-Kun Suk, "Christian Values are Not Limited to Christianity" *Christian Thought* 479 (1998), 21–23 (my translation).

Rather, for the Korean Christians, it is of exceptional significance to be tolerant of people of different religious convictions and practices and to share the Christian faith with respect, forbearance and magnanimity. Jung-Woo Kim correctly points out:

> Since those who believe Jesus Christ as their Lord are saved only by God's grace, it is not biblical to assume superiority over other religious positions (Eph. 2:8). Rather, it is essential to put both the humility of incarnation and the love of the cross into practice. If our convictions lack generosity, tenderness, and mildness, we will never become Jesus' disciples.[8]

The more Christians belittle, disparage and even denigrate different religious beliefs without leniency, the more their attempt to share their faith with them is counter-productive. In order to usher other believers into Yahweh' presence, Christians need to be tolerant and accepting, avoiding razing religious relics indiscriminately. In this respect, the prophetic imagination of what is centred on God's yearning to include all the nations in His people leads us to the affirmation that a responsible Christian must tolerate diverse religions without doing mischief to them.

8 Jung-Woo Kim, "Religious Pluralism and the Interpretation of the First commandment," *Ministry & Theology* 2 (1999), 68.

Conclusion

This research has emerged from the current international debates on the polemical issues (religious pluralism and iconoclastic vandalism), which have recently come to a head in Korea. The specific concern of the thesis has been with the critical implications for the issues in Korea in the light of Isaianic themes, especially their two ostensibly paradoxical facets: particularism and universalism.

The first part of the thesis has offered a broad overview of how two opposing camps, pluralist and evangelical writers, are at odds with each other. It has been shown how contemporary pluralists such as John Hick mount a powerful criticism of an exclusivist stance, and how evangelical camps including D. A. Carson respond with intolerance, disapproval and confrontation to a pluralist worldview. Specifically, this section has elaborated upon the blistering debate on Korean pluralism, since Sun-Whan Pyun, a pioneer of contemporary Korean pluralism was expelled from the Korean Methodist Church in 1992. Likewise, this section has shown how Christian iconoclastic vandalism drives Korean peoples of diverse religions into a frenzy, and enmeshes the Korean Churches in a situation in Korean society.

As a consequence, the second part of the thesis has identified the deep need to assess these issues in the light of the Bible, especially the book of Isaiah in the context of the Korean Churches who hold the biblical Scriptures in high esteem. It has also presented my reading of the book of Isaiah as a whole. As indicated earlier, my biblical approach draws little attention to a historical-critical reading of Isaiah that deals with the book of Isaiah as three independent books such as First, Second and Third Isaiah. My interpretive method is entirely divorced from the historical critics' attempts to reconstruct the textual history in order to explore the intentions of original authors. Rather, my reading strategy places emphasis on Isaianic unitary themes such as the Holy One of Israel or Jerusalem/Zion, which serve as clues for a holistic reading of the book of Isaiah.

More significantly, it has been argued that the unitary themes in Isaiah characterised by particularism and universalism play a central role in evaluating the polemical issues: religious pluralism and iconoclasm. As a consequence, the final part of the thesis was concentrated with the two focal points, particularism and universalism. In chapters 4–6, special emphasis was placed on particularist motifs, such as "the Holy One of Israel," "monotheism" and "the distinct role of Torah," which are prevalent throughout the book of Isaiah. In the book of Isaiah, the sovereign Yahweh is identified with the one Holy God who calls, chooses and commissions Israel as His holy nation which is to exhibit its godliness by putting His divine mandate into practice in the midst of a pagan world that negates the sole existence of God.

It is audaciously claimed in the book of Isaiah that there is no other god but Yahweh! The prophet leaves no place for syncretism or polytheism centred on worshiping pseudo-gods. Finally, in the book of Isaiah, Torah, which serves as the unique medium to deliver the divine revelation of Yahweh, plays a crucial role in assessing Israel's sin and is reckoned the everlasting word of God, which, unlike human words or teachings that recede into the dim past, is relevant for a future time.

On the other hand, in chapters 7–9, attention was drawn to the prophetic manifestations of central universalist themes, such as "Zion," "the New Creation," and "the New Israel," prominent in the book of Isaiah. It is eschatologically envisaged that Zion will emerge as the universal cosmic centre, where all nations will go on a pilgrimage to pay homage to Yahweh with special tributes from every quarter. No longer will access to Zion be exclusively confined to a state like Israel, but will be universally available to all nations that seek to remain loyal to God.

In addition, the New Creation, one of the most universalist motifs, is made explicit in the book of Isaiah, particularly in Isa. 50–66. It is eschatologically anticipated that the old creation will be wondrously transformed into a new creation that yields the ultimate culmination of what is intended by God for the whole world. The emergence of a New Creation will mark the full restoration of the distorted, deteriorated and decaying creation in which humans meet with great setbacks, such as natural calamities, physical and mental diseases, and an absurdity of life. Strikingly, all peoples who long for Yahweh to refurbish the entire universe that Yahweh created will behold an unprecedented age marked by a new heaven and a new earth. No one will have a monopoly on the experience of the event of New Creation. Rather, all the nations that retain their adherence to the God of the New Creation will be ushered in to partake in the cosmic event.

Remarkably, the visionary expression of what is characteristic of the new people of God is panoramically depicted throughout the book of Isaiah. It is spectacularly pictured that God's people will no longer be bound by geographical, national and cultural precincts. Instead, non-Israelites, who abrogate idolatry but retain unswerving commitment to Yahweh, will be incorporated into a people of God, dubbed the "New Israel," and be on a par with the Israelites in God's eyes. It is clearly anticipated that non-Israelites will be actively engaged in the office of worldwide sacrificial service, a point that indicates that the universal priesthood will be qualified for all the nations who are members of God's new people. In this regard, the prophetic imagination of what is portrayed as the New Israel makes it clear that entrance into Yahweh's new universal community will be granted to non-Israelites who long for the appearance of a new heaven and a new earth.

More significantly, each of the chapters (4–9) in the final part has offered a critical assessment of the currently highly contested issues: religious pluralism and iconoclasm. Firstly, chapters 4–6 centred on particularist motifs have presented negative implications for a pluralist position that leaves no room for the uniqueness of Yahweh, to which the Korean Churches retain a singular commitment. As indicated earlier, a liberal pluralist worldview takes up the affirmation that all religious practices and teachings are nothing less than various experiences of the one God, who is the same God manifested in all religions. In other words, this radical position takes the view that all religions are different but equally valid responses to the Ultimate Reality, referred to as 'the unknown God.'

Having followed in the footsteps of the prophet who uncompromisingly claims that there is no god besides Yahweh, however, the Korean Churches, who embrace the biblical books, including the book of Isaiah, as the revealed word of God, have no doubt that Yahweh is not on par with other gods, but indeed the one living God. From a Korean Christian perspective, religious pluralism is dealt with as an inappropriate belief system that has neither part nor lot in the Korean Christian faith, which is deeply committed to the exclusive divinity of Yahweh. Inasmuch as the Korean Christian readers are devoted to the one God, it is impossible for them to espouse liberal pluralist theology that abrogates the distinctive lordship of Yahweh.

Furthermore, the Korean Churches would find it inappropriate to accommodate a liberal pluralist ideology that insists that knowledge of God is not restricted to Torah, the teaching of Yahweh, but is available through other religious teachings or Scriptures. This assertion rests on their belief that God's purpose on behalf of His people is ultimately revealed through Torah, which is clearly set forth in the biblical Scriptures, the locus of God's self-disclosure in words. It should be pointed out, therefore, that Korean pluralist writers who belong to the Korean Churches can on no account disregard the notion of Yahweh's uniqueness that serves as the essential bedrock of the Korean Christian worldview.

On the other hand, chapters 7–9 dealing with universalism in Isaiah have offered a critical evaluation of enthusiasts, who vigorously respond with criticism, condemnation, and violence to other religious teachings and traditions and even focus on the wilful destruction of religious temples and relics. From the perspective of the Korean Christian readers who hold the Bible, including the book of Isaiah, in esteem, non-believers are to be regarded not as a target for cursing but as beneficiaries of sacrificial service so that they may be spontaneously involved in the universal worship of Yahweh. Indeed, the identification of themselves with the people of God has nothing to do with an egotistical, bigoted and fanatical attitude toward other peoples. Rather, the more Christian believers focus on the prophetic manifestation of Yahweh's universal salvific activity toward all the nations, the more they become aware that Christianity ought to respond to non-Christians, including other religionists, with tolerance, respect and leniency. This point leads us to the conclusion that the Korean Christian faith leaves no room for self-righteousness or self-exaltation above people of different religions.

Here it is of considerable importance to deal with the issue of compatibility between the two key central notions in the book of Isaiah (particularism and universalism), since the coexistence of this polarity seems to be incongruous. It can be seen, indeed, that a series of paradoxical concepts are dialectically rooted in the biblical books.[1] Firstly, for instance, one of the dialectical inconsistencies evident in the biblical passages, is between Yahweh's universal dominion over the whole cosmic universe and His particular revelation to His people. It is explicitly spelled out in the biblical Scriptures that while Yahweh is the sovereign creator and the Lord of the cosmos, this God can be known not by intuition, reason or reflection, but only by His divine revelation in word and deed. In other words, in the

1 For a further discussion of dialectical contradictions seen in the Bible, consult Bernhard W. Anderson, *Contours of Old Testament Theology*, 77–78.

biblical texts, Yahweh is identified not only with the universal God who rules over the nations and the whole creation, but also with the unique God whose self-disclosure and presence can be divulged only through His divine revelation.

Secondly, one might find it difficult to avoid the awkward question of how the transcendent God could be immanent in all history and creation. It is overtly claimed in the biblical witnesses that while Yahweh is the Supreme Being who is beyond the phenomenal world to which human consciousness and perception is confined, He is constantly present and at ongoing work in the midst of the whole universe, especially in all human concrete history. Thirdly, God's sovereignty and human will are paradoxically brought into prominence in all of the biblical books. It is true that the course of human history is under the control of Yahweh's sovereign power that could subdue or crush human will, while humans have freedom to make a decision or a response without restraint. Fourthly, one of the most paradoxical dimensions is evidently found in the two crucial natures of Jesus Christ; that is, His divinity and personality. In the traditional belief of the church, Jesus Christ is deemed not only as God the Son, but also as the perfect human, a tenet that has been a keystone of Christian faith that can in no way be recanted.

Above all, as we have noted earlier, these dialectical paradoxes are evident in the book of Isaiah, especially in its two focal points, particularism and universalism. The prophet comes to the categorical assertion that the sovereign Yahweh is the God who is the Holy One of Israel, and the unique Supreme Being. On the other hand, throughout the book of Isaiah Yahweh is described as the God who is restorer of the cosmic centre dubbed Zion, maker of a New Creation, and establisher of a New Israel. One might seemingly find it illegitimate to accommodate these two paradoxical views. Perhaps, it would be a better option to adopt just one of them in order to fit these dialectical ideas to a human perspective.

However, such an interpretation would bias and skew or obscure the overall biblical expressions of the two dialectical motifs and their intentional meaning. Here the living Korean Christian perspective helps us toward an alternative way of dealing with the dialectical paradoxes. For the Korean Churches, the God in whom they claim to believe is the God who is the everlasting Yahweh of Abraham, Isaac, and Jacob revealed in the biblical books. Yet, from a Korean perspective, this unchanging God whose divine manifestation is not restricted to a definite place or state, but universally evident in today's world, now appears in contemporary Korean societies. In other words, the Korean believers are dependent on the lordship of Yahweh shown in the biblical Scriptures, but aver that this same God is not confined to an ethnic group or community; rather, He is continuously present in the midst of pluralistic global communities. While the Korean Christians affirm that no one can have a monopoly on access to the divine presence, they feel it of fundamental importance to remain single-minded toward the Yahweh revealed in the biblical texts.

This Korean simultaneous understanding of the particularity of God's unique existence, and the universality of the scope of His unfailing love reaching to all the nations, sheds light on the possibility of maintaining a grip on the dialectical themes of particularism and universalism. From a Korean viewpoint, though one finds it unacceptable to negate the uniqueness of Yahweh, worshiping Him is a universal possibility. This point leads us to the conclusion that Yahweh is both particular and universal! Thus, this notion of God as representing both particularism and universalism has specific implication for 'the people of God' in Korea, their understanding of these two notions held in tension, and how they view other religions.

Bibliography

Anderson, B. W., *From Creation To New Creation.* Minneapolis: Fortress Press, 1994.

–, *Contours of Old Testament Theology.* Minneapolis: Fortress Press, 1999.

Armerding, C. E., "Images for Today: Word from the Prophets." In *Studies in Old Testament Theology*, (ed.) R. K. J. Robert L. Hubbard Jr., Robert P. Meye. Dallas: Word Publishing, 1992, 169–185.

Arnold, B. T., "Religion in Ancient Israel." In *The Face of Old Testament: A Survey of Contemporary Approaches*, (eds.) David W. Baker & Bill T. Arnold. Grand Rapids: BakerBooks, 1999, 391–420.

Barker, M., *The Older Testament: The Survival of Themes from the Ancient Royal Cult in Sectarian Judaism and Early Christianity.* London: SPCK, 1987.

Barr, J., *History and Ideology in the Old Testament: Biblical Studies at the End of a Millennium.* Oxford: Oxford University Press, 2000.

Barton, J., *Oracles of God: Perceptions of Ancient Prophecy in Israel after the Exile.* London: Longman & Todd, 1986.

–, *Isaiah 1–39.* Sheffield: Sheffield Academic Press, 1995.

–, "Ethics in the Book of Isaiah." In *Writing and Reading the Scroll of Isaiah: Studies of an Interpretive Tradition*, (eds.) Craig C. Broyles & Craig A. Evans. Leiden: Brill, 1997, 67–78.

–, "Historical-Critical Approaches." In *Biblical Interpretation*, (ed.) J. Barton. Cambridge: Cambridge University Press, 1998, 9–19.

Blenkinsopp, J., "Second Isaiah – Prophet of Universalism." In *The Prophets*, (ed.) P. R. Davies, BS 42. Sheffield: Sheffield Academic Press, 1996, 186–206.

–, *Isaiah 1–39: a new translation with introduction and commentary.* New York: Doubleday, 2000.

Brueggemann, W., *Theology of the Old Testament: Testimony, Dispute, Advocacy.* Minneapolis: Fortress Press, 1997.

–, *Isaiah 1–39.* Louisville: Westminster John Knox Press, 1998.

–, *Isaiah 40–66.* Louisville: Westminster John Knox Press, 1998.

Calvin, J., *Isaiah.* Wheaton: Crossway Books, 2000.

Carr, D. M., “Reaching for Unity in Isaiah.” In *The Prophets*, (ed.) P. R. Davies, BS 42. Sheffield: Sheffield Academic Press, 1996, 164–183.

–, “Reading Isaiah from Beginning (Isaiah 1) to End (Isaiah 65–66): Multiple Modern Possibilities.” In *New Visions of Isaiah*, (eds.) Roy F. Melugin & M. A. Sweeney, JSOTSup 214. Sheffield: Sheffield Academic Press, 1996, 188–218.

Carroll, R. P., “Blindsight and the Vision Things: Blindness and Insight in the Book of Isaiah.” In *Writing and Reading the Scroll of Isaiah: Studies of an Interpretive Tradition*, (eds.) Craig C. Broyles & Craig A. Evans. Leiden: Brill, 1997, 79–94.

Carson, D. A., *The Gagging of God.* Leicester: APOLLOS, 1996.

Chah, Y., “Uniqueness of Christianity.” In *Bible and Theology*, (eds.) Sung-Soo Kwon, et al. Seoul: Christian Wisdom Press, 1992, 131–146.

Childs, B. S., *Introduction to the Old Testament as Scripture.* London: SCM Press LTD, 1979.

–, “The Canonical Shape of the Prophetic Literature.” In *Interpreting the Prophets*, (eds.) James Luther Mays & Paul J. Achtemeier. Philadelphia: Fortress Press, 1987, 41–49.

–, *Isaiah.* Louisville: Westminster John Knox Press, 2001.

Clements, R. E., *Old Testament Theology.* Louisville: John Knox Press, 1979.

–, *Isaiah 1–39.* Grand Rapids: Wm. B. Eerdmans Publishing Company, 1980.

–, “A Light to the Nations: A Central Theme of the Book of Isaiah.” In *Forming Prophetic Literature: Essays on Isaiah and the Twelve in Honor of John D. W. Watts*, (eds.) James W. Watts & Paul R. House, JSOTSup 235. Sheffield: Sheffield Academic Press, 1996, 57–69.

–, *Old Testament Prophecy: From Oracles to Canon.* Louisville: Westminster John Knox Press, 1996.

–, “Zion as Symbol and Political Reality: A Central Isaianic Quest.” In *Studies in the Book of Isaiah: Festschrift Willem A. M. Beuken*, (eds.) J. Van Ruiten & M. Vervenne. Leuven: Leuven University Press, 1997, 3–17.

–, “‘Arise, shine, for your light has come’: A Basic Theme of the Isaianic Tradition.” In *Writing and Reading the Scroll of Isaiah: Studies of an Interpretive Tradition*, (eds.) Craig C. Broyles & Craig A. Evans. Supplements to VTS 70. Leiden: Brill, 1997, 441–454.

Clines, D. J. A., *What Does Eve Do to Help? and Other Readerly Questions to the Old Testament.* Sheffield: Sheffield Academic Press, 1994.

–, *On the Way to the Postmodern: Old Testament Essays, 1967–1998.* Sheffield: Sheffield Academic Press, 1998.

Cobb Jr, J. B., "Beyond Pluralism." In *Christian Uniqueness Reconsidered: The Myth of a Pluralistic Theology of Religions*, (ed.) G. D'Costa. Maryknoll: Orbis Books, 1992, 81–95.

Coggins, R. J., *Introducing the Old Testament.* Oxford: Oxford University Press, 1990.

–, "New Ways with Old Texts: How Does One Write a Commentary on Isaiah?" *The Expository Times* 107 (1996): 362–366.

Conrad, E. W., *Reading Isaiah,* OBT (Minneapolis: Fortress Press, 1991).

–, "Prophet, Redactor and Audience." In *New Visions of Isaiah,* (eds.) Roy F. Melugin & M. A. Sweeney, JSOTSup 214. Sheffield: Sheffield Academic Press, 1996, 315–16.

–, "Reading Isaiah and the Twelve as Prophetic Books." In *Writing and Reading the Scroll of Isaiah: Studies of an Interpretive Tradition*, (eds.) Craig C. Broyles & Craig A. Evans. Supplements to VTS 70. Leiden: Brill, 1997, 3–18.

–, "The End of Prophecy and the Appearance of Angels/Messenger in the Book of the Twelve." *JSOT* 73 (1997): 65–79.

–, "Messenger in Isaiah and the Twelve: Implications for Reading Prophetic Books." *JSOT* 91 (2000): 109–124.

Crüsemann, F., *The Torah: Theology and Social History of Old Testament Law.* Minneapolis: Fortress Press, 1998.

Culler, J., "Prolegomena to a Theory of Reading." In *The Reader in the Text*, (eds.) Susan R. Suleiman & Inge Crosman. Princeton: Princeton University Press, 1980, 46–66.

Darr, K. P., *Isaiah's Vision and the Family of God.* Louisville: Westminster John Knox Press, 1994.

Davies, P. R., *In Search of 'Ancient Israel'*, JSOTS 148. Sheffield: Sheffield Academic Press, 1992.

D'Costa, G., *Theology and Religious Pluralism.* New York: Basil Blackwell, 1986.

–, "Christ, The Trinity, and Religious Plurality." In *Christian Uniqueness Reconsidered: The Myth of a Pluralistic Theology of Religions*, (ed.) G. D'Costa, FMFS. Maryknoll: New York, 1992, 16–29.

Dever, W. G., "Archaeology, Ideology and the Quest for an 'Ancient' or 'Biblical' Israel." *Near Eastern Archaeology* 61:1 (1998): 39–52.

Dumbrell, W. J., "The Purpose of the Book of Isaiah." *TynBul*, 36 (1985): 111–28.

–, *The Faith of Israel: Its Expression in the Books of the Old Testament.* Leicester: APOLLOS, 1993.

–, *The Search for Order: Biblical Eschatology in Focus.* Grand Rapids: Baker Books, 1994.

Dupuis, J., *Toward a Christian Theology of Religious Pluralism.* Maryknoll: Orbis Books, 2001.

Durham, J. I., "Isaiah 40–55: A New Creation, A New Exodus, A New Messiah." In *Yahweh/Baal Confrontation and Other Studies in Biblical Literature and Archaeology: Essays in honour of Emmett Willard Hamrick*, (eds.) Julia M. O'Brien and Fred L. Horton, Jr. Lewiston: Mellen Biblical Press, 1995, 47–56.

De Moor, J. C., *The Rise of Yahwism: The Roots of Israelite Monotheism.* Leuven: Leuven University Press, 1990.

Eco, U., *The Role of the Reader: Explorations in the Semiotics of Texts.* London: Hutchinson, 1985.

–, *Interpretation and Overinterpretation.* Cambridge: Cambridge University Press, 1992.

Fish, S., *Is There a Text in This Class? The Authority of Interpretive Communities.* Cambridge: Cambridge University Press, 1980.

–, "Literature in the Reader: Affective Stylistics." In *Reader-Response Criticism: From Formalism to Post-Structuralism*, (ed.) J. P. Tompkins. Baltimore and London: The Johns Hopkins University Press, 1980, 70–100.

Gaiser, F. J., "'To Whom Then Will You Compare Me?': Agency in Second Isaiah." *Word & World*, XIX (1999): 141–152.

Gammie, J. G., *Holiness in Israel,* OBT. Minneapolis: Fortress Press, 1989.

Gilliangham, S. E., *One Bible, Many Voices: Different Approaches to Biblical Studies.* Grand Rapids: William B. Eerdmans Publishing Company, 1998.

Gnuse, R. K., *No Other Gods: Emergent Monotheism in Israel.* Sheffield: Sheffield Academic Press, 1997.

Goldingay, J., *God's Prophet, God's Servant.* Carlisle: The Paternoster Press, 1994.

Gowan, D. E., *Theology of the Prophetic Books: The Death and Resurrection of Israel.* Louisville: Westminster John Knox Press, 1998.

Grayson, J. H., "The Shinto Shrine Conflict and Protest Martyrs in Korea, 1938–1945." *Missiology: An International Review* XXIX (2001): 287–305.

Hanson, P. D., *Isaiah 40–66.* Louisville: John Knox Press, 1995.

Harmon, A., "Edward Joseph Young." In *Biblical Interpreters of the 20th Century: A Selection of Evangelical Voices*, (eds.) Walter A. Elwell & J. D. Weaver. Grand Rapids: Baker Books, 1999, 189–201.

Herbert, A. S., *The Book of the Prophet Isaiah: Chapters 1–39.* Cambridge: Cambridge University Press, 1973.

Hick, J., *God Has Many Names.* Philadelphia: The Westminster Press, 1982.

–, "A Pluralist View." In *Four Views on Salvation in a Pluralistic World*, (eds.) Dennis L. Okholm & Timothy R. Philips. Grand Rapids: Zondervan, 1996, 27–59.

Holladay, C. R., "Contemporary Methods of Reading the Bible." In *The New Interpreter's Bible.* Nashville: Abingdon Press, 1994, 134–35.

House, P. R., *Old Testament Theology.* Downers Grove: IVP, 1998.

Iser, W., "Interaction between Text and Reader." In *The Reader in the Text*, (eds.) Susan R. Suleiman & Inge Crosman. Princeton: Princeton University Press, 1980, 106–119.

–, "The Reading Process: A Phenomenological Approach." In *Reader-Response Criticism: From Formalism to Post-Structuralism*, (ed.) J. P. Tompkins. Baltimore and London: The Johns Hopkins University Press, 1980, 50–69.

Jarick, J., "Prophets and Losses: Some Themes in Recent Study of the Prophets." *The Expository Times* 107 (1995): 75–77.

Jensen, J., *The Use of Torah by Isaiah.* Washington, D. C.: The Catholic University of America, 1973.

Jun, H., "Religious Pluralism and the Uniqueness of Christ." *Ministry & Theology* 8 (1991): 158–75.

–, "Religious Pluralism in Evagelistic Perspective." In *Bible and Theology*, (ed.) Sung-Soo Kwon, et al. Seoul: Christian Wisdom Press, 1992, 1992.

–, *Religious Pluralism and Mission Strategies Toward Other Religions.* Seoul: The Korea Society for Reformed Faith and Action, 1993.

Kaiser, O., *Isaiah 13–39.* London: SCM Press, 1980.

–, *Isaiah 1–12.* London: SCM Press, 1983.

Kaiser Jr., W. C., "The Torah Speaks Today." In *Studies in Old Testament Theology*, (eds.) Robert L. Hubbard Jr., Robert K. Johnston, Robert P. Meye. Dallas: Word Publishing, 1992, 117–134.

–, *Mission in the Old Testament: Israel as a Light to the Nations.* Grand Rapids: Baker Books, 2000.

Kang, S., *Religious Pluralism and Salvation.* Seoul: The Christian Literature Society of Korea, 1997.

Kim, J., "Religious Pluralism and Korean Indigenous Theology." *Ministry & Theology* 7 (1992): 61–70.

–, "Paul's Theology of the Cross and Pluralism in Religions." In *Bible and Theology*, (ed.) H.-B. K. Sung-Soo Kwon, et al. Seoul: Christian Wisdom Press, 1992.

Kim, J., "The Conflict between the Mythical Tangun and The Historical Tangun and the Extent of Religious Respect." *JBS* 9 (1999): 3–6.

Kim, N., *Shinto Nationalism and The Korean Churches.* Seoul: SaeSoon Press, 1990.

Kim, S., *Jesus and Paul.* Seoul: The Chammal Publishing House, 1993.

Kim, Y., *The Culture Theology of the Korean Christian.* Seoul: Sung Kwang Publishing Company, 1992.

–, *The 21st Century and Reformed Theology (II): The Postmodernism and Reformed Theology.* Seoul: The Presbyterian Church of Korea, 1998.

Kim, Y., *A History of the Korean Church.* Seoul: The Korea Society for Reformed Faith and Action, 1998.

Knitter, P. F., *No Other Name?* London: SCM Press, 1985.

–, "The Christian Theology Must Be the Dialogue Theology." In *Christian Thought* 8 (1994): 88–105.

Kwon, S., *Biblical Hermeneutics.* Seoul: Chongshin Publishing Company, 1991.

Laato, A., *History and Ideology in the Old Testament Prophetic Literature: A Semiotic Approach to the Reconstruction of the Proclamation of the Historical Prophets*. CB. Stockholm: Almqvist & Wiksell International, 1996.

–, *"About Zion I Will Not Be Silent": The Book of Isaiah as an Ideological Unity.* Stockholm: Almqvist & Wiksell International, 1998.

Lang, B., *Monotheism and the Prophetic Minority: An Essay in Biblical History and Sociology*. Sheffield: Almond, 1983.

Lee, D., *Asian Religious and Christianity.* Seoul: Christian Literature Crusade, 1998.

–, *Contemporary Theology of Mission.* Seoul: Christian Literature Crusade, 1998.

Lee, S., "Rev. Kichul Ju's Resistance against Shinto Shrine Worship." *Journal of Christian Thought* 4 (1997): 197–232.

Lemche, N. P., *The Canaanites and Their Land.* Sheffield: Sheffield Academic Press, 1991.

–, "The Origin of the Israelite State – A Copenhagen Perspective on the Emergence of Critical Historical Studies of Ancient Israel in Recent Time." *JSOT* 12/1 (1998): 44–63.

Levenson, J. D., *Sinai and Zion.* Minneapolis: Winston Press, 1985.

Lohfink, N., *Great Themes from the Old Testament.* Edinburgh: T. & T. Clark LTD, 1982.

Longman III, T., "Literary Approaches to Old Testament Study." In *The Face of Old Testament Studies: A Survey of Contemporary Approaches*, (eds.) David W. Baker & Bill T. Arnold. Grand Rapids: Baker Books, 1999, 97–115.

Martens, E. A., "Embracing the Law: A Biblical Theological Perspective." In *Bulletin for Biblical Research* 2 (1992): 1–28.

McGrath, A. E., "A Particularist View: A Post-Enlightenment Approach." In *Four Views on Salvation in a Pluralistic World*, (eds.) Dennis L. Okholm & Timothy R. Phillips. Grand Rapids: Zondervan Publishing House, 1996, 149–180.

–, *A Passion for Truth: The Intellectual Coherence of Evangelicalism.* Leicester: APOLLOS, 1996.

Melugin, R. F., "Figurative Speech and the Reading of Isaiah 1 as Scripture." In *New Visions of Isaiah*, (eds.) Roy F. Melugin & M. A. Sweeney. JSOTSup 214. Sheffield: Sheffield Academic Press, 1996, 282–305.

–, "The Book of Isaiah and the Construction of Meaning." In *Writing and Reading the Scroll of Isaiah: Studies of an Interpretive Tradition*, (eds.) Craig C. Broyles & Craig A. Evans. Leiden: Brill, 1997, 39–55.

Mettinger, T. N. D., "In Search of the Hidden Structure: YHWH as King in Isaiah 40–55." In *Writing and Reading the Scroll of Isaiah: Studies of an Interpretive Tradition*, (eds.) Craig C. Broyles & Craig A. Evans. Leiden: Brill, 1997, 143–154.

Miscall, P. D., "New Heavens, New Earth, New Book." In *Reading Between Texts: Intertextuality and the Hebrew Bible*, (eds.) D. N. Fewell. Louisville: Westminster/John Knox Press, 1992, 41–56.

–, *Isaiah.* Sheffield: JSOT Press, 1993.

–, *Isaiah 34–35: A Nightmare/A Dream.* Sheffield: Sheffield Academic Press, 1999.

Motyer, A., *Isaiah: An Introduction and Commentary.* Leicester: IVP, 1999.

–, *The Prophecy of Isaiah.* Leicester: IVP, 1994.

O'Connell, R. H., *Concentricity and Continuity: The Literary Structure of Isaiah.* Sheffield: Sheffield Academic Press, 1994.

Ollenburger, B. C., *Zion The City of the Great King.* Sheffield: JSOT Press, 1987.

Oswalt, J. N., *The Book of Isaiah: Chapters 1–39.* NICOT. Grand Rapids: Eerdmans, 1986.

–, *The Book of Isaiah: Chapters 40–66.* NICOT. Grand Rapids: Eerdmans, 1998.

Panikkar, R., *The Intrareligious Dialogue.* New York: Paulist Press, 1978.

–, *The Unknown Christ of Hinduism.* Maryknoll: Orbis Books, 1981.

Park, C., "The Model and Nature of The Church." In *How Should the Contemporary Church be Born-again?*, (eds.) Young-Chul Kong & Kue-Jung Jung. Seoul: DaeJangKan Press, 1991.

Park, Y., *A History of Presbyterian Theological Thought in Korea: Korean Protestantism and Biblical Authority.* Seoul: Chongshin Publishing Company, 1992.

Phillips, W. G., "A Particularist View: An Evidentialist Approach." In *Four Views on Salvation in a Pluralistic World*, (eds.) Dennis L. Okholm & Timothy R. Phillips. Grand Rapids: Zondervan Publishing House, 1996, 211–245.

Provan, I. W., "Ideologies, Literary and Critical: Reflections on Recent Writing on the History of Israel." *JBL* 114, no. 4 (1995): 585–606.

–, "In the Stable with the Dwarves: Testimony, Interpretation, Faith, and the History of Israel." In *Windows into Old Testament History*, (eds.) V. Philips Long, David W. Baker & Gordon J. Wenham. Grand Rapids: Eerdmans, 2002, 161–197.

Pyun, S., "Other Religions and Theology." *The Theological Thought* 47 (1984): 687–717.

–, "Introduction: Korean Religions as a Theological Subject." In *Religious Pluralism and a Theological Subject*, ed. Korea Association of Christian Studies, 3–6. Seoul: The Christian Literature Society of Korea, 1990.

–, "My Theological Background." In *Religious Pluralism and Korean Theology: Essays in Memory of Dr. Pyun's Retire*, ed. Publication Committee, 15–30. Chunan: The Korean Theological Study Institute, 1993.

–, "A Dialogue with Religions During 100 Years and Its View." In *Korean Religion and Korean Theology: Essays in Memory of Dr. Lyu's 70th Birthday*, (ed.) Publication Committee. Chunan: The Korean Theological Study Institute, 1993.

–, *Dialogue Between Religions and Asian Theology: Pyun Sun-Whan Collection I*, (ed.) Pyun Sun-Whan Archive. Chunan: The Korean Theological Study Institute, 1996.

–, *Search for Korean Theology: Pyun Sun-Whan Collection III,* (ed.) Pyun Sun-Whan Archive. Chunan: The Korean Theological Study Institute, 1997.

Rendtorff, R., *The Old Testament: An Introduction.* London: SCM Press Ltd, 1985.

–, *Canon and Theology,* OBT. Minneapolis: Fortress Press, 1993.

–, "The Book of Isaiah: a complex Unity: Synchronic and Diachronic Reading." In *Prophecy and Prophets: The Diversity of Contemporary Issues in Scholarship*, (ed.) Y. Gitay, Semeia Studies SBL, 1997.

Roberts, J. J. M., "Isaiah in Old Testament Theology." In *Interpreting the Prophets*, (ed.) James Luther Mays & Paul J. Achtemeier. Philadelphia: Fortress Press, 1987, 62–74.

Roberts, K. L., "'Our Eyes Will See the Beauty of the King': The Esthetics of Kingship." *Word & World*, XIX (1999): 117–124.

Sawyer, J. F. A., *Isaiah,* DSB. Philadelphia: Westminster Press, 1984.

–, "'Blessed be My People Egypt' (Isaiah 19.25): The Context and Meaning of a Remarkable Passage." In *A Word in Season*, (eds.) David J. A. Clines & Philip R. Davies. JSOTSup 42. Sheffield: Sheffield, 1986, 57–71.

–, *Prophecy and the Prophets of the Old Testament.* Oxford: Oxford University Press, 1987.

–, *The Fifth Gospel: Isaiah in the History of Christianity.* Cambridge: Cambridge University Press, 1996.

Schwöbel, C., "Particularity, Universality, and the Religions." In *Christian Uniqueness Reconsidered: The Myth of a Pluralistic Theology of Religions*, (ed.) G. D'Costa, FMFS. Maryknoll: New York, 1992, 30–46.

Segovia, F. F., "'And They Began to Speak in Other Tongues': Competing Modes of Discourse in Contemporary Biblical Criticism." In *Reading From This Place*, (eds.) Fernando F. Segovia & Mary Ann Tolbert. Minneapolis: Fortress Press, 1995, 1–32.

Seitz, C. R., "Isaiah 1–66: Making Sense of the Whole." In *Reading and Preaching the Book of Isaiah*, ed. C. R. Seitz. Philadelphia: Fortress Press, 1988, 105–126.

–, *Zion's Final Destiny: The Development of the Book of Isaiah.* Minneapolis: Fortress Press, 1991.

–, *Isaiah 1–39.* Louisville: John Knox Press, 1993.

–, *Word Without End: The Old Testament as Abiding Theological Witness.* Grand Rapids: William B. Eerdmans Publishing Company, 1998.

Silva, M., "Contemporary Theories of Biblical Interpretation." In *The New Interpreter's Bible*. Nashville: Abingdon Press, 1994, 116–120.

Skilton, J. H., "Oswald T. Allis." In *Biblical Interpreters of the 20th Century: A Selection of Evangelical Voices*, (eds.) Walter A. Elwell & J. D. Weaver. Grand Rapids: Baker Books, 1999, 122–130.

Smith, M., *Palestinian Parties and Politics That Shaped the Old Testament.* London: SCM, 1971.

Stacey, D., *Isaiah: Chapters 1–39.* London: Epworth Press, 1993.

Sweeney, M. A., "The Book of Isaiah in Recent Research." *CR: BS* 1 (1993): 141–162.

–, "The Book of Isaiah as Prophetic Torah." In *New Visions of Isaiah*, (eds.) Roy F. Melugin & M. A. Sweeney, JSOTSup 214. Sheffield: Sheffield Academic Press, 1996, 50–67.

–, *Isaiah 1–39 with An Introduction to Prophetic Literature.* Grand Rapids: William B. Eerdmans Publishing Company, 1996.

–, "Prophetic Exegesis in Isaiah 65–66." In *Writing and Reading the Scroll of Isaiah: Studies of an Interpretive Tradition*, (eds.) Craig C. Broyles & Craig A. Evans. Leiden: Brill, 1997, 455–474.

Tate, M. E., "The Book of Isaiah in Recent Study." In *Forming Prophetic Literature: Essays on Isaiah and the Twelve in Honor of John D. W. Watts*, (eds.) James W. Watts and Paul R. House, JSOTSup 235. Sheffield: Sheffield Academic Press, 1996, 22–56.

Thompson, T. L., *Early History of the Israelite People from the Written and Archaeological Sources*. Leiden: Brill, 1992.

–, *The Bible in History: How Writers Create a Past*. London: Jonathan Cape, 1999.

Tompkins, J. P., "An Introduction to Reader-Response Criticism." In *Reader-Response Criticism: From Formalism to Post-Structuralism*, (ed.) J. P. Tompkins. Baltimore and London: The Johns Hopkins University Press, 1980, ix–xxvi.

Vangemeren, W. A., "Isaiah." In *Baker Commentary on the Bible*, (ed.) W. A. Elwell. Grand Rapids: Baker Books, 1989, 471–514.

Vanhoozer, K. J., *Is There a Meaning in This Text? The Bible, the Reader and the Morality of Literary Knowledge*. Leicester: APOLLOS, 1998.

Watts, J. D. W., *Isaiah 1–33*, WBC 24. Waco: Word Books, 1985.

–, *Isaiah 34–66*, WBC 25. Waco: Word Books, 1987.

–, *Isaiah*, WBT. Dallas: Word Publishing, 1989.

–, "Images of Yahweh: God in the Prophets." In *Studies in Old Testament Theology*, ed. R. K. J. Robert L. Hubbard Jr., Robert P. Meye. Dallas: Word Publishing, 1992, 135–168.

Webb, B. G., "Zion in Transformation: A Literary Approach to Isaiah." In *The Bible in Three Dimensions: Essays in Celebration of Forty Years of Biblical Studies in the University of Sheffield*, (eds.) David J. A. Clines, Stephen E. Fowl, Stanley E. Porter, JSOTSup 87. Sheffield: Sheffield Academic Press, 1990, 65–84.

Westermann, C., *Isaiah 40–66*. London: SCM Press, 1969.

Whaling, F., "Theories of Religion." In *The Blackwell Encyclopaedia of Modern Christian Thought*, (ed.) A. E. McGrath. Oxford: Blackwell, 1993, 549.

Whitelam, K. W., *The Invention of Ancient Israel: The Silencing of Palestinian History*. London: Routledge, 1996.

Whybray, R. N., *Isaiah 40–66*. Grand Rapids: Eerdmans, 1981.

Williamson, H. G. M., *The Book Called Isaiah: Deutero-Isaiah's Role in Composition and Redaction*. Oxford: Oxford University Press, 1994.

–, *Variations on a Theme: King, Messiah and Servant in the Book of Isaiah*. Carlisle: Paternoster Press, 1998.

Willis, J. T., "Exclusivistic and Inclusivistic Aspects of the Concept of the People of God in the Book of Isaiah." *Restoration Quarterly* 40 (1998): 3–12.

Wuthnow, R., *Rediscovering the Sacred: Perspectives on Religion in Contemporary Society.* Grand Rapids: Eerdmans, 1992.

Yee, G. A., "The Author/Text/Reader and Power: Suggestions for a Critical Framework for Biblical Studies." In *Reading From This Place: Social Location and Biblical Interpretation in the United States*, (eds.) Fernando F. Segovia and Mary Ann Tolbert. Minneapolis: Fortress Press, 1995, 109–120.

Young, E. J., *The Book of Isaiah,* Volumes 1–3. Grand Rapids: Eerdmans, 1965–72.

Bible in History

Series List

Vol. 1 Joseph Alobaidi: *Le commentaire des psaumes par le qaraïte Salmon ben Yeruham. Psaumes 1–10. Introduction, édition, traduction.* 1996.

Vol. 2 Joseph Alobaidi: *The Messiah in Isaiah 53. The commentaries of Saadia Gaon, Salmon ben Yeruham and Yefet ben Eli on Is 52:13–53.12. Edition and translation.* 1998.

Vol. 3 Emmanuel Uchenna Dim: *The Eschatological Implications of Isa 65 and 66 as the Conclusion of the Book of Isaiah.* 2005.

Vol. 4 Se-Hoon Jang: *Particularism and Universalism in the Book of Isaiah. Isaiah's Implications for a Pluralistic World from a Korean Perspective.* 2005.